The Japan Idea

Cover: Detail, wallpaper sample, 19th century
Embossed leather with gold leaf and painted decoration, Japan
George Walter Vincent Smith Art Museum
Springfield, Massachusetts

The Japan Idea

Art and Life in
Victorian America

by William Hosley

Wadsworth Atheneum
Hartford, Connecticut

*The Japan Idea: Art and Life
in Victorian America*

This volume was published in conjunction with
The Japan Idea – the exhibition – held at
Wadsworth Atheneum 600 Main Street
Hartford, Connecticut 06103
from October 21 to December 30, 1990

The research, exhibition, and part of the cost of
printing the catalog were made possible by grants from

Fidelity Investments through the Fidelity Foundation
The Japan World Exposition Commemorative Fund
United Technologies Corporation
The Women's Committee of the Wadsworth Atheneum
Yamaichi International (America) Inc.
Loctite Corporation
The Mary Livingston Griggs and Mary Griggs Burke Foundation
Konica Business Machines USA, Inc.
Connecticut Commission on the Arts
Kazunao Takeuchi
Acura of Avon
Schaller Acura

Copyright © 1990 Wadsworth Atheneum and William Hosley
All rights reserved
Library of Congress Catalog Card Number 90-071054
International Standard Book Number 0-918333-07-5

Edited by Guthrie Sayen
Captions and Research Assistance by Karen L. Blanchfield
Indexed by Kathleen D. Bagioni
Design by Peter Good Graphic Design
Printed and Bound by Eastern Press

All photographs supplied by lending institutions or by
Joseph Szaszfai, unless otherwise noted

Contents

Director's Foreword   6

Lenders to the Exhibition   8

Author's Preface and Acknowledgments   10

Introduction   14

I.   Matthew C. Perry and the Opening of Japan   17

II. Selling Japan in the West:
     The Centennial and Beyond   29

III. American Taste and the Arts of Japan   47

IV. Japan in the Artist's Eye   80

V.   Architecture and the Japanesque Interior   103

VI. American Industry Responds   117

VII. British Pottery Invades America   154

VIII. Women's Art & Popular Culture   161

IX. Aftershocks   183

X.   Color Plates   185

Endnotes   201

Index   208

Foreword

This publication and the exhibition it documents trace the immediate impact of Japan on American civilization in the last third of the nineteenth century. This impact was most readily evident in decorative arts for use and adornment in the American home. All media, from glass and metal to textiles and wall coverings, porcelains, and cloisonné, reflected the pervasive influence. The "Japanese craze," as the Victorians called it, was particularly centered in New England.

The basic thrust behind the excited American discovery of Japan was the belief that Japan represented a purer, more spiritual civilization, in touch with nature and spared the ravages of an industrialized society. The originality of the exhibition and catalogue aims to show how long, how deep, and how complex the American-Japanese connection has been, how America embraced the Japanese influence long before Sony, Toyota, and Hitachi arrived on the world scene.

The Japan Idea: Art and Life in Victorian America brings into focus and consciousness all manner of objects of daily living which long have been neglected or misunderstood, and demonstrates to a contemporary audience how these two great nations were connected more than one hundred years ago.

The centennial exhibition, held in Philadelphia in 1876, gave ten million Americans of all classes the opportunity to see Japanese objects, and this widespread exposure to Japanese craftsmanship intensified the American public's embrace of Japanese aesthetics, then considered to be the epitome of good taste.

The Japan Idea brings together Japanese goods imported to America in the late nineteenth century – including woodblock prints, cloisonné, lacquer and porcelains – and objects made in America (both by industry and individuals) in response. Americans admired, appropriated, and adapted Japanese iconography and design. This is evidenced by greeting and trade cards, sheet music, ceramics, hardware, silver, glass, textiles, wallpaper, and furniture – even a commode. The Japan idea permeated works by Winslow Homer, Mary Cassatt, and John Twachtman, as well as those by such lesser known artists as John O'Brien Inman and the hundreds of amateur women whose "China painting" and needlework proliferated in the late nineteenth century.

The Atheneum's indefatigable and innovative curator of American decorative arts, William Hosley, conceived and organized this landmark exhibition of more than two hundred objects, which will be seen only at the Wadsworth Atheneum. He also wrote this insightful catalogue. We are grateful to him and his assistant, Karen Blanchfield, who contributed her considerable organizational, research, and writing skills.

In addition to the Wadsworth Atheneum staff, two other groups made this project possible. More than eighty lenders shared their objects with us during the fall of 1990; their cooperation is greatly appreciated. We are also heartened by the generosity of a group of sponsors, both Japanese and American, who came together to cover the many expenses involved in such an endeavor. *The Japan Idea* received major support from Fidelity Investments through the Fidelity Foundation. Generous support was also provided by the Japan World Exposition Commemorative Fund, United Technologies Corporation, the Women's Committee of the Wadsworth Atheneum, Loctite Corporation, Yamaichi International (America) Inc., the Mary Livingston Griggs and Mary Griggs Burke Foundation, and Konica Business Machines USA, Inc. The Atheneum would also like to thank the Connecticut Commission on the Arts and Kazunao Takeuchi.

Patrick McCaughey
Director

Lenders to the Exhibition

Adirondack Museum, Blue Mountain Lake, New York
Helen Allen Textile Collection, Madison, Wisconsin
The Arkansas Arts Center, Little Rock, Arkansas
Laura H. Banta
Thomas Beckman
Joel Bogart
The Brooklyn Museum, New York
Brown and Corbin Fine Art, Lincoln, Massachusetts
Dr. Charles Burden
Jay Cantor
Castle Tucker House Museum, Wiscasset, Maine
Wilson and Helen Chatfield
The Cleveland Museum of Art
Concord Antiquarian Museum, Concord, Massachusetts
The Connecticut Historical Society, Hartford, Connecticut
Cooper-Hewitt Museum, The Smithsonian Institution's
  National Museum of Design, New York City
Fred Cray
The Currier Gallery of Art, Manchester, New Hampshire
Mr. & Mrs. David Dangremond
Daughters of the American Revolution Museum,
  Washington, D.C.
The Detroit Institute of Arts
Essex Institute, Salem, Massachusetts
Everson Museum of Art, Syracuse, New York
John Quentin Feller, Ph.D.
Henry Ford Museum and Greenfield Village,
  Greenfield, Michigan
Mr. & Mrs. Morris Greenberg
Hall Memorial Library, Ellington, Connecticut
Hartford Public Library
Helen Hersh & Charles Sporn

Helen Hersh, Hamish Hog Antiques, Brooklyn, New York
Mugnier Higgins Antiques, New Castle, Delaware
Frederick Hill, Berry-Hill Galleries, New York City
Historical Design Collection, Inc., New York City
Historical Society of Cheshire County, Keene,
   New Hampshire
Ipswich Historical Society, Ipswich, Massachusetts
The Jones Museum of Glass and Ceramics, Sebago, Maine
Kimball-Jenkins Estate, Concord, New Hampshire
Kingman Tavern Historical Museum, Cunningham,
   Massachusetts
Mrs. Horace B. Learned & Mrs. H.C.L. Colt
Maine Historical Society, Portland, Maine
Maine State Museum, Augusta, Maine
Meriden Historical Society, Meriden, Connecticut
The Metropolitan Museum of Art, New York City
Thomas Michie
Minnesota Historical Society, St. Paul, Minnesota
Mount Holyoke College Art Museum, South Hadley,
   Massachusetts
Museum of American Textile History, North Andover,
   Massachusetts
Museum of Art, Rhode Island School of Design,
   Providence, Rhode Island
Museum of Fine Arts, Springfield, Massachusetts
Mystic Seaport Museum
The Newark Museum, Newark, New Jersey
New Bedford Glass Museum, New Bedford, Massachusetts
New Hampshire Historical Society, Concord,
   New Hampshire
New York Historical Society, New York City
Orange Historical Society, Orange, Connecticut

John Osgood
The Parrish Art Museum, Southampton, New York
Peabody Museum of Salem, Salem, Massachusetts
Philadelphia Museum of Art
Portland Museum of Art, Portland, Maine
Post Road Gallery, Larchmont, New York
Rhode Island Historical Society, Providence, Rhode Island
The St. Louis Art Museum
Kevin Stayton
The Stowe-Day Foundation, Hartford, Connecticut
George Walter Vincent Smith Art Museum, Springfield,
   Massachusetts
Smith College Museum of Art, Northampton,
   Massachusetts
The Stone House Museum, Belchertown, Massachusetts
The Strong Museum, Rochester, New York
Robert Tuggle and Paul Jeromack
The Mark Twain Memorial, Hartford, Connecticut
Jane Voorhees-Zimmerli Art Museum, Rutgers University,
   New Brunswick, New Jersey
Wallingford Historical Society, Wallingford, Connecticut
Paul Walter
Walters Art Gallery, Baltimore, Maryland
Watkinson Library, Trinity College, Hartford, Connecticut
Ann Woodhouse
Worcester Historical Museum, Worcester, Massachusetts

Author's Preface and Acknowledgments

"Style percolates down"—a favorite aphorism of *Vogue's* legendary founder Condé Nast— feels as disquieting today as it did in 1975 when I came across it for the first time. And yet it is an assumption at the heart of the art historian's insatiable quest for sources of influence. Art history is a strange business that celebrates creativity and imagination and then invalidates it by seeking chains of influence. Gregory Hedberg, my former boss and the person who first encouraged me to explore "The Japan Craze," used to talk quite convincingly about the "burden of culture" on great cities like Paris and New York. Because everyone looks there—the national media seems to look nowhere else—great centers of culture develop a compulsion toward perfection so inhibiting that genuine innovation is stifled or at least confined to some impertinent niche on the sidelines. Hedberg's favorite example of this was French Impressionism, a movement nurtured and developed in the provinces. But even a cursory glance at the history of technology and innovation provides many related examples.

I mention this because I am proud that the inspiration for this exhibition originated not in a desire to reinterpret or expand what is already an abundant literature on *japonisme*, but in a small side gallery exhibition titled *Japan The Fad*, organized by the Brattleboro Museum and Art Center in Vermont during the spring of 1987. Under the directorship first of Rod Faulds and later Allison Devine and Dolores Root, the Brattleboro Museum operated one of the best exhibition programs in New England. *Japan The Fad* (no catalog) was just one of many great ideas that bubbled up out of the water there.

Japan The Fad took social history and popular culture as its point of reference, and in a seventeen by thirteen foot room, with less than thirty objects to display, mapped out an argument with style, humor and intelligence, that effectively called into question the whole notion of *japonisme*, with its implicit Franco-determinist emphasis. *Japan The Fad* did not argue that Japanese influence in western culture began in the United States, rather than France. In fact, it ignored the whole question of what-started-where, when, and who-influenced-whom, and cut straight to the more interesting notion that, by immersing oneself in the detritus of an idea, we will understand it more fully. Brattleboro's selection of *both* elite and popular arts, of historical documents and graphic depictions of historical events was a fine but humble demonstration of how ideas can be set in motion. The Atheneum lent some of its collection to *Japan The Fad,* which is how I got involved with it. My only regret, or I should say, my great opportunity, was that Brattleboro was unable to produce a companion catalog and explore their concept in detail.

So perhaps, style - or rather, new ideas - actually percolate up, not down. The Atheneum's appropriating Brattleboro's exhibition concept may lead to its reaching a larger audience and ultimately, being swallowed by still bigger fish. That seems natural.

The Japan Idea bounced around the Atheneum's exhibition planning sessions for about a year. In 1988 the Atheneum's new director, Patrick McCaughey, organized a lecture series to showcase for the public (and, no doubt, to learn for himself) what his curatorial staff was doing. In keeping with the spirit that has prevailed every step of the way with this project, I offered to lecture on something I had not formerly studied but hoped to learn more about. After *Japan The Fad* opened my eyes to the topic, I discovered that the deepest, darkest corners of the Atheneum's basement storage vaults contained this network of widely dispersed stuff that no one ever looked at or displayed, but which appeared related to some of the ideas about Japan and the Victorians examined in Brattleboro. I hope you are not shocked to imagine that a museum, almost 150 years old, has "stuff" that only the registrar keeps track of and then only like so many dusty books on a shelf that are cataloged, but which no one reads. That is the joy of working for an old museum. I hope it does not sound presumptuous to suggest that the Atheneum (founded 1842), or any museum its age, has forgotten more than we will ever know. How could it be otherwise when history encompasses so many more nows than we have now?

The Japan Idea began with a core collection of books and objects found in the Atheneum library and eight of its dozen storage areas, each falling under the jurisdiction of a different department head. The tendency of museums and universities to segregate knowledge into disciplines and media areas such as "prints" or "silver" has done much to inhibit the kind of interdisciplinary study that this project represents. Add on the alarming tendency of museums to eradicate their own institutional memory by selling off formerly prized treasures, and you can imagine the difficulty we faced in finding objects to tell the story of *The Japan Idea*. This is a story some have chosen not to remember.

Such is life in a big museum. I, however, am luckier than most. Either due to parsimony or good old-fashioned Yankee conservatism, the Wadsworth Atheneum is unusual, even among institutions its age, for retaining so much of the collection that was important to it a century ago. If there were ten museums in the Northeast of the Atheneum's age and archaeological integrity our search for objects could have been wrapped up in six weeks. It took longer.

My luck was still running high the day Karen Blanchfield, then a junior in college, inquired about a summer internship. It is so hard to find bright people interested in art who have not been soured by the artifice of art history. Karen completed the internship and returned a year later as a curatorial assistant with a refreshingly open mind, and a strong appetite for learning. Without her, *The Japan Idea* would have remained an idea only. Karen was involved at every stage and with almost every function of this project. Even now, as I am writing this from a quiet perch far from the buzz and hum of the museum, Karen is tying up loose ends, papering the object files with interpretive information, preparing text for captions and labels, overseeing the production and assembly of photographs, and working with Cecil Adams, Jack Tracz, Edd Russo, Linda Ayres, and the Atheneum's crack exhibition design team trying to give *The Japan Idea* form.

Karen and I were ably assisted by a host of associates and friends at the Atheneum. Patrick McCaughey, the Atheneum's director, is a tremendous decision maker who leads into objectives with insight and courage. Although Karen and I really worked hard to keep expenses down, nothing this size comes cheap. We have been blessed by a host of sponsors, some old friends and some new. Those who joined on first (United Technologies and Loctite) and those who joined on for the largest share (The Japan World Exposition Commemorative Fund and the Fidelity Foundation) made this effort possible. Putting together a team of sponsors is a tough job. It was handled with grace and ingenuity by Patrick, the development director Muriel Fleischmann, her associates Hugh Crowley and Patricia Sprague, who are the most resourceful practitioners of their art I have had the pleasure to work with. Not having to worry about money is a rare blessing.

The multi-source loan exhibition is an endangered species, especially at the regional level. Insurance costs, "professional standards," shipping, installation, and book printing have become so expensive that exhibitions of this size and format may soon be impossible to undertake, unless one counts their visitors in six-figure increments. Nonetheless, here we are, and although we relied on consultants for some things, the Atheneum's staff proved essential in several key areas: Mary Ellen Goeke, the registrar, orchestrated the insurance and logistics and proved immeasurably patient and resourceful in indulging some of the more innovative approaches to shipping required by our diverse lenders. Linda Ayres, a renowned scholar in American art, now spends much of her time as our cool-witted air-traffic controller. Getting a network of departments to perform as a team is really difficult, and Linda's oversight of conservation, education, registration, and exhibition design and installation has given the Atheneum a strength it never has when each department marches to its own drum.

Most importantly, I would like to thank the Atheneum's librarian, John Teahan, my most valued sounding board and friend, whose instincts and boundless curiosity have been of immeasurable value to me both with *The Japan Idea* and all of my Atheneum projects over the past decade.

The Japan Idea benefited from both formal and informal relations with consultants and research assistants. Among my colleagues in the fields of American art, domestic life, and material culture, I'd like to single out Christopher Monkhouse and Thomas Michie of the Museum of Art, Rhode Island School of Design, for their moral and intellectual support and for Tom's remarkable analysis of Japanese pattern books. Michael Ettema of the Henry Ford Museum, Jay Cantor of Christie's, Alice C. Frelinghuysen of The Metropolitan Museum of Art, Sally Mills of the deYoung Museum in San Francisco, Kevin Stayton at The Brooklyn Museum, Donna-Belle Garvin at New Hampshire Historical Society, Ruth Caccavole at Tiffany Archives, Anita Ellis at the Cincinnati Art Museum — these are colleagues and friends who shared their time and insight with enthusiasm and grace. Bill and Arlene Schwind, John Holverson, Dorothy Lee Jones, Ed Churchill, and Earle Shettleworth—the Maine contingent—proved exceedingly resourceful in locating objects and documents of great value to us. Finally, I would like to thank Jane Spillman at The Corning Museum of Glass for putting us onto Georgette Lee, whose survey of advertisements, period literature, and the trade catalogs of Japanese-style glass manufacturers, was our best sounding of the extraordinary depths attained by the Japan idea. During the first phase of research Linda S. Cohen spent long hours taking notes on Victorian periodicals and Cindy Cormier, now with the Atheneum's education department, spent several months compiling images and information on American painters involved with the Japan idea.

Among Japanese art scholars I am especially grateful to Barbara Ford of The Metropolitan Museum of Art, Anne N. Morse of the Museum of Fine Arts, Boston, Jack Thayer, Elaine Vukov and John Grimes of the Peabody Museum, Salem, Emil Schnorr and Karen Papineau of the George Walter Vincent Smith Museum, Springfield, and Hiram Woodward of the Walters Art Gallery, Baltimore. They all indulged graciously my forays into their files and storage areas. Lee B. Johnson of the Freer Gallery in Washington and the Japanese art scholar Julia Meech of New York both spent time in Hartford cross-checking our selections and brainstorming about some of the ideas here explored. Correspondence with Clay Lancaster early in the project provided an invigorating association with one of the pioneers in the study of Japanese influence in the arts.

The Japan Idea marks the first time I have relied heavily on art and antique dealers for guidance and information. It proves a point. When you tread new ground in the field of art, the dealers and collectors really do seem to get there - wherever there is - first! One of my greatest stimulants was the contagious enthusiasm of the dealers and collectors who are out there reassembling the Japan idea in all of its wildest and most intriguing permutations. For all that is said about great fortunes being made in dealing art, that are not already trendy or highly valued is a labor of pure love. Collecting and dealing stuff that is off cycle is not a quick buck, but it is a noble one. Helen Hersh, Bill and Arlene Schwind, Robert Tuggle, Margot Johnson, Paul Walter, Mimi Findlay, Jeffrey Brown, Priscilla St. Germain, Helen Fusscas, Sylvia Greenberg, and Denis Gallion—thank you for everything. You're amazing.

I write and lecture about small local-history museums, the traditional historical societies you find in towns across America. Each year my wife and I add a dozen or more to a list that now numbers in the hundreds. Not all of them are great or have great things'. but their collective holdings tower over those of major museums and in many respects are more interesting. For rarity and variety of collections and quality of documentation, historical societies are unmatched. And yet too many of these organizations are struggling for their survival. Total the annual budgets of one thousand of them and it would still be far less than any one of several of our largest museums! Their loss is our loss because they have done the best job of preserving the stuff of our American culture. Among our lenders to *The Japan Idea*, I'd like to single out historical societies in Meriden and Wallingford, Connecticut, Orange, Ipswich, Cummington, and Belchertown, Massachusetts, and Cheshire County, New Hampshire, and Woolwich, Maine.

I'd like to close these acknowledgments on the highest possible note by mentioning my wife, Christine Ermenc. In addition to providing moral support, Christine is also my best colleague. When we met at Winterthur in the late 1970s, I could not figure out why someone with her ability had chosen to go into museum education, a field curatorial types like myself regarded as glorified child care. Was I ever wrong! What I have learned from Christine as I have witnessed her founding and providing vision for her department at the Connecticut Historical Society is that education is a museum's highest purpose. If we are not in the education business, it would puzzle a fiend to know what business we are in. If our work is not conceived in educational terms, what redeeming perspective shapes it? This, and much more, I have learned from a wife who has shared my work and shaped my goals and life like no one else.

I should also mention my father-in-law, Prof. Joseph Ermenc, whose "Tech 20" course at Dartmouth on the history of technology was a legendary and pioneering example of interdisciplinary study, conceived long before the trend. The capacity of this engineer-historian-polymath to see the big picture on many fronts has been a joyous and liberating factor in my work. With a family like this, anything is possible.

William Hosley
Enfield, Connecticut
July 1990

Introduction

In the not very distant day when we shall receive envoys... from the inhabitants of Mars... to our own international expositions, these exhibits will probably not differ very much from our own than do those of the Empire of Japan in the present Chicago show.... The European or the American who enters these galleries... recognizes at once a new order of things and a new world.... [an] air of having come from somewhere beyond the stars.[1]

Thus begins the chapter describing Japan's presence in one of the many international expositions that marked and measured Victorian society's ever steady pursuit of progress. At first reluctant and reclusive, Japan's relationship with the Victorians stands as one of the most poignant and revealing interactions of the age. Imagine a culture so malleable that it could reverse centuries of self-imposed isolation to become a major factor in international trade and the standard-bearer of modernization in the East. The Japan that Americans discovered, first through words and pictures and later in its dazzling displays at the international expositions, was a nation that both confirmed and denied their most cherished ideals. The qualities of pride and prejudice, admiration and envy, and sensitivity and appropriation are just part of the range of emotions and attitudes that colored the West's dealings with this, its most exotic and unusual ally and friend. The story of Japan and Victorian America is a story of two cultures bound together by their pursuit of prestige and power in a highly competitive and changing world. As two of the newest entries in a race long dominated by Europe, Japan and the United States were both upstarts and outsiders. But even as rivals, they shared values.

Fascination with Japan and the acknowledgment of its influence in Western art – the study of Japanism (or its French equivalent *japonisme*) – began almost from the moment of contact between East and West.[2] But this was never the entire story. Although Japan became a major factor in the aesthetic debates that raged during the last quarter of the nineteenth century, the collision of East and West was felt more widely and deeply than in the narrow channel of the fine arts. This was especially true in the United States where "the Japan craze" shaped popular culture for more than a decade, affecting everything from music and theater to advertising and home furnishing. Although its response lagged behind Europe's, the United States

Map of Japan, 1876
Philadelphia, Pennsylvania
Exhibition Catalog
Japanese Section, Centennial Exposition
Wadsworth Atheneum

formed a bond with Japan that was direct, distinctive, and strong. *The Japan Idea* is the story of that bond and the record of its material culture. By enlarging the notion of Japanism to incorporate all manifestations of the phenomenon, *The Japan Idea* is defined more broadly and its power appears more sure.

This book and its companion exhibition were developed for the purpose of bringing together a cross section of ideas and things that would tell the story of Victorian America's encounter with the arts of Japan. Having bitten off a project that could rightly occupy years of study, the purpose here is not to have the final word but to lay the groundwork for a broader and more pluralistic consideration of the phenomenon of Japanism and its American context. To create visual juxtapositions and provoke thoughts and emotions that might lead to greater public interest in the history of Japanese-American relations seem like a worthy endeavor. As important as our relationship with Japan has become today, it is astonishing how infrequently the history of that relationship is invoked. That the United States and Japan were enmeshed in a mutually beneficial relationship a century ago appears to have largely escaped notice. One of the objectives of *The Japan Idea* is to hold up again this not so distant mirror so we can better understand our differences and our mutualities.

The story begins with the historic opening of Japan to the West in 1854 by the American naval commander Matthew C. Perry and continues with the Meiji Restoration of 1868 which launched Japan's embrace of westernization and foreign trade. Japan's performance at the United States' International Exhibition of Arts, Manufacturers, and Products of the Soil and Mines (hereafter called the Centennial Exhibition) in 1876 presaged a twenty-year national pre-occupation with Japanese art which crested during the 1880s when American industry, art, and popular culture lined up behind a movement the Victorians dubbed "the Japan craze." Where Victorian Americans at mid-century knew little more about Japan than its place on the map, a generation later Americans of all classes and backgrounds exhibited a cultlike fascination with the distant island nation. How this transformation occurred and what it meant to those involved is the story behind *The Japan Idea*.

I. Matthew C. Perry and the Opening of Japan

In 1638, at the height of the Age of Exploration, the island of Japan expelled all Europeans from its midst and entered a period of profound national seclusion that would last two centuries. Japan's break with the West – then represented by a few Jesuit missions and Portuguese traders – was dramatic, brutal, and complete. The missionaries were expelled and forty thousand Christian converts were massacred.[3] For more than two centuries Japan remained sealed from outsiders. Its people were prohibited from leaving and the occasional fisherman stranded on foreign shores was not allowed to return. The profoundly xenophobic Tokugawa shogunate reigned over as prosperous and peaceful a time as Japan had ever known. At its zenith, on the eve of the modern era, Japan was a nation without war or poverty sustained by a moral economy that gave rise to an extraordinary florescence of art and artisanry. Isolated and independent, the Japanese culture that the Victorians encountered was almost its mirror opposite.

Repeated attempts to breach Japan's isolation succeeded only in deepening the nation's fear of foreigners. European states harboring colonial aspirations played the nations of the Far East, Asia, and North Africa like so many cards. The Opium War (1840) engulfed China in a humiliating struggle that stripped her of authority over her own trade and forced her to accept drugs as payment for export goods, thus demonstrating the ruthlessness of the West's appetite for expansion, especially when dealing with "heathen" cultures. By mid-century Westerners stared hungrily at Japan. Czar Nicholas I organized an unsuccessful Japan expedition in 1852, and it became increasingly clear within Japan that the time to deal with mounting foreign aggression had come.

On the other side of the world was the United States which marked its arrival at mid-century by completing its advance to the Oregon Territory and the Pacific Ocean and by wresting Texas from its Mexican neighbor. Nonetheless, as a new face on the world stage, the United States was less threatening to the Japanese. It lacked Europe's tradition of global imperialism and embraced ethnic and religious pluralism.

Fearing the inevitable collapse of its policy of seclusion, the Tokugawa shogunate was already vulnerable and internally divided on the issue when in July 1853 the United States naval squadron under the command of Commodore Matthew C. Perry arrived at Edo Bay (now Tokyo), with smokestacks gushing black fumes and heavy black guns mounted for battle (color plate 1). Through a masterful demonstration of gunboat diplomacy the Perry expedition succeeded in negotiating treaties that were the basis for Japan's historic opening to the West. Perry was prepared for diplomacy or war: he could wine, dine, and entertain Japanese officials as a prelude to negotiations, or he could pound the capital with cannon as a prelude to invasion. The squadron was a water-borne festival complete with a French chef, an Italian bandmaster, a Negro minstrel show, and a veritable museum of American progress and industry. Thus, armed with both carrots and sticks, the United States pressed the initiative to an historic conclusion.

The squadron remained idle at Edo Bay for several days as the Japanese mobilized their defenses and prepared to respond to the sudden foreign threat. The Japanese instructed Perry to go to Nagasaki, the only sanctioned port of entry for foreign vessels. Perry refused. He had a letter from the President of the United States which the emperor must receive; otherwise it would be taken as an insult with consequences that could not be gauged. On July 14, Perry and a delegation of naval officers and crewmen landed (color plate 2), remaining long enough to deliver the letter (fig. 1) and obtain assurance that he could return at some future date for an answer. Perry then steamed off toward Hong Kong.

Perry's wisdom in allowing the Japanese time to consider their options was a masterly stroke of diplomacy. Having familiarized himself with the limited Western literature on Japanese history, religion, and trade, Perry was better prepared to confront Japan on its own terms than any Westerner before him. The effect of Perry's initiative was to throw the government of the ruling shogun, Ieyasu, into turmoil. Already weakened by infighting, corruption, pervasive nepotism, and its own isolation, the shogun was forced to confer with the feudal lords, or daimyos, who ruled Japan's regional domains with the ruthlessness of absolute sovereigns. The powerful daimyo of Mito circulated a memorandum urging the lords of neighboring domains to prepare for war, while blaming the shogun for Japan's weakness. The memorandum also hinted at the need to reinvest the emperor with his traditional authority and power, thus beginning a struggle that ultimately led to the restoration of Japan's ancient monarchy.

As outlined in President Fillmore's letter, the United States sought limited but specific advantages. Perry allowed almost a year for Japan to study the proposal and respond. The United States sought protection for American whaling vessels lost in Japanese waters, permission to enter Japanese ports to obtain supplies, and a coaling station for the Pacific steamline then shuttling between San Francisco and China. The United States denied any intention of seeking exclusive trade privileges while pointing out its independence of the British Empire, the feared and despised malefactor in the Opium War. Finally, Perry advanced the cause of mutual trade, arguing that with only twenty days travel by steamer separating California and Japan the potential for gain was boundless.

Commodore Perry's naval squadron spent the next seven months in the eastern Pacific conducting sideline diplomacy in Hong Kong, Siam (Thailand), and at other Asian ports. Perry's waiting game, unprecedented in East-West relations, proved to be the right strategy for dealing with the slow-turning mechanism of Japanese bureaucracy. Although the changes put in motion by Perry's arrival would take almost fifteen years to climax, the most important change – the negotiation of Japan's opening to the West – occurred during the seven months of waiting.

Japan and the United States each had something the other needed, and although the form and content of the relationship did not take shape until years later, the first encounter struck a tone that would reverberate for the next half-century – indeed continues to reverberate today. History provides rare instances of sudden transformation. Change more often creeps quietly. For Japan, the American naval squadron's arrival was a pivotal moment from which there was no exit and no turning back. The rules must change. The time for accommodation had arrived.

The government of the shogun, weakened by the decline of its military strength and quietly resented for its century-old usurpation of the emperor's authority, was overwhelmed by the responsibility for so momentous a decision. Although difficult for Westerners to understand, Japan's dual system of governance is fascinating. Basically, the emperor is Japan's conscience and soul. The shogun was its political and military head. In the United States, a sort of vague and rarely exercised notion of the sovereignty

What's New In Ceramics

Schedule of Speakers
October 26, 1990

1:00-1:10 — **Richard Martin**
Executive Director of the Shirley Goodman Resource Center
Introduction

1:15-1:50 — **Robert Koehl**
Assistant Professor of Classical Archeology, Hunter College
The Forms and Functions of Aegean Bronze Age Rhyta

1:55-2:30 — **Marilyn Karmason** with **Joan B. Stacke**
Authors of Majolica: A Complete History and Illustrated Survey
Victorian Majolica Revisted

2:35-3:10 — **Martin Eidelberg**
Professor of Art History, Rutgers University
Vollard's Artistic Ceramics

3:10-3:35 — Break

3:35-4:10 — **Marcia Favrot**
Artist and Art Historian
Saint-Porchaire Pottery: New Approach, New Theories

4:15-4:50 — **Norman Weiss**
Adjunct Professor, Columbia University School of Architecture
and
Linda Rosenfeld Shulsky
Adjunct Professor, New School for Social Research, Parsons School of Design
China and Italy: Ceramic Design Anomalies in the 16th Century

4:55-5:30 — **George Szabo**
Director, Place des Antiquaires and Adjunct Professor, F.I.T. Graduate Programs
Italian Maiolica: Place Setting to Social Setting

5:30 — Wine Reception

What's New In Ceramics

Friday, October 26, 1990
Fashion Institute of Technology
Shirley Goodman Resource Center
Sixth Floor

The fee for the symposium is $25 for each participant ($15 for students with valid I.D.)

Space is limited, reserve early.

Name _____

Address _____

City, State, Zip _____

Telephone (Area Code) _____

Number of Tickets Requested _____

Name of Guest _____

Total Amount Enclosed _____

Please make checks payable to:
Fashion Institute of Technology

Mail your check along with this completed form to:

Office of the Executive Director
Shirley Goodman Resource Center
Room E304
Fashion Institute of Technology
Seventh Avenue @ 27th Street
New York, New York 10001-5992

What's New In Ceramics

Presented by the
Shirley Goodman
Resource Center at F.I.T.
212.760.7970

Ceramics carries the message of the culture from which it sprang. It has its place in architecture (Della Robbia), painting (Pellipario), and sculpture (Kändler and Boucher), and yet for all this richness frozen by fire in time, there has been less focused attention given to ceramics than needs to be. There is much yet to be discovered by careful review of documents or bringing together a group of objects never before seen together for comparison or analysis.

It is with great pleasure and a feeling of timeliness that the Shirley Goodman Resource Center at the Fashion Institute of Technology provides a forum for those working in the field of ceramics to present their ideas and for those in the audience to celebrate their interest and commitment.

On the Cover:
Minton & Co., Majolica Ewer, 1871. Sculpted by Hughes Protât.. Illustrated in Majolica: A complete History and Illustrated Survey, (Harry N. Abrams, Inc., 1989)

What's New In Ceramics

Friday, 26 October 1990

Shirley Goodman Resource Center
Sixth Floor
Fashion Institute of Technology
Southwest Corner of Seventh Avenue
@ 27th Street

Shirley Goodman Resource Center
Room E304
Fashion Institute of Technology
Seventh Avenue @ 27th Street
New York, New York 10001-5992

The Wadsworth Atheneum Presents
"The Rising Sun In the Gilded Age: The Japanese Influence on Victorian America"

9:00 a.m.	Registration and Coffee
9:30 a.m.	Introductory Remarks, Patrick McCaughey, Director, Wadsworth Atheneum
9:30 a.m.	*The Japan Idea: Art and Life in Victorian America* William Hosley, Curator of American Decorative Arts, Wadsworth Atheneum and organizer of the exhibition
10:30 a.m.	*The Reopening of Japan: East Meets West* Harold Bolitho, Prof. of Japanese Studies and Director of the Edwin O. Reischauer Institute of Japanese Studies, Harvard University
11:30 p.m.	*Japonisme Comes to America* Julia Meech, Ph.D, Art Consultant of Japanese Fine Arts
12:30 p.m.	Lunch break
2:00 p.m.	*Women's Role in the Spread of American Japonisme* Jane Converse Brown, Ph.D, Lecturer, University of Wisconsin
3:00 p.m.	*Japanese Influence on American Silver* Charles Venable, Associate Curator of Decorative Arts, Dallas Museum of Art
4:00 p.m.	*"Rabid just now on the J.": American Painters' Response to Japanese Art* Sally Mills, Associate Curator of American Paintings, The Fine Arts Museums of San Francisco

This symposium made possible by a grant from the Connecticut Humanities Council.

(plate 1-color reproduction, page 186)
Passing the Rubicon
July 11, 1853
Detail of color lithograph
WILLIAM HEINE
Mystic Seaport Museum

Matthew C. Perry's historic opening of Japan to the West was documented by the staff artist, William Heine, who captured the scenery and ceremony of the trip in watercolor sketches which were issued commercially as a set of deluxe lithograph prints by Eliphalet Brown Jr. of New York. The fact that the voyage merited the appointment of an official artist attests to its recognized importance and the anticipated curiosity of Americans back home. Together with the illustrations and narrative accompanying Perry's official account of his journey—published shortly after his return—these images provided Americans with their first glimpses of Japan.

of the people serves a similar purpose. It had been so long since the emperor had exercised his authority, that the shogun had lost sight of his accountability to that authority. The late summer of 1853 was characterized by acrimonious debate and swollen pride. The feudal lords of the regional domains, the daimyos, were sucked into the vacuum created by the shogun's irresolute handling of the situation. Having encouraged a formerly intolerable level of openness and debate, the shogun now found himself swamped in discord. With the shogun's authority being challenged from all sides, the more powerful and prosperous daimyos, especially those from Satsuma and Mito, gained a decided advantage in shaping Japan's response to the Perry initiative. Inexperienced in the ways of the West and unsure of just what kind of threat Perry represented, the daimyo of Mito moved decisively to assuage the nation's threatened sovereignty by calling for resistance to all foreign demands. Consensus for resistance mounted and defensive preparations were being made when suddenly, in late August, Shogun Ieyoshi was found dead, an event that only reinforced a sense of the shogunate's impotence.[4]

The late shogun was replaced by his son, Iesada, thus leaving the powerful shogunal bureaucracy intact. In spite of resistance from the feudal lords, Commodore Perry returned on February 13, 1854, to

(plate 2-color reproduction, page 187)
First Landing of Americans in Japan
July 14, 1853
Detail of color lithograph
WILLIAM HEINE
Mystic Seaport Museum

(1) *The Message of the Admiral of the United States to the Shogun*
1855
Colored wood engraving on rice paper
Japan
ANONYMOUS
Graphics Collection, The Rhode Island Historical Society

Japanese artists recorded their impressions of the visiting Americans soon after Perry's arrival. Just as Japanese costumes and ceremonies confused and awed the American delegation, the Americans were the subject of much speculation on the part of the Japanese. Here Perry and two of his officers are awkwardly portrayed in naval uniforms, never before seen in Japan. The unknown Japanese artist seems to have been fascinated by the details of the Americans' clothing.

(plate 3-color reproduction, page 187)
Landing of Commodore Perry, Officers, and Men of the Squadron
March 8, 1854
Detail of color lithograph
WILLIAM HEINE
Mystic Seaport Museum

find the Japanese ready to negotiate. As the squadron's three steam frigates and four sloops of war slid into Edo Bay, both sides were ready for an historic encounter.

The formal meeting and exchange of papers between Commodore Perry and the imperial commissioners took place on March 8, 1854, at Kanagawa, a village near Yokohama at the mouth of Edo Bay (color plate 3). Buttressed by technological superiority, the stagecraft of Perry's landing, with its pronounced display of ritual and order, left little doubt about which side manned the controls.

Pageantry is the kinder and gentler side of military power. Perry led three hundred of his officers and staff in a procession flanked by two rows of armed, flag-bearing, uniformed soldiers in starched white slacks and gloves. At bay was a phalanx of gunboats. Military might was on one side and an overture of friendship and comity on the other. Well rehearsed in the Japanese ritual of gift exchange, Perry put on a show that was at once inspirational and intimidating. Furnished with a budget of $20,000 (equivalent to more than half a million dollars today) to procure gifts for the emperor, Perry offered up a veritable museum of American progress in industry and the arts. Among the most prized offerings were the double-elephant folio engravings of John James Audubon's *Birds of America* (1827-38) (fig. 2) and the equally stupendous folio-size lithographs of Audubon's *Quadrupeds of North America* (1839-48) (fig. 3), valued then at an astronomical $1,000 each.

(2) *Iceland Falcon*, 1837
Plate CCCLXVI, Number 74 of
The Birds of America Folio
Double-elephant aquatint engraving on paper
London, England
JOHN JAMES AUDUBON (1780-1851)
Printed and colored by Robert Havell
Wadsworth Atheneum

(3) *Soft-haired Squirrel*, 1845-1848
Plate XIX, Number 4 of
The Viviparous Quadrupeds of North America Folio
Imperial folio lithograph on paper
Philadelphia
JOHN JAMES AUDUBON (1780-1851)
Printed and colored by J.T. Bowen
Wadsworth Atheneum

The gifts which accompanied Perry to Japan were mostly representative of America's growing technological and industrial might. The deluxe editions of Audubon's Birds of America *and* Viviparous Quadrupeds of North America *were an important exception. These exquisite, bound illustrations suggest the direction of American art at mid-century and testify to the extraordinary ability of one of the nation's greatest observers of nature. Valued then at $1,000 for each set, these pictures were perfectly suited to satisfying the Japanese curiosity about American wildlife.*

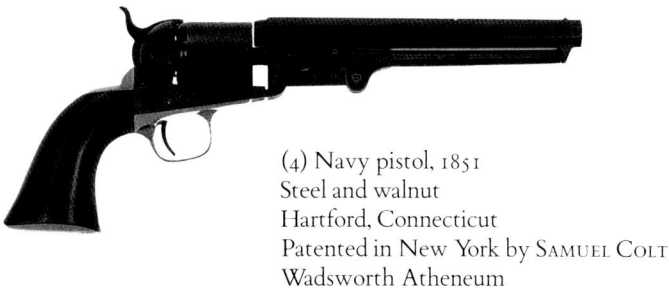

(4) Navy pistol, 1851
Steel and walnut
Hartford, Connecticut
Patented in New York by SAMUEL COLT
Wadsworth Atheneum

As Commodore Perry steamed toward his historic encounter with Japan during the winter of 1853, his cargo included an assortment of treasures intended as gifts to be exchanged in goodwill with the Japanese. Among the gifts were 50 Navy pistols, like the example illustrated here, 25 Army pistols, and 25 pocket pistols of varying length. The United States government bought some and the rest were personally offered by Samuel Colt as gifts for the Japanese officials, interpreters, and the Emperor. The standard Navy pistol retailed for $25, a princely sum at the time. More importantly, Colt's gift embodied the qualities of American technological superiority that awed the Japanese and led to their eventual accommodation of American demands.

(5) Box, about 1854
Lacquer
Japan
Wadsworth Atheneum

This lacquer box is representative of the quality of work the Japanese regarded as suitable for gift exchange with the Perry expedition. Included as part of the crate of goods earmarked for Samuel Colt, this box does not reveal the extraordinary capabilities of Japan's lacquer industry on the eve of its opening to the West.

American inventiveness was represented by a quarter-scale locomotive and track, a case of firearms from the legendary inventor and arms manufacturer Samuel Colt (fig. 4), a daguerreotype camera, and a telegraph machine, a gift from the artist and inventor Samuel F.B. Morse. The collaboration between business and government enabled Perry to make a much grander gesture than would have been possible relying on government resources alone.[5]

The Japanese reciprocated on March 24 with gifts regarded at the time as a poor response to what they received on March 13th. But considering the context, the exchange was respectable and revealing. Where the American gifts emphasized technology and invention, the Japanese gifts introduced Americans to the phenomenon of Japanese art, forming an impression that would linger and grow into an obsession in the decades that followed. Certain gifts were earmarked for President Franklin Pierce (President Fillmore left office between the time of the expedition's planning and completion), among them an exquisite lacquer box and writing case, a bronze incense burner, and a bolt of embroidered silk. Comparable gifts were offered to Commodore Perry and his officers, and some special gifts (figs. 5, 6, 7, 8) were addressed to American industrialists like Samuel Colt, whose gift of firearms, laden with symbolic meaning to the militarily backward Japanese, was greeted with excitement and delight.[6]

The ceremonies at Kanagawa continued with the formal translation and reading of the American petition and the shogun's formal reply. The shogun's imperial commissioners affirmed that, although meeting the American proposals would violate the laws of Japan's imperial ancestors, the "urgency" of the times demanded that Japan "entirely comply with the proposals of your government concerning coal, wood, water, provisions and the saving of ships and their crews in distress."[7] The proposal to open trade, however, was denied "in the name of the emperor," who was excluded from negotiations and, in fact, may not have been truly aware of what the shogun was proposing.

On March 27, with negotiations completed, Commodore Perry honored the Japanese commissioners with a banquet on board the ship Powhatan. There the Japanese feasted on a meal prepared by the expedition's French chef, listened to

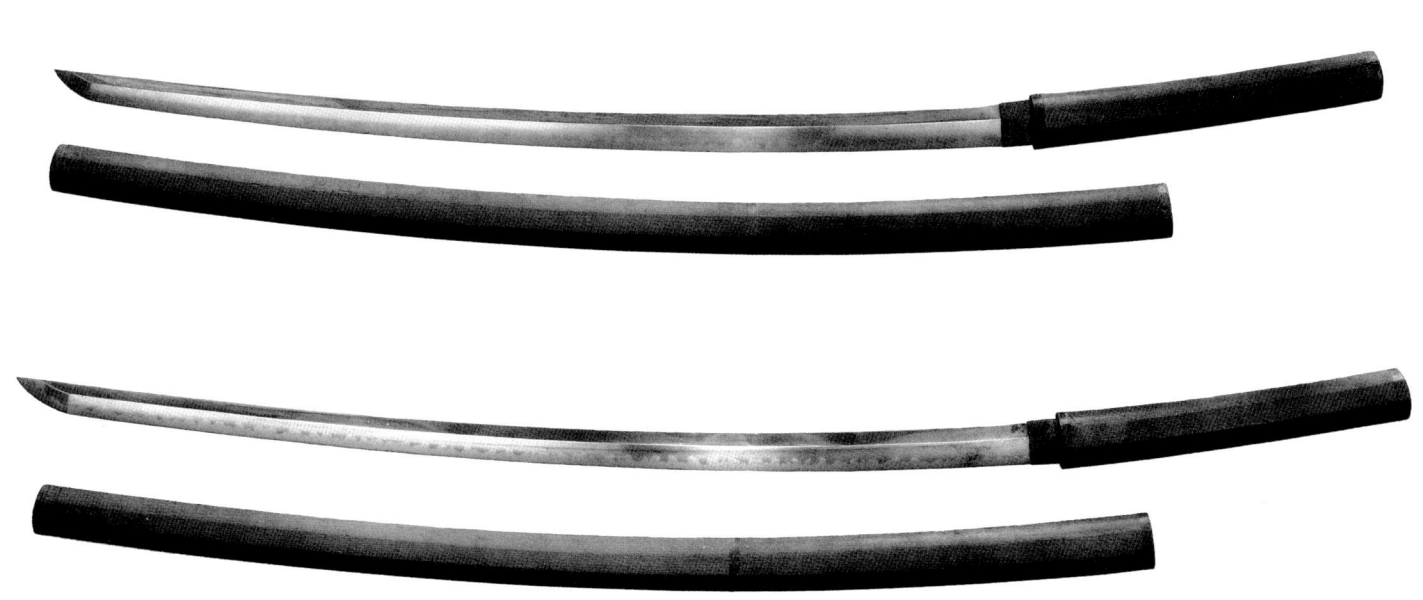

(6) Samurai swords, 1853
Steel blade, unfinished spruce mounts
Japan
Top sword designed by TAKENAKA KUNIHIKO
Wadsworth Atheneum

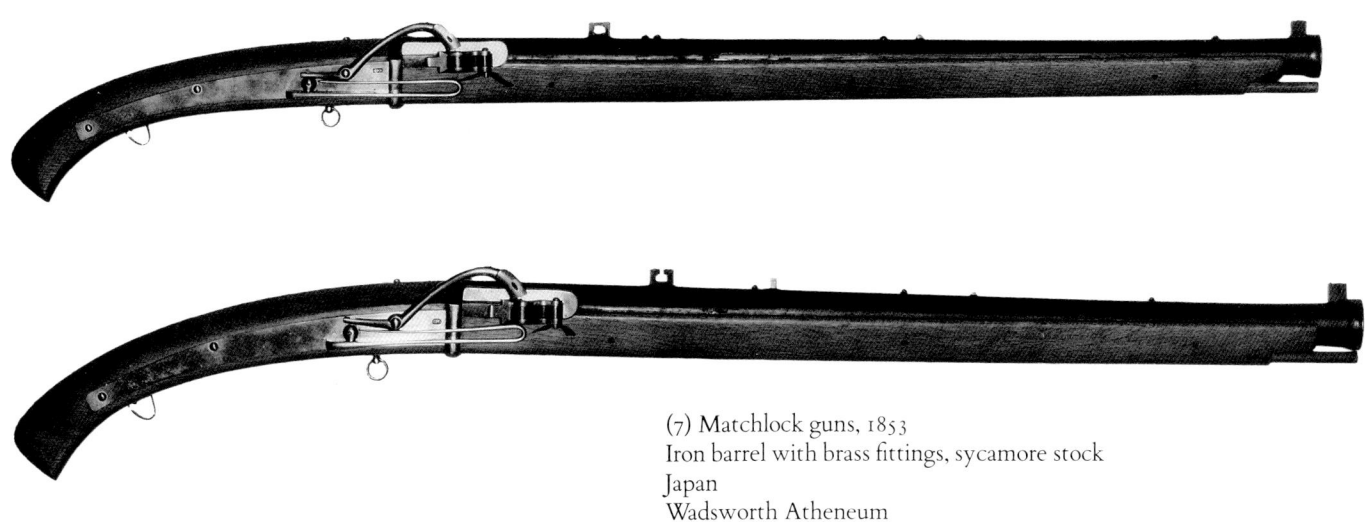

(7) Matchlock guns, 1853
Iron barrel with brass fittings, sycamore stock
Japan
Wadsworth Atheneum

Throughout his life, Hartford arms merchant Samuel Colt cherished the firearms and swords given to him by the Japanese to reciprocate for the revolvers and pistols that he sent with Commodore Perry as gifts for the Japanese emperor and dignitaries. Colt's collection of rare, exotic, and technologically innovative weapons was one of the finest in America during the 1850s.

Matthew C. Perry and the Opening of Japan   25

(8) Wall hanging, about 1854
Silk and silver metallic brocade
with paper backing
Japan
Wadsworth Atheneum

The gifts exchanged between the Americans and Japanese on March 24, 1854 were among the first examples of Japanese art brought to the United States. The choicest gifts were designated for the President of the United States—several are preserved today in The White House Collection. This silk brocade wall hanging was earmarked for the Hartford arms tycoon Samuel Colt, whose gift of firearms had so pleased and impressed the Japanese.

music performed by its Italian bandmaster, and were entertained by the Negro minstrel troupe. By closing on a multinational note, Perry showcased America's cosmopolitanism as well as the richness of its indigenous culture. European cuisine and entertainment revealed America's worldliness as assuredly as the arts of its native blacks revealed its folk culture. The melding of folk and cosmopolitan struck a note of self-reflexive irony that underscored the United States' participation in and independence from European culture. This appears to have intrigued the Japanese and set the tone for a relationship that ultimately recognized their mutual exclusion and shared isolation from the mainstream.

The treaty was signed on March 31, 1854, eight and a half months after Perry's first landing on Japanese shores, sixteen months after he embarked from the naval yards at Norfolk, Virginia, and worlds away from anything either nation knew before their historic encounter. Commodore Perry's triumph in Japan was due to practicing the art of war without waging it. No European nation had ever dealt with Japan so subtly. The opening of Japan was a milestone in American history and its greatest diplomatic achievement during the nineteenth century. Japan, the flower of the East, was ready to bloom.

* * *

The influence of Japanese art and culture – the Japan idea – did not blossom immediately. Neither the United States nor Japan was equipped to deal with their changing relationship. Commodore Perry returned to a nation preoccupied with its internal squabbles and even closer to civil war than when he left two years earlier. Japan entered a period of tumultuous change that impeded even the simplest national initiatives. Although in the fall of 1856, the United States became the first Western nation to install an ambassador in Japan, contact between the two nations was limited and the American press and public remained largely indifferent to the new relationship. The treaty concessions granted the United States were soon extended to the major trading nations of Europe, thus blunting whatever advantage the United States might have enjoyed.

In Japan the action shifted to modernization and its dismantling of feudalism. In the West we often think of feudalism as ending with the Middle Ages. In fact vestiges of feudalism still existed in the West as recently as the nineteenth century. The American Revolution was in part about throwing off a quasi-feudalistic system of privilege as was the Civil War almost a century later.[8] The West's intolerance of Japan's feudal government was undoubtedly aggravated by its not so distant memories of the same thing. Dismantling that system took time.

The American gifts to the Emperor were not especially appreciated even if they pointed the way to Japan's future. Those Japanese who were aware of the changes afoot were conflicted and ambivalent. Years later the American Japanophile William Elliot Griffis recalled seeing the shogun's collection of "presents brought by Commodore Perry lying, many of them, in mildew, rust, or neglect."[9] In addition to their symbolizing Japan's weakness in the face of foreign aggression, the gifts designated for the emperor were tainted by the shogun's usurpation of imperial authority. The historic realignment of this relationship, the restoration of the monarchy and the end of the Shogunate and feudalism, was the most dramatic outcome of Perry's visit. The shogun's submission to American demands was convincing evidence that Japan had grown weak and vulnerable. Those who opposed the treaty clamored for restoration of the emperor's power. Hostility toward foreigners was intense. Although its ports were open to trade, Japan earned a reputation as one of the most dangerous diplomatic posts in the world. Fanatics routinely assaulted and murdered foreigners on the streets, and no faction within government appeared quite stable.

During the fall of 1866 the young shogun Iemochi died at his castle in Osaka. The following February the emperor Komei also died.[10] The deaths of the shogun and emperor cleared the way for the resolution of internal conflict, the end of feudalism, the restoration of the emperor's governing authority, and the advent of modernization. During the winter of 1867 Mutsuhito, the fifteen-year-old son of the late emperor Komei, succeeded him as reigning emperor. Backed by the increasingly well-organized daimyos, the young emperor gained the support needed to abolish the shogunate, unify a divided government, and reassert his authority. In November 1867, Yoshihisa, recently installed successor to the late shogun Iemochi, resigned, transferring all authority to the emperor, thus allowing the nation to rally around a single unified government. Several months later the emperor broke all historic precedent by inviting the representatives of foreign powers then stationed in Japan to present themselves before him.[11] Equally unprecedented was the decision to remove the emperor's castle from its traditional site in Kyoto to a new location, the former center of the shogun's government at Edo, renamed Tokyo in honor of the change. In further commemoration the era of the young emperor was given the honorific name Meiji, meaning Enlightened Peace. In April 1868, His Majesty, surrounded by the leaders of the Revolution, took an oath that perfectly illustrates the transformation at hand. He declared, "The uncivilized customs of former times shall be broken through . . . and learning shall be sought . . . throughout the world to establish the foundation of the Empire."[12]

Japan's program of modernization provides one of the most startling examples of structural reform in history. Led by the emperor, the Meiji reforms were carefully thought out and speedily executed. Japan acknowledged its weakness by reorganizing its entire political structure with unprecedented decisiveness. By embracing modernization and the Western ideal of progress, Japan became a symbol of triumph of Western values. Having been last, Japan was now first in the eyes of the West and one of the only nations in the history of colonialism to embrace wholeheartedly the values of its oppressors.

Victorian tabloids were filled with commentary on the changes afoot. In 1871 the Boston magazine *Every Saturday* ran an editorial that described the "sudden rising of Japan out of darkness into the light of civilization" as "more like romance than reality. . . . The whole world should feel an abiding interest in this Oriental Empire . . . passing through a second birth which must result in its permanent prosperity and happiness."[13] Japan's rapid westernization was alternately reassuring and disturbing. Accustomed to subjugating developing nations, neither Europeans nor Americans were quite prepared to deal with a nation that, once forced into a relationship, would seek to control it. Japan did not go compliantly into the new world order. She arrived on the Western stage ready to compete.

Japanese modernization took many forms. Within a decade of the Restoration, telegraph lines, railroads, gaslit streets, coastal lighthouses, and Western-style architecture had become a common sight in Japan's urban centers. Western-style museums were created, and Western education was adopted. A generation of young Japanese scholars was sent to American and European colleges and universities.[14] Many returned to fill key roles in government and industry. Government leaders, from the emperor on down, affected a Western manner, lived in Western-style houses, wore Western clothes, and embraced modernization. At its extremes government officials advocated conversion to Christianity and intermarriage with Westerners "to improve the race."[15]

It is ironic that Japan emerged as a symbol of Western anti-modernism at the same time she was exchanging her traditions for modernization. "The Japan craze" of the 1870s and 1880s was fueled by misperceptions and nostalgia. Part of what made Japan's modernization possible was its success in catering to the West's desire for art, consumer goods, and symbols of its premodern culture. By means created by modernization Japan was able to sell the idea of its traditional culture to the West and in so doing gain status and power among Western nations. The paradox of this fragile relationship was to characterize Japan's engagement with the West for a half-century and explains why even today it is difficult to separate myth from reality in our dealings with Japan. Had the Japanese fully understood the paradox of this relationship, its impact would have been less powerful. The fact is, Japan truly embraced westernization. Until shocked by Western Japanophiles into arresting its loss, Japan appeared perfectly willing to discard centuries of art and tradition as the detritus of a discredited age.

With the end of feudalism many of Japan's old nobility were forced by hard times to sell their art treasures and ceremonial armor. As early as 1876 it was recognized that Western collectors had already scooped up much of Japan's best art. Even today there are more and better examples of eighteenth- and early nineteenth-century Japanese art in Europe and America than in Japan.[16]

II. Selling Japan in the West: The Centennial and Beyond

With the opening of Japan to the West, a generation of Japanese art critics, collectors, and pundits was born. These people, here called the Japanophiles, played an important role in selling the idea of Japan to the West. The Japan idea was theirs, and it is as much about the anxieties and needs of Victorian intellectuals as the culture it purports to represent. The idea of Japan was calculated to intoxicate Western readers by appealing to their deepest desires.

Japan offered both a diagnosis and a cure for the Victorian's growing cultural malaise. The throbbing pulse of industrialization had taken its toll. Victorian intellectuals were disillusioned by the effect of so much change, growth, and "progress." The encounter between Japan and the West led each to act upon latent instincts that simmered anxiously within. For Japan it was the fear of foreign imperialism and that nation's well-founded suspicion that it could no longer defend itself. Victorians feared that, in spite of abundance, the quality of life had somehow declined; economic growth had not brought real progress. Like lovers, Japan and the West were eventually drawn toward one another by a yearning for wholeness and fulfillment. Between the United States and Japan that yearning was intensified by their shared status as developing nations just arriving on the global playing field theretofore dominated by Europeans.

Whatever one cares to call it – Japanism, *japonisme*, the Japan craze, the Japanese art movement, or the cult of Japan – the concept was first popularized by art historians searching for the origins of modernism, the ideology whose battle cry is "art for art's sake." In modernism, artists remain aloof from the larger concerns of society, devoted first and foremost to the development of their individuality. Art historians of the modernist school search for sources of influence, an act that ironically deprives artists of the very quality attributed to them, their individuality of artistic expression. Yet it was in this search for influences that modernism and Japan first collide. Art historians were the first to develop a field of study around Japan's influence on Victorian culture. One of their goals was to explain how Japanese art influenced the French impressionists, the nineteenth-century counter-culture darlings of the modernist movement.

It is no coincidence that the field of art criticism matured in the midst of the Japan craze of the 1870s and 1880s. The Japan idea was shaped, packaged, and sold to the West through a remarkable and informal – perhaps even unconscious – collaboration between Western art critics, Japanophiles, and Japanese entrepreneurs. Even before the Meiji Restoration solidified Japan's commitment to westernization and trade, a network of predominantly British and American critics adopted Japanese art as a mantra which, with proper and regular chanting, would bring about much needed reforms in Western art. As a group these art critics and social pundits were almost unanimously enthusiastic about Japan. Among the most influential were Sir Rutherford Alcock, Charles Wyllys Elliot, Christopher Dresser, Edward S. Morse, James Jackson Jarves, and William Elliot Griffis. By means of newspaper and magazine articles, public lectures, books, and museum exhibitions, the

Japanophiles shaped public opinion, thus playing a crucial role in selling Japan to the West.

Japanese art goods were singled out for praise soon after the initial treaties were signed. Within a decade of Commodore Perry's arrival, Sir Rutherford Alcock, the first British consul general in Japan, gathered together a collection of Japanese decorative arts which he exhibited at the International Exhibition at London in 1862, marking the first time the arts of Japan were exposed to a broad Western audience.[17] Alcock was well suited to his duties in what was widely regarded as one of the most dangerous consulates in the British system. An imaginative and resourceful risk taker, Alcock was one of the few early diplomats to throw himself into the study of his foreign post. He mastered the language and read the published reports of the Dutch and American visitors who preceded him. As the first Westerner to climb Mount Fuji, Alcock gained notoriety for asserting the right of diplomats to freedom of travel inside Japan. Inquisitive and acquisitive, he became a devoted student of Japanese culture while collecting hundreds of examples of native arts and crafts.

Like most Victorian Japanophiles, Alcock's deep personal involvement and firsthand observation of Japan caused him to question the values and ideals of his own culture. The collection he assembled and exhibited in London in 1862 served as an introduction to the arts of Japan and a rebuttal of the ethnocentricity of Western art-goods manufacturers, who were astonished by such strong work from a nation totally outside the industrial loop.[18] Although previous international expositions (notably London, 1851; New York and Dublin, 1853; Munich, 1854; and Paris, 1855) provided grand displays of industrial products and machinery, London's 1862 exhibition included the most complete line of fine and decorative art ever shown before. Nations competed in everything from sculpture and paintings to embroidery and ceramics. Competition was fierce and the critics were keen to take note of new trends and innovations. By citing Japan as an example of the "progress in civilization of a people . . . . unaided by contact . . . with the European race," Alcock loosed the opening volley in what would be a long campaign of Western self-recrimination.[19] The contrast in cultures was indeed stark and provided critics of industrialization with an argument that challenged the West's most basic measures of progress.

Alcock's *Japanese Court* at the London exposition featured almost one thousand objects divided into nine media categories such as lacquerware, pottery, basketwork, and textiles.[20] Although modest in scale and not widely promoted, the *Japanese Court* provided an introduction to Japanese art for many of the exhibition's over six million visitors. It was there that British artists and architects like Christopher Dresser, William Burges, and Edward Godwin, as well as the expatriate American painter James McNeill Whistler, first discovered the arts of Japan. As one of Britain's leading medievalists, the architect William Burges was the first to associate Japanese craftsmanship and naturalistic ornament with the much-venerated art from Britain's medieval past, then regarded by aesthetes as a golden age.[21]

In a pattern that became all too familiar, the collections exhibited in the *Japanese Court* were dispersed once the exhibition closed. Alcock's collection was mostly bought for resale by the Oriental Warehouse department of Farmer and Rogers' fashionable emporium in London. The following year Alcock published *The Capital of the Tycoon: A Narrative of a Three Years' Residence in Japan* (1863), the first major English language publication about Japan. Fifteen years later he helped introduce Americans to Japanese art in a series of articles for (Appleton's) *Art Journal*. With those initiatives, Japanism was born and a process set in motion by which the idea of Japan would be sold to the West.

The Japanophiles were romantics. Even the scientists among them, like the zoologist Edward S. Morse of Salem, Massachusetts, were motivated by an aversion to modern life and an aching desire to reform standards of art and society. Although not among the first Americans to visit and write about Japan, Morse is among the most interesting. His *Japanese Homes and Their Surroundings* (1886) remains one of the classic works on Japanese craftsmanship and domestic life, a topic he probed with unsurpassed anthropological thoroughness. His collections, now housed at the Peabody Museum in Salem and the Museum of Fine Arts in Boston, are unique in all the world for their ethnographic specificity and for the completeness with which the material culture of everyday life in nineteenth-century Japan is documented.

Morse was first drawn to Japan in 1877 to collect

marine life from the Japanese seas. In three visits over seven years (1877–1883) Morse traveled extensively in Japan, taught at the newly founded Western-style University of Tokyo, conducted archaeological excavations, and, most of all, collected, a task at which he excelled.

The Victorians were the most adept and resolute taxonomists in modern times. The registration systems and many of the collection categories found in museums today are a direct inheritance from an age that made a kind of secular religion out of the identification and classification of nature. The taxonomic skills and instincts of the period are astonishing and were eventually enlarged beyond nature to include art and a full representation of cultural artifacts. Morse's training in science prepared him well for his role as an anthropologist. Although not the first, he was the most thorough student of Japanese life in his time and the only one to earn a national following in the United States. Widely respected as a career zoologist, Morse is best remembered today for his writings and teachings about Japan.

Morse's legacy is not without conflict and contradiction. Having documented Japanese ceramic production by assembling a collection of more than five thousand objects[22] (Museum of Fine Arts, Boston), many acquired at the source of manufacture, Morse was the West's leading expert in the field and one of the few who actually visited the sites where the pottery was made. He was not, however, an aesthete and became openly contemptuous of what he saw as the highly subjective, ahistorical, and changeable tastes of Western connoisseurs. For Morse, the question of aesthetic excellence was not only irrelevant but offensive.[23]

In spite of his passion for empirical analysis, Morse's writings are strewn with testy value judgments that reveal his deeper sentiments, while shedding light on the forces at play among the Japanophiles. Citing a legendary Japanese antiquarian who devoted his life to preserving and documenting for posterity "any art or accomplishment that might be going out of the world," Morse became almost obsessed with the deleterious effect westernization was having on Japanese culture. He wrote that "nothing can be of greater importance than the study of those nations and peoples who are passing through profound changes ... as a result of their compulsory contact with the vigorous, selfish, and mercantile nations of the West."[24]

Morse shared the values of art-reform critics who found in Japan a suitable model for their cause. Morse's firsthand observations of Japan provided fuel for his ever more corrosive assaults on Western interior design and modes of manufacturing. Lauding the Japanese for an aesthetic based not on conspicuous display and wealth but on simplicity and nature, Morse noted that in Japan a "comfortable house, fit for the habitation of a family of four or five," may be built cheaply. The Japanese family lived "without the slightest ostentation" and with a refinement unknown in the West.[25] In a barbed comparison he further added that the "monstrous bills for carpets, curtains, furniture, silver, dishes ... often entailed upon young housekeepers at home ... are social miseries that the Japanese happily know but little about." He described

rooms in America encumbered with chairs, bureaus, tables, bedsteads, workstands ... dusty carpets and suffocating wall-paper ... tables with carved cherubs .... against whose absurd contours one knocks his legs ... carpets which have depicted ... a simpering and reddened maiden being made love to by an equally ruddy shepherd.... [These are] hardly proper surfaces to tread upon with comfort, though one may take a certain grim delight in wiping his soiled boots upon them.[26] Morse was unambiguous in concluding that "the Japanese show infinitely greater refinement in their methods of house-adornment than we do."[27] That the arts and architecture of Japan would appeal to such a sensibility helps explain how the Japan idea grew.

Morse acknowledged Japan's immense popular appeal. As the person who coined the phrase "the Japan craze," Morse was refreshingly evenhanded in acknowledging the range of its impact and applications. He described how the arts of Japan "at first so little understood modified our own methods of ornamentation until frescoes and wallpapers, wood-work and carpets, dishes and table-cloths, metal work and book-covers, christmas cards and even railroad advertisements were decorated, modelled and designed after the Japanese style."[28]

Twenty years after Commodore Perry's historic encounter, however, most Americans knew little and cared less about the remote island nation. With few exceptions Japan remained a minor footnote in an American's education in world history and art. This changed emphatically and dramatically in 1876.

The coincidence of Japan's emergence with the great age of international expositions made it possible for Japan to sell itself to the West with efficiency and style. Where aesthetes and intellectuals marveled at the *Japanese Court*, tucked away in a corner of the London Exhibition of 1862, Japan's presence at subsequent world's fairs was extravagant and conspicuous. Although *japonisme* is usually cited as beginning with the French artist Felix Bracquemond's "discovery" of the color woodblock prints of Hokusai, which circulated among his Parisian art circle in 1855, Japanese art did not reach France in force until after the Paris Exposition of 1867. Intercourse between Japan and the West was relatively insignificant until after the Meiji Restoration in 1868 and only then would the Japan craze take root and blossom.

The next great international exposition and the first where the Japanese government organized a formal display was Vienna in 1873. Vienna is important from an American perspective because it was the world's fair up and running while the United States was planning the exposition that commemorated its centennial. The United States Centennial Commission sent representatives to Vienna to study everything from toilet facilities and security to the specifications and types of exhibit buildings and the problems of financing.[27] Records of the London Exhibition of 1862 were also studied so that the commission was well prepared when formal planning began. Thirty months before opening day the challenge must have looked at least as awesome to the commissioners looking ahead as their achievement appears to us in looking back.

The Centennial's role as a watershed in American life has not been overstated. Contemporary observers were quite aware of the profound affect so great a concentration of international commerce and culture might have on the nation. A journalist for the *Philadelphia Inquirer* noted that the Centennial exposition had "stirred up the sluggish blood of dwellers in the backwoods" and great cities by introducing "more cosmopolitan ideas." "The pulse of this new life," the journalist continued, "can be felt in the nation's veins.... The millions who have visited Philadelphia this year, many of whom were never out of their native villages before, will not be content to go home and sink into another twenty years' sleep."[30] And awakened they were. Centennial fever induced a flurry of new enterprises, and more than any other event of the century was the impetus behind America's new-found competitiveness and the booming market for consumer goods and art products.

Japan's participation at the Centennial has been neatly chronicled by Dallas Finn, who cited it as the event that fixed Japan in the national consciousness.[31] Japan's exhibits were characterized by good planning, broad ambitions, backstage machinations, and good luck. Planning for the Centennial did not get underway quickly or smoothly. Although Congress authorized a celebration of the nation's one hundreth anniversary in 1871, invitations to exhibiting nations were not sent out until 1873, and as late as 1875 few of the participants had registered their plans. Japan's Centennial Commission, however, was organized as a department of the Ministry of the Interior, which enjoyed strong political and financial backing from the new Meiji government, and English and American advisors were selected to assist the commission in assessing Western tastes. From the outset Japan's goal was unmistakably commercial. Although anxious for recognition, Japan was even more determined to make sales and develop markets for its export goods.

With the experience of Vienna behind it, Japan's Centennial Commission lobbied manufacturers to increase production of items suitable for sale and display in the United States. Within a year of agreeing to participate, Japan had opened an office in Philadelphia to coordinate operations in the United States. Already assigned more than fourteen thousand square feet in the main exhibition building, the Japanese approached the Centennial's general manager about obtaining an acre of land "for the erection of Japanese houses to be used as a bazaar for the sale of Japanese goods." Mindful of the prestige in a good location, a separate appeal conveyed Japan's desire for land near the British buildings.[32]

Although the exact scope of activity can only be surmised, it appears that artisans and manufacturers throughout Japan threw themselves into the production of exhibition-quality goods. How this may have affected the structure of Japan's art-products industry is uncertain, but it is known that Japan's exhibit at the Centennial included goods that were created specifically with the American market in mind. It is, therefore, likely that a certain amount of reorganization of the industry was required.

Reporting in October 1875 to John A. Bingham, the American foreign minister in Tokyo, Japan's minister of foreign affairs boasted of his nation's success at collecting "natural and artificial products of the whole country" and "encouraging its people to exhibit their skill upon fine work for the exhibition." As many as thirty thousand "products of the provinces," valued at $222,000 (equal to about six million in 1990), were amassed, together with $30,000 in exhibit materials from Japan's department of education. An additional $300,000 was budgeted for staff, display, and materials for two entire buildings to be shipped around the world. Although the Meiji government coordinated the efforts, only about one-eighth of the budget was government funded. The rest was drawn from private sources, including more than two hundred exhibitors.[33] The total freight was estimated at thirteen hundred tons, an amount so great that Bingham felt the need to ask the American shipping industry to help with the expense. The Pacific Mail Steamship Co. offered to carry Japan's freight across the ocean at half the normal rate while the Central Pacific Railroad Co. volunteered to ship the goods from their point of entry at San Francisco free of charge![34] As America ushered in the new year, its grand celebration was shaping up to be a real sensation. Japan's full-throttle involvement was one of the things that would make this exposition special, the most spectacular the world had yet seen.

Media coverage of the Centennial began long before its May opening. Newspapers from across the nation dispatched writers who filed weekly dispatches on the exhibits and events. The Japanese made great copy almost from the moment they arrived. In February *Frank Leslie's Illustrated Newspaper* featured "scenes and incidents" from the Japanese building site on the Centennial grounds.[35] Illustrations depicted Japanese workmen in traditional dress preparing meals, studying books and charts, assembling a house frame, warming their hands around a fire, and sawing and finishing timbers with archaic tools. Spectators crowded around the site to watch in amazement as buildings were raised and assembled by methods as foreign and primitive as the buildings themselves.

Almost two hundred structures were crowded into the northwest corner of Philadelphia's Fairmont Park (fig. 9). What an astonishing vista this must have presented. Here was a spectacle, a panoramic survey of all that was new and exciting: art, cuisine, furnishings, architecture, machinery, exotic horticulture, and folk life from around the world. Some of America's boldest and most innovative manufacturers of glass, iron stoves, and sewing machines erected independent buildings to showcase their achievements. Others exhibited their products in dramatic, architectural displays in the main exhibition building. An avenue along the northwest corner of the grounds was lined with exhibit buildings sponsored by the various American states, each spending extravagantly to outdo the others and dazzle foreign and native visitors. The architecture was eclectic and colorful. There was high Gothic for Pennsylvania and the Italian-villa style for New York. Connecticut erected a neo-colonial saltbox, while Mississippi adopted a rustic Polynesian theme; a log cabin built of sixty-eight different woods native to Mississippi, eaves fringed with moss, and a balcony made from the natural, unfinished roots and limbs of trees. The Avenue of the States was one of the most exciting attractions at the Centennial, which undoubtedly fueled the sense of pride and competitiveness. A century had not cured Americans of their fierce state and local pride, and this sparring for eminence became a notable subtext for the festivities.

Japan was prominently represented in four separate locations on the Centennial grounds, in the main and agricultural buildings and in two traditional structures shipped from Japan and assembled onsite the winter before. The dwelling house (fig. 10) of the Japanese Centennial Commission and exhibits staff occupied a prominent location and was widely admired as an example of Japan's traditional housing. Its lower story of open latticework screening and its roof covered with black and white tiles presented an architectural novelty unlike anything in America. In spite of complaints, the Japanese dwelling was not open for public viewing. Centennial visitors had to content themselves with other Japanese exhibits, like the Japanese Bazaar (fig. 11).

The bazaar was conceived as a commercial enterprise and was stocked with goods by a consortium of unidentified Japanese merchants. Even the most prized and spectacular of the Japanese exhibits were eventually sold, and at least one critic

(9) Birdseye view of Centennial exhibition, 1875
Lithographic print
Philadelphia, Pennsylvania
Drawn by THEODORE POLENI
Printed by THOMAS HUNTER
Watkinson Library, Trinity College

This view of the Centennial grounds was produced more than a year before the exhibition opened in hopes of attracting exhibitors from the American states and around the world. By opening day in May 1876, the grounds filled up. A year earlier, the Centennial Commission was able to provide a preview of the major state sponsored buildings, including Agricultural Hall, Machinery Hall, the Ladies Pavilion, Horticultural Hall, and the Main Building.

(10) Japanese dwelling, Philadelphia Centennial Exposition, 1876
Lithographic print
Philadelphia, Pennsylvania
Published by THOMAS HUNTER
Courtesy of The Athenaeum of Philadelphia

(11) Japanese bazaar, Philadelphia Centennial Exposition, 1876
Lithographic print
Philadelphia, Pennsylvania
Published by THOMAS HUNTER
Courtesy of The Athenaeum of Philadelphia

(12) Japanese pavilion, Philadelphia Centennial Exposition, 1876

(13 a) Folding fan, 1876
Paper on bamboo ribs
Japan
Wadsworth Atheneum

(13 b) Folding fan, 1876
Paper on bamboo ribs
Japan
New Hampshire Historical Society

Folding fans were favorite souvenirs of the many visitors to the Japanese bazaar at the Centennial. Several versions were available, all made in Japan. These fans were especially appealing because they were affordable, portable, and fancifully decorated in the Japanese taste.

condemned Japan's conspicuous price tags. Although the contents of the bazaar were not judged as were the exhibits in the main building, most Centennial visitors found it an ideal source of affordable trinkets and souvenirs. An illustration of the interior of the bazaar (fig. 12) shows hanging paper lanterns above tables decked with bronze figures and walls lined with paper fans. Standing on the floor were an assortment of folding screens. Reviews also cited ivories, gold lacquer, porcelain, and bamboo canes – goods considerably cheaper and less ostentatious than those featured in the main building.[36] Although sales figures are unknown, souvenir fans made especially for the Centennial (fig. 13 a,b) are so common in museum collections today that it would not be surprising to learn than one hundred thousand or more were sold. Surrounded by a bamboo fence on grounds appointed with a lotus pool, stone lanterns, enormous bronze sculptures of storks, and bansai trees, the Bazaar (fig. 14) offered a comfortable spot to sit, drink tea, and scan shelves filled with a seemingly inexhaustible supply of art goods and merchandise. Americans mingled with their Japanese hosts, whose cleanliness and patient service contrasted with other Centennial concessionaires.[37]

Japan's most dazzling accomplishment was its display in the main building. This building was the Centennial's major focal point and certainly as grand a structure as stood anywhere in America on opening day in 1876. Exceeding one-third of a mile in length and 464 feet wide, the building was erected at a cost of $1.6 million and covered more than twenty-one acres of exhibition space![38] If the stakes were high for the world's competing nations, this was the arena in which their sparring occurred.

Draping their seventeen thousand square feet of space with intersecting rows of colorful sixteen-lobed chrysanthemum banners and bunting, Japan's Centennial Commission staged a dramatic and novel exhibit (fig. 15). At its center stood a raised octagonal platform with an enormous pyramid of porcelain vases (color plate 4) and a bronze fountain. Cases were stuffed with the most elaborate examples of Japanese metalsmithing, including urns and fountains, lidded cups, and the inevitable stork mounted on the back of a turtle. In the adjoining aisles were cases of exquisite black lacquer, intricately carved ivory, an enormous Western-style wardrobe made of ebony, carved to

(14) Japanese bazaar, Philadelphia Centennial Exposition, 1876
photograph

(15) Empire of Japan exhibit, Philadelphia Centennial
Exposition, 1876
Main Exhibition Hall
photograph
Philadelphia Centennial Archives

Selling Japan in the West: The Centennial and Beyond 37

(plate 4-color reproduction, page 188)
Pair of covered jars, 1875
Decorated porcelain
Arita, Japan
Koransha porcelain works
Ichiryusai Uchimatsu, decorator
Wadsworth Atheneum

These enormous jars were purchased from the Japanese exhibition at the Centennial by Elizabeth Colt, then involved in forming collections for display in her Hartford mansion, "Armsmear." The stunning size and dazzling gilt-accented decoration showcase the flawless workmanship characteristic of the Japanese decorative arts on display at the Centennial. Eager to make a lasting and favorable impression, the Japanese commissioned large-scale pieces, such as these, exclusively for the fair. The jars were manufactured by the Koransha porcelain factory in Arita, Japan, which later emerged as a major exporter of art goods bound for the United States.

resemble stands of bamboo and lotus flowers (fig. 16). With the West anxious to enlarge its vocabulary of naturalistic ornament, Japanese art was a revelation that provided a new visual language of birds, animals, sea creatures, and flowers. Monkeys and dragons, cranes and chickens, elephants and eagles, chrysanthemums and cherry blossoms; these are just a few of the motifs that Americans discovered at the Japanese display.

The press responded with predictable inconsistency. Some writers were awed by the achievements of a primitive and isolated "heathen" nation. More responded by mocking or giggling at anything foreign or strange. America may have been flush with money, but it was still extremely homogenous and culturally immature.

Victorian Americans, well acquainted with vigorous ornament and eclectic design, were nonetheless unprepared for so large a body of material so new and different. Reviewers introduced readers to the basics of Japanese craft while citing prestigious patronage. A writer for Philadelphia's *Public Ledger* described Japan's pottery as "some of the most gigantic and elaborate pieces" at the Centennial and noted that a "case containing a representative collection of . . . Japanese pottery has just been purchased for the South Kensington Museum, London" at a cost of $4,000.[39]

Japan fanned the flames of public enthusiasm by issuing an English-language catalog (fig. 17) that spoke directly to Western perceptions and prejudices. So what if Japan's image did not accord with its reality, the image is what sold. In a flattering echo of Victorian art critics then pounding for reforms, the catalog noted that "the Japanese artisan is still very much like those of medieval Europe working in his own peculiar way, assisted only by a very few assistants, and being himself both artist and artisan." In noting that "very few workshops" in Japan employed "more than 30 or 40 persons" and that "heavy machinery . . . is not used," Japan's Centennial Commission painted a picture of unspoiled innocence, ideally matched to the reform initiatives then taking root throughout the West.[40]

Here it was in a nutshell, the gospel of anti-modernism being mirrored back at its preachers. The glorification of the small-shop craftsman and the implication that the machine age, with its

(16) "Selections From The Japanese Exhibit" (Appleton's) *Art Journal*, 1876

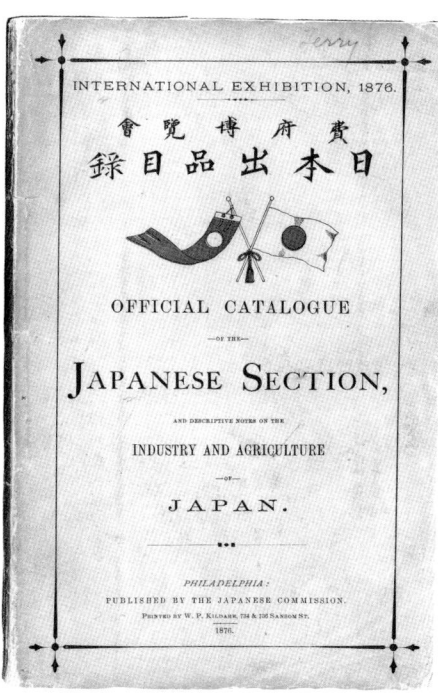

(17) Exhibition catalog, 1876
Japanese Section, Centennial Exposition
Philadelphia, Pennsylvania
Wadsworth Atheneum

This catalog, complete with a map of Japan, an essay on Japanese art, and a description and floor plan of the Japanese exhibit in the main building of the Centennial, is a rare and important document. The catalog belonged to Stephen Terry, a Hartford ceramics collector, whose annotated notes in the margins document the impact of the Japanese exhibit on America's early collectors.

(18) Pair of monumental vases, about 1890
Cloisonné enamel
Japan
Wadsworth Atheneum

This enormous pair of cloisonné vases was used as furnishings in a late-nineteenth-century Hartford mansion and is representative of the most garish and monumental products made in Japan for the American market. No exact record of purchase survives, but the vases are typical of work made around 1890 and may have been purchased at the World's Columbian Exposition, held in Chicago in 1893.

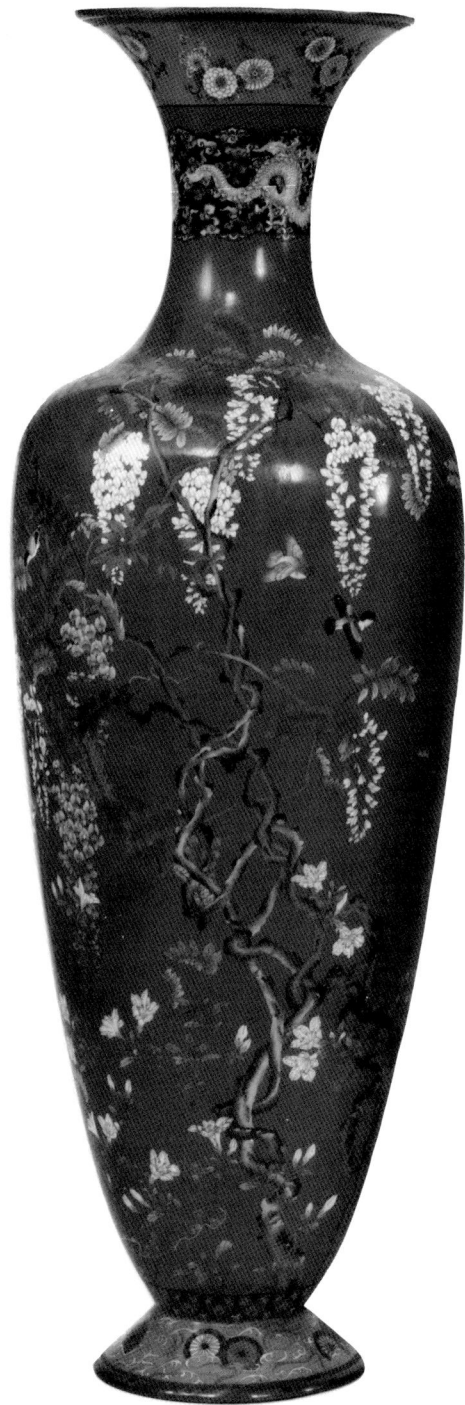

did not own one. Asserting that "Japanese paper fans … are largely superseding the fans manufactured in other countries," Vantine stocked "over five hundred different styles," a fact given perspective when one realizes that, however slightly they might vary, the Japanese fan industry strenuously avoided repetition of design. Artistic fans, even cheap ones, were never two alike.

Vantine stocked folding screens, decorative hanging wall scrolls, the still popular reed curtains for porch use, paper lanterns galore, paper umbrellas up to 18 feet in diameter!, toys and dolls and – my favorite – a category called novelties which included a wire-and-silk "spider and web." Had enough? Vantine also operated a silks and upholstery department that offered yard goods, custom-work and standard lines of curtains, table covers, piano scarfs, portieres, kimonos, and "gents' smoking jackets." That is not to mention a full line of baskets and cheap lacquer boxes.

Here it was, one-stop shopping at its best, the whole cornucopia of Japanese art goods spilling out at Broadway and 18th. A.A. Vantine & Co. was one of almost two dozen Japanese import houses in New York alone. It dominated the middle market and thus is perfectly emblematic of the Japan craze at its apogee.

The Japan craze would not have taken off without the critical support of the art-book and periodicals industry. The explosive growth in art publishing during the 1870s and 80s parallels the Japan craze, and they were mutually reinforcing. Both depended on an increasingly status-conscious, culturally insecure, and affluent middle class, determined to join the consumer revolution begun by their counterparts in Europe. Prescriptive literature on fine and industrial art and home furnishings overflows with insecurity about appearances, the right look or gesture, the right manners and mores, and, of course, the right furnishings and wallpaper. As late Victorians fine-tuned their awareness of status markers and etiquette, the gulf between urban and rural, elite and pedestrian, and polished and unpolished widened, creating tremendous anxiety and pressure on those close to the margin. Enter an arsenal of how-to books and equally didactic but less pandering literature meant to furnish the reader with the trappings of this new "aesthetic" culture.[61] The art-publishing industry was the medium, and the Japan idea was the message.

The Japanophiles like Alcock, Morse, Dresser, and Griffis built their reputations by strategic use of the media. They were not alone. Jane Converse Brown, whose unpublished dissertation is the single best source on the relationship between art publishing and the Japan craze has compiled some astonishing statistics.[62] In a painstaking survey of late Victorian periodicals she analyzed 2,882 items of literature on the Japanese style and art movement and, based on the frequency of new entries, identified the period 1885-1889 as the "height the 'craze'" which "peaked in 1889 with 186 references."[63] That was a lot of coverage a century ago – it would be even now when, despite tremendous growth, the art-publishing industry was small compared with today. Articles by American and British art critics, artists, travel writers and cultural pundits blanketed America's enormous reading public in the comfort of the Japan idea.

Art magazines, founded mostly between 1874 and 1884, were the most persistent in promoting Japanese art. *The Decorator and Furnisher, The Art Amateur,* (Appleton's) *Art Journal, The Art Interchange, American Architect and Building News,* and *American Art Review* were popular American entries in an increasingly vital Anglo-American periodical trade. Better circulating variety magazines and women's magazines like *Harper's Bazaar, Godey's Lady's Book, Century, Scribner's Monthly, Frank Leslie's Illustrated Weekly Newspaper, Saturday Magazine,* and *Atlantic Monthly* brought the Japan idea into hundreds of thousands of American households, diversifying its audience with features that touched issues as widely ranging as children's education and moral reform to pottery collecting and the competitiveness of American industry. Even *Scientific American,* which then billed itself as "a weekly journal of practical information, art, science, mechanics, chemistry and manufacturers," jumped on the bandwagon. Indeed, some of the most interesting features on Japan, Japanese technology, and American industrial arts were first published there.

Books on Japan and Japanese art circulated widely and included some of the most lavishly illustrated and expensively printed books of their era. A recent bibliography lists more than one hundred books in English and French published during the nineteenth century, and this does not include domestic-advice books, travel guides, histories, and related literature.[64] Although information on print runs and distribution is unavailable, the works that turn up or are cited most frequently today include Aime Humbert's *Japan and the Japanese* (1874), James J. Jarves's *Glimpse of the Art of Japan* (1876), William Elliot Griffis's *Mikado's Empire* (1877), Sir Rutherford Alcock's *Art and Industries in Japan* (1878), Thomas W. Cutler's *A Grammar of Japanese Ornament* (1880), Christopher Dresser's *Japan: Its Architecture, Art, and Art Manufacturers* (1882), George Ashdown Audsley's *Ornamental Arts of Japan* (1883), Edward S. Morse's *Japanese Homes and Their Surroundings* (1886), Sir Edwin Arnold's *Japonica* (1892), Felix Ragamey's *Japan in Art and Industry* (1893), and a breathtaking ten-volume deluxe work titled *Japan: Described and Illustrated by the Japanese. Written by Eminent Japanese Authorities and Scholars* (1897-1898). All these titles were widely available in the United States, and even the French and English publications were reprinted here.

Domestic-advice books and women's art manuals, although not primarily about Japanese art, inevitably referred to it in the most explicit and reverential tones. As a genre of literature that flourished in the United States, books like Walter Smith's *Examples of Household Taste* (1876), Constance Cary Harrison's *Women's Handiwork in Modern Homes* (1882), Clarence Cook's *The House Beautiful* (1878), and George Ward Nichols's *Art Education Applied to Industry* (1878) played a major role in selling the Japan idea to elite and middle-class America.

In the extreme the promotion of Japan's art culture spawned a mania for travel to Japan. Although American-Japanese tourism was inconsequential until the late 1880s, the published travelogues of artists and writers and the creation of Western tourist amenities led to a boom in Asian travel during the 1890s. The fact that the middle class embraced the Japan idea did not prevent elites from creating their own status system. Collecting rare and unusual art objects was the ultimate status marker of the day. Traveling to Asia, in 1890!? Very chic and very expensive.

Anyone familiar with the ambience of a flea market can picture the image suggested by the traveler who in 1893 wrote:
not until you reach Japan do you discover what the craze for Japanese "curios" really is. The second thought, if not the first, of almost every globe-trotter who comes to the land of the Morning Sun, is to procure some Japanese artistic antiquities, either to add to the beauty and interest of his own home or to excite the envy of other collectors....When two tourists meet almost the first question they put to each other is "have you bought much?" Everybody buys something.[65]

Murray's *Handbook for Travellers in Japan*, a sort of Victorian *Michelin* guide, suggests just how expansive the amenities for Western tourists to Meiji Japan had become. For tourists that like to experience foreign cultures without giving up any of their familiar customs and comforts, Yokohama, the traditional port of entry for all foreign vessels, was a delight. A veritable theme park of Japonica, Yokohama was the perfect mix of East and West. In seventy pages of advertisements, Murray's *Handbook* provides a keyhole glimpse of this intriguing hybrid environment. Resort hotels that looked like they were plucked out of the White Mountains in New Hampshire were operated by a dizzying mix of French, British, American, and Japanese proprietors. There were also exporters and retailers galore, banks, porcelain factory outlets, silver and silverplate, bookstores, photographic studios, and western-style pharmacies. In Kyoto, the favorite destination for art collectors, a dozen dealers in art goods placed advertisement in Murray's.[66] Clearly, the ultimate act at the height of the Japan craze was to go there and shop like mad.

III. American Taste and the Arts of Japan

The Japan idea revolved around a constellation of objects that Victorian Americans described as "art." So completely were these things associated with the popular notion of art that Japan took on an almost metaphorical identity. At the height of the Japan craze few would have denied that Japan = art. What was this stuff that caused all the commotion? We've seen a little of it at the Centennial and in the various ceramic, bronze, and paper objects at A.A. Vantine & Co. But don't go to the library and take out a book on Japanese art if you want to see what Victorian America saw, because what present-day Japanophiles call Japanese art bears little resemblance to what Victorians saw when they crossed the threshold of Vantine's.

The elimination of export wares from the history of Japanese art was not an occurrence unique to that field of study. Having criticized what I call the "scorched-earth" policy of modernism – the entrenched and institutionalized ideology of traditional art history – I was pleased to come across a recent essay by Robert Rosenblum that articulates the forces at work behind the bowdlerization of nineteenth-century art in all fields. Arguing the case in an introduction to the collection at the new and controversial Musée d'Orsay in Paris, he summarized the formerly suppressed but still shocking story of the advent of modern art. Describing it as a "civil war between avant-garde and conservative factions that was fought and won by the partisans of Modernism," Rosenblum cites the creation of a "noble dynastic table" that "vigorously rejected and often maligned . . . what appeared irrelevant to their cause."[67] Ahistorical, anticultural, and, ultimately, just plain antisocial, the orthodoxy of modernism was one of absolutes in which diversity of taste was intolerable. Once in command, the adherents of modernism laid waste to everything that did not conform to their rigid system of values. "They reduced to nearly invisible rubble the infinite acres and tons of art that, at its best, presumably led nowhere and was therefore inconsequential and, at its worst, . . . actively impeded the triumphal course of Modernism."

What has this got to do with Japanese art? Everything. The Japan idea, at least the Victorian's idea of Japanese art, was mangled, manipulated, and suppressed by the modernists. Talk about scorched earth! Only one of the three major Japanese collections assembled by Victorian art museums (Metropolitan Museum of Art, New York) is still intact, and even there the early accessions are rarely shown. The two other great collections (Museum of Fine Arts, Boston and the Philadelphia Museum of Art) have been pillaged, their contents neglected and dispersed, and their memory nearly expunged from the record. Since collecting Japanese art was one of the major goals of American art museums during the nineteenth century, it is small wonder that the best treasures – the material that epitomized the Japan idea – found its way early into public collections. It is hard to believe that it is now almost impossible to find any of the tens of thousands of Japanese art objects that remained in the United States after the Centennial. The fact that American and British museums engaged in collection building at the Centennial suggests what the accession records at Boston and Philadelphia confirm with agonizing clarity: the best of what Victorians saw in Japanese art entered the public domain, only to be abandoned and discarded once the Japan craze ran its course.[68]

The triumph of fine arts over applied, industrial, and decorative arts was an important facet of the modernist agenda. James McNeill Whistler's often quoted battle cry of "art for art's sake" was a frontal assault on the whole notion of industrial art with its commercial overtones and implied subordination of aesthetics. For most educated Americans art was industrial and decorative art. The thought of separating the aesthetic quality of art from its moral and utilitarian functions would have struck Victorians as bizarre. And yet, the fact that the Japan idea was embodied in the decorative arts did not stop modernists from adopting it as inspiration for an aesthetic ideology that repudiated decorative art. Having devoured the message the modernists killed off the parent and kidnapped the child.

The dominance of decorative arts in the discussions of the arts of Japan is indicated by turning to Sir Rutherford Alcock's *Catalogue of Works of Industry and Art, Sent from Japan* (1862), which described objects displayed at London's international exposition of 1862. Prints and paintings, listed in the seventh of nine categories, were clumped together with carvings in wood and ivory.[69]

Japanese decorative arts hit all the hot buttons with Victorian Americans. For those who feared that industrialization was undermining the secular cult of progress, Japanese art provided a perfect antidote to the West's suffering and pointed the way for reform. The Japan idea was in essence the idea of anti-modernism and reform.

It is no coincidence that the qualities attributed to the arts of Japan were opposite to those found in western art of the time. Beaming with innocent ethnocentricity, Victorian literature on Japanese art projects a highly romanticized, almost mythical image. Recognized in hindsight as a distorted picture of the economy of art production in Meiji Japan, this literature is as revealing for what it says about Victorian aspirations as for its teaching about the real Japan. The attributes assigned to Japanese art are those already associated with England's heroic medieval past, which art-reform critics began actively promoting even before their encounter with Japan. Small wonder that the British architect William Burges was quick to point out similarities between Japanese principles of design and Britain's medieval style, when he reviewed the *Japanese Court* at the London exposition of 1862.[70] American critics also associated Japanese art with a mythic past, one of whom suggested a comparison with the pilgrim fathers. In essence the Japan idea was more about confirming traditional values than creating new ones.

Western critics believed Japanese art was the product of a moral economy characterized by small family shops and labor practices that validated the dignity of the individual worker. It was an ethic that opposed specialization and the division of labor. The unity of art and artisanry, variation in ornament, and the use of traditional tools and technologies became positively charged. The Japan idea developed into a kind of shorthand for the affirmation of tradition. As one writer put it "conservatism and hatred of innovation are inborn characteristics of the Japanese."[71] For those afraid that Western progress had gone too far, these were exactly the qualities desired.

The British design theorist Christopher Dresser in his influential writings on Japanese art explored the relationship between Shinto, Japan's native religion, and the ideals of artisanry. Dresser explained Japanese art as a natural expression of its religion, a religion that venerated constancy and tradition, openness and honesty. Citing the symbol of the mirror – the "great emblem of the Shinto religion" – Dresser explained that the principle where "thoughts and actions should be open and visible" was "rigidly carried out in the construction of every Shinto temple" and in all Japanese art. "Honest workmanship" was manifest in "all good Japanese works," which "are as well finished in the parts that are unseen as in the parts that are seen." "Here is a tray," he continued, "on the under surface of which is a spray [of flowers] as carefully drawn as the figures on the upper surface." Noting the influence of Buddhism in "that strange love of all created things which characterizes the Japanese," Dresser defined the "harmony between man and the lower creatures" as the foundation of Japan's natural ornamental style.[72]

Western reformers attributed declining standards of art to the dehumanizing conditions of labor. From the small, single-proprietor craft shops of the preindustrial era had emerged the modern factory with its time cards, mind-numbing repetition, and division of labor. Small wonder that the old ways, now splendidly reaffirmed in the discovery of Japanese art, would be invoked as a new standard. George Audsley summed it up by describing "the conditions under which the old artists and artificers cultivated their special talents" as "those most favorable to the production of perfect works of art." "Free from all cares," the Japanese artisan "expended the most loving care upon each object.... Time was of no account to them; and their masters were well content to watch the gradual development of ideas.... It was under such circumstances that all the great artists worked for centuries prior to the suppression of the feudal system." In Japan "the artist and workman are one individual, and the mind and hand go together in all he does."[73]

Edward Morse, in an acerbic aside, railed at the comparison between American and Japanese artisanry:

A somewhat extended experience with the common everyday carpenter at home leads me to say ... that in matters pertaining to their craft the Japanese carpenters are superior. . . . Not only do they show their superiority in their work, but in their versatile ability in making new things.... It is a notorious fact that most of the carpenters in our smaller towns ... are utterly incompetent to carry out any special demand made upon them ... in most cases their fathers were not carpenters, nor will their children be; and herein alone the Japanese carpenter has an immense advantage over the American, for his trade, as well as other trades, have been perpetuated through generations of families.... When I see one of our carpenter's ponderous tool-chests ... and contemplate the work often done with them ... and then recall the Japanese carpenter with his ridiculously light and flimsy tool-box ... [I am] forced to the conviction that civilization and modern appliances count as nothing unless accompanied with a moiety of brains and some little taste and wit. It is a very serious fact that now-a-days no one in our country is acquiring faithfully the carpenter's trade ... due to the fact that machine-work has supplanted the hand-work of former times.[74]

The idea of Japan as a living medieval culture was an important factor in gaining acceptance for its art. As early as the Centennial Japan recognized the power of this argument. Even though it contradicted their campaign of westernization, Japan's promotional material emphasized the antiquated, preindustrial roots of its art economy: "The Japanese artisan is still very much like those of medieval Europe, working in his own peculiar way, assisted only by a very few assistants, and being himself both artist and artisan. This of course has had the fortunate effect of preserving to the industrial productions their striking features of originality."[75]

Christopher Dresser, one of the first Western critics to visit Japan, applauded the diversity and skill of the Japanese artisan noting that "the potter who 'throws' the clay generally turns it, bakes it, glazes it, and ... decorates it." He observed "as much pride ... manifested by the maker in completing a little cup, [or] a lacquer box ... as there is in one of our great artists contemplating an historical painting."[76] For reformers like Dresser, money and commerce were the corrupting influence, and no great art could be produced by time-serving artisans: "There is a vast difference between toil undergone for the sake of mere money-making, and the production of the most perfect works of which man is capable. No thought of gain enters the mind of the great artist while he is engaged upon his work.... In buying from [a Japanese artisan] ... I found that he could not count money, and that he had little or no idea of its value."[77] How accurately this idealistic image conveys the reality of art production in Meiji Japan is questionable. What is certain is that antimaterialism and anti-industrial rhetoric was a central component of the Japan idea.

As important as the ideology were the goods, which Victorians praised without reserve. Recognizing that industrial arts and household furnishings had almost eclipsed the fine arts as a focus of critical interest it comes as no surprise that Japanese arts in wood, metal, lacquer, ceramic, and textiles occupied center stage throughout the Japan craze. James Jackson Jarves, the American expatriate art critic and son of a New England glass manufacturer, asserted the preeminence of decorative arts in the arts of Japan, noting, "Statuary, in the European meaning of the word, they do not possess anymore than they do easel paintings or fine architecture."[78] What Jarves and his contemporaries found instead was "an understanding and knowledge of the capabilities of materials greater than that of any European people, ... an artistic paradise of an original character, which

Europe does not rival," and an extraordinary "tendency in Japanese artists to cope with mechanical difficulty."[79]

Victorian art critics gushed with enthusiasm: "No other race understands better the vital exigencies of ornamentation, or is more skillful in manual practice." The arts of Japan exhibit "absolute excellence, rare invention, pure taste, accurate finish, [and] entire adaptability," especially when contrasted with the West. "Our homes are crammed with inappropriate objects, neither useful nor beautiful.... Money is worse than thrown away in heaps of uncomfortable trash ... wrongly conceived, structurally ... false as regards grammar of ornament, ... [and] meretriciously ugly."[80]

The moral superiority of Japan's art economy was linked with a profound sensitivity to the natural world which amazed Americans only recently awakened to the beauty of their own land. Artists of the Hudson River school espoused the divinity of nature and became intense observers of their surroundings. But nothing in the experience of Western artists prepared them for the depth of engagement with nature exhibited in Japanese art. Japanese artists were described as "very close observers of the habits and customs of smaller animals, such as birds, fish, insects, etc."[81] The artist "watches the birds, animals, fishes and insects around him in his village ... and thus the book of nature is translated into decorative art with the freedom and fidelity which has so astonished the Western world.... The habit of seeing the plants and flowers of nature as they are – not as depicted in books of botany – is one that comes after long, patient, loving study."[82] From Japan the West heard a distant echo of its own growing commitment to truthfulness in art and direct observation of nature. These were the values that would power the impressionist movement on both continents. These were the values in which Japan surpassed all the world.

Americans were fascinated by the symbolism and grammar of ornament in Japanese art. Although many of its decorative motifs and conventions of composition were Chinese in origin, it was Japan that introduced this decorative language to the West during the Meiji period. No other culture at the time was so immutably linked with a specific vocabulary of ornament as the Japanese. Symbols and motifs found over and over again on everything from lacquer trays to silk kimonos emerged as shorthand for the Japan idea. With the exception of complex geometric diapers (diamond-shaped borders), almost all of the motifs found in Japanese art are representations of nature.

The vocabulary of Japanese art is extensive. Through selective imitation, American artists and industrial arts manufacturers helped popularize some motifs more than others. The most frequently used became decorative clichés. Who cannot recall the image of a stork, leg raised with beak drooping, which adorns everything from pottery and piano scarfs to advertising cards and window panes in Victorian America? Birds were highly favored by Japanese artists, and in the hands of renowned illustrators like Hokusai they assumed an astonishing range of postures and attitudes. Victorian critics were quick to note how the Japanese lived in harmony with "the lower creatures." Edward Morse observed the Japanese custom of allowing birds to build nests inside their homes! - noting that the "presence of the bird in the house is regarded as a good omen."[83] Even today, it actually does appear that birds and animals are less afraid of people there.

In addition to the ubiquitous cranes and storks we find ravens, wrens, owls, hawks, kingfishers, and assorted geese and waterfowl. Among the fish and sea creatures, wild carp were the most commonly depicted. As a symbol of courage and strength, the image of the carp struggling against a turbulent stream is one of the most enduring in Japanese art. Crabs, lobsters, and tortoises are also commonly depicted, the latter being a symbol of longevity. No other culture has incorporated insect life into its decorative vocabulary as widely as the Japanese. The spider and its web, a motif virtually unknown in Western art, became a popular cliché of the Japan craze. Black flies, dragonflies, and butterflies were also frequently depicted. A plaque or vase encrusted with insect life provided amusement and delight. Although monkeys, bats, and deer appear occasionally as ornament in Japanese art, animals were not as popular in Japan as in the United States and England, where horses and domesticated dogs have been immortalized by artists for centuries.

In all of nature it was the Japanese artist's handling of flowers and trees that had the most enduring impact on the West. The viewing of spring cherry blossoms remains to this day a favorite national pastime in Japan. What intrigued Americans the most was the ornamental value the Japanese assigned to familiar fruit trees – cherry, apple, peach, and plum – usually valued in the West only for their harvest. Americans became so enamored with the Japanese idea of flowering trees and changing foliage that they created their own rituals of leaf peeping and flower-blossom rendering. As recently as the 1910s and 1920s Wallace Nutting – one of America's most prolific art photographers – produced and sold hundreds of thousands of tinted photographs depicting the flowering fruit trees of New England.

Depictions of trees were not restricted to flowering fruit blossoms. The Japanese were also enamored with the pine tree, a symbol of longevity and everlasting youth, the bamboo tree, a symbol of uprightness and usefulness, and the florid coloration of autumn maple leaves. In fact, the Japan craze enlarged America's whole vocabulary of floral decoration. Azaleas, honeysuckles, cattails, lotuses, peonies, morning glories, wisteria, and, of course, chrysanthemums and irises were some of the many flowers that became synonymous with Japanese art. Each season had its symbolic flower, weather patterns, and trees. Depictions of the seasons are some of the strongest images in Japanese art. The subtle shifts in light, color, and foliate plumage, so poignantly expressed in Japanese art, tightened the West's embrace of nature and inspired its commitment to intense and direct observation.

Natural landscape features were carefully observed and depicted. Waterfalls, mountains, ocean waves, clouds, and misty landscapes offered varied ornamental possibilities. Mount Fuji, as symbolic of Japan as the Statue of Liberty is of the United States, was captured from every vantage point, in all seasons, and in every kind of weather. For the impressionist artists of the late nineteenth century, the ability to express a range of moods, atmospheres, and perspectives in one evocative setting validated claims that Japan was the original aesthetic culture.

Finally, but significantly, the Japan idea embraced a rich vocabulary of meteorological phenomenon. Driving rain, lightning, and cracked ice are three motifs that were handled with great sensitivity and imagination by Japanese artists. Indeed, it was the abstract rendering of cracked ice and lightning that introduced fractured picture planes and layered composition to Western art, thus forming a basis for the development of cubism, futurism, and other early experiments with abstraction.[84] The cracked-ice, or crackled-glaze motif was interpreted widely and liberally, emerging during the 1880s as aesthetic shorthand for the whole phenomenon of random occurrence in nature. In the more extreme instances of pure composition and abstraction – the border details on cloisonné and the layers of pattern in woven silks – Japanese art veers sharply away from the tradition of literal representation. Although virtually all Japanese ornament has some basis in nature, the combination of foreshortened perspective, impressionistic rendering, and abstraction provided a door through which the Western artists passed into the modern age.

The compositional conventions of Japanese art were almost totally foreign to the West. Within the tradition of pure representation, a favorite Japanese compositional device was to juxtapose motion against still features in nature. These juxtapositions often became clichés in the hands of Western artists and industrial arts manufacturers. Birds in the grass, netted carp, owls or geese against the full moon, storks in a moving stream, sea waves crashing against the rocks, and a dragon amidst the clouds – these are a few of the most popular representational themes in Japanese art.

The appearance of randomness and accidental effect is one of the most mannered and intriguing compositional devices in Japanese art. What could be more unlike the West's tradition of rationalism and time-work discipline than a society where the artist is described as "a creature of impulse" working "free from all cares?"[85] Like the Renaissance notion of sprezzatura – the art that conceals art, or planned spontaneity – the Japanese reverence for randomness and accidental effect has an oxymoronic quality filled with irony and humor. This quality is most pronounced in the manipulation of ceramics, where ornamentation is controlled through a process of planned accident. Where Britain's nineteenth-century ceramics industry, the world's most developed, prided itself in the perfection of repeatable standards of excellence, Japanese potters took advantage of chance effects created by combining glazes and by random juxtaposition of ornament. Where factories in the Staffordshire region of England cranked out hundreds of each pattern, Japanese potters prided themselves in never repeating themselves. This attitude was expressed in related arts and, indeed, in the whole bourgeois culture depicted in the famed ukiyo-e prints of the floating world.

The debate about how Japanese composition and design were transmitted to the West will not be resolved here. But given the predominance of the decorative arts in the Japan craze and given the fact that many of the compositional conventions associated with Japan's much-heralded woodblock prints were also employed in the crafts, and, finally, given the fact that the artists most interested in Japan tended to collect everything – not just prints – the possibility that decorative arts were the primary medium of transmission must be considered.

For the majority of Americans, a simple fan or a Satsuma vase was all they were likely to see, much less own, in the way of Japanese art goods. Those who attended the Centennial saw more, but woodblock prints were not featured there. It was not until the 1890s that Americans gained ready access to the ukiyo-e prints. Since figural representation is far more prominent in ukiyo-e prints than in the crafts, Japanesque qualities of posture, facial expression, and dress were not as influential at the height of the Japan craze as at the turn of the century when prints were actively collected. But most of the compositional conventions found in prints are also evident in the allied arts: the absence of shading and Western perspective, the bird's-eye vantage point employed in landscapes, the exaggerated spatial extension that renders foreground subjects with an abstract, truncated closeness, the preference for balance over symmetry, the complete invalidation of the Western ideas of borders and frames, and the irregular division of space. Japanese art further invoked a new sense of color. The Western palette of subdued primary colors seemed weak and unexciting when compared with the discordant combinations of secondary and tertiary colors characteristic of Japanese art. Metallic colors, vulgarized by excessive use in Western sculpture and decorative arts, also acquired a new cachet.

To understand Western interpretations of Japanese art, it is important to know what Victorian Americans recognized as Japanese art. Driven to improve the competitiveness of America's industrial arts, it is not surprising that Victorians seemed more interested in craftsmanship and materials than aesthetics. Nineteenth-century literature on Japanese art is frequently arranged by medium: lacquer, bronze casting, ivory and wood carving, fanmaking, etc. With the exception of print collecting, almost nothing in the current literature addresses the question of what Americans actually owned and collected.[86] Since Japanese export objects are still held in low esteem by Asian art scholars, it proved difficult to round up a representative selection of documented works. The objects illustrated here were chosen either because they have a known history of ownership in nineteenth-century America or because they represent the kind of thing illustrated and discussed in nineteenth-century literature on Japanese art. Whenever possible we selected objects for which both conditions apply. Those chosen are not necessarily "the best" of what Meiji Japan produced nor were the owners especially famous. Our goal was to provide as objectively as possible a cross section of what Victorian Americans imagined when they thought of Japanese art.

* * *

Japanese metalwork was described by Victorian critics as "greater than that of any European people" and as "the only perfect metal-works . . . the world has yet produced." Citing patronage of armor and sword manufacturers by Japan's traditional warrior class, metalwork was recognized as one of the premier arts in traditional Japan.[87] Japan's enormous cast bronze sculptures attracted crowds and critical reviews at world's fairs from Vienna to Chicago. Christopher Dresser exclaimed: "The processes employed for the enrichment of metal-work in Japan are more numerous than in any other country. . . . No people but the Japanese have understood the value of colour in metal. . . . In many of their works we see gold, silver, copper, zinc, black-metal, tea-urn bronze, green bronze, and other metals." Of special interest was the Japanese metalsmith's ability to mix metals together in one object using processes such as inlay, applied castings, and mechanical fusion (figs. 19, 20 a,b). Where the West traditionally valued silver and gold for the material, the Japanese were described as "the only people who do not think of the material. . . . To them iron, zinc, bismuth, gold, silver and copper are only so many materials with which things of beauty may be produced."⁸⁸ As we shall see, Japan's metallurgical sophistication caused Western silver manufacturers to completely rethink their craftsmanship and design.

In addition to vases and wall plaques (fig. 21), Japan's metalsmiths produced enormous cast bronze statuary and intricately worked small sword guards

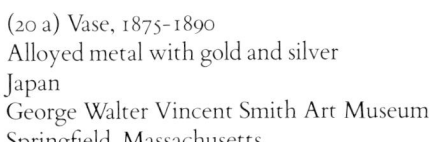

(20 a) Vase, 1875-1890
Alloyed metal with gold and silver
Japan
George Walter Vincent Smith Art Museum
Springfield, Massachusetts

Mixed metal work, a Japanese specialty, symbolized Japan's superiority in metalsmithing. The basic concept of mixed metal was successfully imitated by the American silver manufacturers Tiffany and Gorham. This vase combines metals and alloys to form colorful pictures and patterns never before seen in this country.

(20 b) Vase in shape of bamboo, 1875-1890
Alloyed metals
Japan
George Walter Vincent Smith Art Museum
Springfield, Massachusetts

American craftsmen were impressed and intrigued by their Japanese counterparts' skill and ingenuity. Of particular interest was the Japanese artisan's ability to imitate shapes and textures using different mediums. Here, a bamboo stalk is fashioned out of metal, complete with leaves. Other examples of using one material to suggest another include ceramic "baskets" and woodgrained metals.

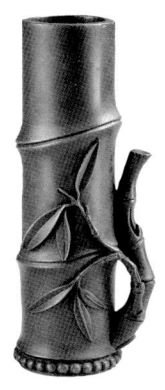

(19) Vase, 1875-1890
Alloyed metal with gold and silver
Japan
George Walter Vincent Smith Art Museum
Springfield, Massachusetts

Japanese artists' metallurgical skills astonished the West. This vase exhibits the technique of inlaying multi-colored metals by a method known as tetsu.

(21) Wall plaque, 1875-1885
Bronze with gilded decoration
Japan
Courtesy of The Brooklyn Museum
Gift of Mr. and Mrs. E.S. Griswold in memory of her father, John Sloane

Bronze was a popular metal, suitable for large sculptures or smaller objects like wall plaques. The Victorians were attracted to naturalistic designs like this jumping carp because they represented a pure regard for nature and a culture untainted by the complications of the industrialized west. This plaque was part of the furnishings of the house built for John Sloane on Fifth Avenue in New York in 1882.

American Taste and the Arts of Japan   53

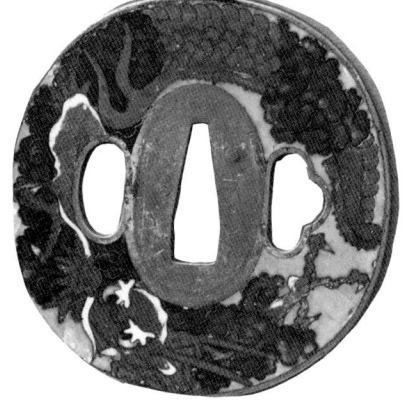

(22) Tsuba, 1870-1890
Mixed metals
Japan
The Walters Art Gallery (top row)
George Walter Vincent Smith Art Museum (middle row)
Wadsworth Atheneum (bottom row)

Tsuba, or sword guards, were ideally suited for curio cabinet displays. Of all the Japanese arts, tsuba best represented the quality of variability that Victorians admired. A collector might own one hundred of them with no two alike. The six shown here were selected to show a range of stylistic types from the simple iron cut-out bamboo guard, to the colorful cloisonné, and the elaborate mixed metal guards.

known as tsuba. Tsubas were lauded by Western critics from the beginning of the Japan craze, but they were not prominently advertised by Japanese export houses and do not appear to have been widely collected until the 1890s. Collections formed toward the end of the Japan craze, notably those of William T. and Henry Walters of Baltimore and George Walter Vincent Smith of Springfield, Massachusetts, contain dozens of tsuba, which their owners mounted on boards and exhibited in glass cases like jewels (fig. 22). With collectors seemingly oblivious to the desecration of swords for their exquisite guards, Japanese metalsmiths eventually entered into the production of tsuba solely to accommodate surging demand. Tsuba were perfect objects for mass accumulation, and Victorians relished the assembling of collections where no two were alike.

Whenever Japan selected art products for public display, bronze castings inevitably took center stage (fig. 23). Critics marvelled at the contrast between the extreme ostentation of the objects and their humble mode of manufacture in workshops described as "no better than ordinary blacksmith's shops."[89] A reviewer at the Centennial praised Japanese cast bronze as "the most marvelous objects here" and described a method of production involving wax models "painted with hundreds of coats" of a sand-and-glue mixture, which, once hardened, served as a mold into which molten bronze was poured for casting.[90] Another report described bronzes "so abounding in the drollest conceits, and the most grotesque shapes of birds, beasts, and human beings . . . that no description of them is possible without . . . engravings or photographs." Japanese hosts informed curious visitors that one of their largest vases involved 2,250 days of steady labor. From the creation of the molds to the finishing off of the casting with chasing, engraving, and polishing, few objects made by man could boast more or better workmanship.[91]

The Japanese metalsmith's emphasis on cheap base metals and alloys such as copper and bronze heightened the Westerner's appreciation for these materials, which they traditionally regarded as only suitable for utilitarian use. Although gold and silver had a place in Japanese metalsmithing, the output of bronze exceeded all other metals combined. The tradition of bronze casting in Japan dated back one thousand years. The bronze family included an

(23) Sculpture and stand, about 1880
Bronze and teak base
Japan
Private Collection

Visitors to both the Centennial Exposition and the 1892 World's Columbian Exposition in Chicago marveled at the monumental bronzes displayed in the Japanese sections. This sculpture was probably exhibited at one of these world's fairs where it was purchased for use in a Boston residence. Supported by seven scaly dragons and embellished with fish, a feathered eagle with outstretched wings, and two pictorial scenes, this piece is a testimony to the highest level of artisanry achieved in Japanese bronze sculpture during the nineteenth century.

(24) Wall plaque, about 1880
Cloisonné enamel
Japan
Courtesy of The Brooklyn Museum
Gift of Mr. and Mrs. William E.S. Griswold in memory of her father, John Sloane

Victorian collectors delighted in the mythical figures depicted in Japanese art. Books such as Henri Joly's Legend in Japanese Art *(1908) helped collectors identify the symbols and figures that abound in Japanese art. As explained in Joly's introduction, "Collectors and lovers of Japanese objets d'art . . . all confess to the attraction exerted upon them by the subjects depicted, the symbolism of the composition, the hidden meaning of some scene." This plaque, which was purchased as part of the furnishings for the Brooklyn townhouse of John Sloane about 1880, shows Fujin, the god of the winds, amid a crack of lightning that forms a sharp diagonal, typical of Japanese decoration.*

astonishing array of alloys: a reddish-purple material called *shakudo,* made of copper mixed with traces of gold and silver; a velvet-textured, silver-gray alloy called *shibuichi;* and a green-tinted alloy called *seido,* made of copper with traces of lead and tin.

Critics lamented what they described as the "degeneration in Japanese art" after the opening of the treaty ports and the abolition of feudalism. After the Meiji Restoration art patronage was transferred from the feudal nobility to a large but less wealthy market of foreign collectors. For more than twenty years the West remained the primary market for Japan's artistic treasures. The so-called relics of feudalism were liquidated by the families of the former nobility, often forced by poverty into selling heirlooms they had possessed for centuries. By the late 1880s the supply of native treasures, once considered unlimited, was nearly exhausted. As native industries began to revive during the late 1870s, Western tastes were accommodated. Yet it is apparent that some of the traditional arts were practiced much as always. Meiji bronze and lacquer, for example, are not easily distinguished from antique work. Both were marketed and collected side by side, and although the more caricatured productions were unquestionably modern hybrids of Japanese and Western taste, even work made "in 'lines' by the gross, to suite the demands of foreign trade," had much in common with traditional work.[92]

Of all the branches of Japanese metalwork, the production of cloisonné, or enameled copper, was the most profoundly affected by trade with the West. Among the traditional arts introduced from China and Korea, cloisonné was one of the least developed during Japan's feudal era. In style and craftsmanship cloisonné remained characteristically Chinese, featuring bright reds and yellows on a turquoise ground, which the Japanese regarded as a "weird combination of absurd colors."[93] For reasons that remain unexplained, the Japanese did an about-face during the early 1870s by embracing and expanding their production of cloisonné vases (color plate 5), plaques (fig. 24), and related Western forms. Influenced by the advice and technical know-how of a consulting chemist named Gottfried von Wagner, Japan transformed its cloisonné industry into a major export enterprise. Wagner later advised the Japanese commissions that prepared exhibits for Vienna and Philadelphia, suggesting that further research into the role of Western advisors

(plate 5-color reproduction, page 189)
Globe-shaped covered jar, about 1890
Cloisonné enamel
Japan
School of Namikawa Yasuyuki (1845–1927)
Wadsworth Atheneum

An original bill of sale from the Hartford art store of A.D. Vorce documents the purchase of this jar by a Hartford collector in 1891. By the 1890s, fine examples of Japanese cloisonné could be purchased in almost any American city. The sides of the jar are decorated with traditional dragon and phoenix motifs, and the cover is circled with butterflies. Namikawa's work is known for superb craftsmanship and minute detail.

(25) Covered jar, about 1880
Cloisonné enamel
Japan
Wadsworth Atheneum

This jar is representative of the first wave of Japanese cloisonné that hit American shores. Its garish colors and the extraordinary intricacy of its borders and patterning are typical of the qualities Westerners liked best.

might prove useful in determining how the reorganization of Japan's art industries was accomplished.[94]

Once committed to its development, Japan rapidly surpassed the Chinese as the world's premier cloisonné manufacturer. In the catalog of its exhibit at the World's Columbian Exposition, held in Chicago in 1893, Japan's cloisonné manufacturers were praised for making "such strides that her enamels have left their Chinese predecessors at an immeasurable distance, and stand easily at the head of everything of the kind the world has ever seen."[95] Technical innovations were so rapid between 1875 and 1890 that assigning dates to objects presents difficulties. Work from the Kyoto school, with its intricate patterns of exposed copper cloisons and large central medallions framed with exquisite diapers and arabesques, attracted a wide following at the height of the Japan craze. By 1890 this type of work was supplanted by products of the cloisonless school, noted for concealing the copper cloisons which outline the design and hold the liquid enamel in place during firing. Removing the cloisons allowed the enamel colors to fuse together, creating a seamless, more pictorial effect.[96] This was the look imitated by many American art potteries during the late 1890s. For garish color and faultless technique, nothing appealed more to the Victorian sensibility than the new products of Japan's cloisonné industry (fig. 25).

Japan's advance into world markets was driven by the success of its lacquer work which set a standard unmatched for centuries. The aura of rarity, exclusivity, and intrigue that surrounded this most venerated and indigenous of Japanese arts added to its allure. Long before Japan opened its doors to the West, its lacquer was known and treasured by European royalty.[97] At the beginning of the seventeenth century it was so highly esteemed that lacquer produced elsewhere in Asia, as well as the many European and American imitations, were lumped together under the rubric "Japanned work." Victorian artists and critics regarded lacquer as the acme of artistic achievement, noting that "among the Art Industries of Japan, that of lacquering undoubtedly holds the first place not only as furnishing occupations to thousands...but also as displaying skill, patience, and in many cases the highest kind of artistic excellence."[98] For variety of ornament, mastery of workmanship, practicality of function, novelty of technique, and complexity of design, Japanese lacquer had no equal (figs. 26, 27, 28).

Attuned more to technique than aesthetics, Victorian critics marveled at the complex sequence of operations involved in lacquer manufacturing. From the extracting of sap from the lacquer tree (rhus vernicifera), to its painstaking application and polishing in dozens of layers, to the final ornamentation, the production of lacquer could not have been less like the bang-it-out attitude of industrial arts manufacturers in the West.

Victorians were not insensitive to the aesthetic achievement of Japanese lacquer. The British design theorist Christopher Dresser maintained that "while we have here the elements of gaudiness . . . [lacquer] presents a refinement of effect, as well as finish, which few European's works possess. If we use gold freely we usually get a meretricious effect, and by the inlaying of pearl we almost invariably secure vulgarity; but with the Japanese, the lustrous surface of mother-of-pearl is so skillfully used as to produce repose."[99]

(26) Writing box (Suzuribako), about 1880
Lacquer
Japan
George Walter Vincent Smith Art Museum
Springfield, Massachusetts

Lacquer was the most technically advanced of the Japanese arts and the least like anything produced in the West. Collectors loved it and forms like this writing box became objects of intense desire by sophisticated American collectors like George Walter Vincent Smith. Often exquisitely decorated both inside and out, as in the case of this writing box, it is easy to understand their appeal. The background surfaces are nashiji *(particles of gold sprinkled over the lacquer), the leaves and flowers by the side of the stream are gold and colored* takamakie *(raised gold decoration) and* kirigane *(inlaid gold leaf). The technique* ji-maki, *or sprinkling the lacquer with gold dust, created designs that were rich-looking, yet delicate.*

American Taste and the Arts of Japan

(27) Small cabinet on stand, about 1875
Lacquer with brass hinges and drawer pulls
Japan
Wadsworth Atheneum

On the vanguard of taste, the Goodwin family was among the first in Hartford to incorporate Japanese and Japanese style objects in furnishing their home. This cabinet, which features typical Japanese design motifs, such as flying storks, fruit blossoms, and fans, is typical of the application of traditional Japanese arts in the production of Western forms. It was owned at "Woodlands," the Goodwin family estate.

(28) Cosmetic box (Kobako), early 19th century
Lacquer
Japan
Mount Holyoke College Art Museum
Bequest of Emma Dickinson, Class of 1867

Although this box dates from before the opening of Japan to the West, it could easily have entered the United States during the 1880s, when many fine older examples of Japanese decorative arts were sold to Americans, both in Japan and in the many shops specializing in Japanese novelties that prospered in American cities during the Japan craze. It is a magnificent example of the lacquer art.

The methods and styles of lacquer ornament were indeed remarkable. Silver, gold, and bronze powders built up on thicknesses of plaster, created fields of pattern, both flat and in high relief. Bits of precious metal, mother-of-pearl, and ivory were occasionally embedded in the surface (fig. 29). Foundations of wood, cardboard, ivory, shell (fig. 30), and even ceramic suggest the versatility of application. Keenly attuned to variety in ornament, one critic described with wonder a lacquer box with "102 distinctly different patterns" of ornament applied to the many drawers and compartments, each of a different shape.[100] Most astonishing of all was the apparent indestructibility of work that appeared so delicate and fragile. Traveling in Japan today, one is struck with the incongruity of lacquer's use in cooking and serving foods and spirits. Oil, acid, and alcohol may be spilled on it; boiling hot foods dispensed from it; and sharp utensils used without scratching it. As was said in 1880, "the old lacquer of Japan is almost indestructible." And yet it is basically just a heavily finished wooden box, not fired ceramic or cast metal. Nothing like this existed in the West. As a case in point, the Victorians loved to recite the story of the ship *Nile*, which sunk off the coast of Japan in 1874 carrying a cargo of art goods. Eighteen months later the freight was brought up, and the lacquer, "although filled with water," was "absolutely undamaged." These same objects were later displayed for promotional purposes in New York.[101]

Victorian critics liked to grouse about how trade with the West was corrupting Japan's traditional arts. Although this argument had two sides, there is no question that the arts of Japan adapted to market conditions and was thus altered. Typical sentiment suggested that "demand in Europe and America for the products of the country has aroused the cupidity of the Japanese, who now work for money, and, naturally, cannot afford to devote the time and care to their tasks that they used to give when they were executed for the glory of the craft."[102] In fact the Japan trade created a vastly enlarged market for Japanese art goods, and while most of what was produced was for the middle market, Victorian America was hardly at a loss for millionaires able to sink outrageous sums into art collecting.

The Japan craze coincided with the most intense outbreak of ceramic fever, before or since. Talent and

(29) Charger, about 1885
Lacquer and inlaid ivory, shell, and mother of pearl
Japan
Wadsworth Atheneum

Acquired in Hartford by a collector in 1891, this charger is an exceptional example of the type of Japanese craftsmanship so admired by Americans. The inlay of shell, ivory, and mother of pearl in the center panel and intricate pattern of overlapping storks (all labor-intensive, hand-made details) contrasts sharply with the generic, factory-produced goods saturating the American market.

(30) Lacquered ostrich egg on stand, 1875-1885
Lacquered egg shell
Japan
Wadsworth Atheneum

Novelty items like this gold-lacquered egg were enthusiastically purchased to decorate the shelves of well-appointed parlor cabinets and collectors' cases. Its original owner, Samuel P. Avery, was an avid collector and dealer of Japanese art.

American Taste and the Arts of Japan 61

(31) Advertising broadside, about 1885
H. R. Moore and Company
Woodblock printed paper
Japan
DeWitt Historical Society of Tomkins County, N.Y.

The Japanese art movement coincided with and profited from the advent of advertising as a cost-effective way of promoting merchandise. Broadsides like this one, advertising Japanese art objects, disseminated information to an eager American public. Mass marketing enabled vendors like H. R. Moore to reach many households and likewise allowed the Japan craze to enter many more homes than would have been possible a decade earlier.

capital poured into the ceramics industry, attracting collectors, aesthetes, and a considerable public following. Painters, sculptors, and architects dabbled in ceramic design, some even forsaking their careers to pursue it professionally. Ceramic art was regarded with painting as the highest of possible artistic callings, a status it has never enjoyed since. After raw silk, Japan exported more ceramic goods than any other commodity. In promotional material by Japanese art importers (fig. 31) like A.A. Vantine & Co. twice as much space was devoted to pottery as any other material.

Because few Westerners visited Japanese potteries before the reforms of the Meiji Restoration transformed the industry, and because few export records survive it is hard to know what was made and used in Japan versus what was exported to the West. No other area in Japanese art studies is so fraught with controversy. Edward Morse, one of the few Westerners who did visit potteries before the export explosion, always distinguished between domestic and export goods, affirming the superiority of the former and the degradation of the latter.

The Morse collections (Peabody Museum, Salem, Massachusetts, and Museum of Fine Arts, Boston) remain unequaled, even in Japan, as repositories of regional pottery production. Yet it is hardly representative of the Japan trade and deliberately omits proof of the increasingly westernized tastes of the Japanese themselves. Consider the source. In an age legendary for its national chauvinism, Morse wrote how "we read daily in our papers the details of the most blood-curdling crimes ... But we go to another country and perhaps find a new species of vice ... howl at the enormity ... send home the most exaggerated accounts, malign the people without stint, and then prate to them about Christian charity."[103] While not entirely inaccurate, this comment reveals deep misgivings about the West and invites questions about the hidden motives behind Morse's interpretations of Japanese pottery and culture. The fact is, the Japanese appear to have liked and used the "vulgar" export products they made "for the barbarians." Even today Japan's role in Western society is portrayed as manipulative and two sided with the not too subtle implication that the "real" Japan is somehow different. Then as now it smacks of cynicism and racism to suggest that the Japanese are merely opportunists with no real attachment to the foreign side of their increasingly hybrid culture.

Such are the issues raised in the study of pots and pans. Belief in the decline of Japan's native art after 1868 has been accepted so uncritically that it is very difficult to secure reliable information about what was actually being made and used both in Japan and America. In seeking to erase evidence of the West's influence on Japan, the literature on Japanese art has distorted Japanese culture. We must therefore turn again to the art itself which represents a body of dry facts that are undeniable.

In the field of Japanese ceramics no subject is more cloaked in mystery, folklore, and symbolism than the much-discussed but elusive Satsuma ware. Editorials on Satsuma spilled forth in the art books and journals of Victorian America. Almost everyone seemed to have an opinion on this much-venerated Japanese pottery. Edward Morse warned of fakes and forgery; Christopher Dresser worried about the imitation of Satsuma at Awata; and everyone seemed anxious to know the difference between old and new, as if such knowledge was a baptism in the mystery and art of connoisseurship.[104] Unable, even now, to consistently and accurately explain the nuances of connoisseurship that obsessed Victorians, it is perhaps clearer if we accept that Satsuma became a code name for an entire species of art and that art was everywhere.

A few characteristics should be observed. Satsuma, although made from the same kaolinic clays as true porcelain and finished with a feldspathic glaze, is more properly categorized as faience, which is heavier bodied, has a thick crackled glaze, and lacks the translucency of true porcelain. Where the glaze is fused to the body in true porcelain, Satsuma glaze is more like a skin: it can chip and separate from the body. Satsuma is cream colored – connoisseurs argued that imitations made in Awata were yellower – and heavily ornamented with red, green, purple, and gilt patterns of birds, flowers, and diapers, arranged to give the appearance of random order.

Satsuma's allure owes partly to political history and national pride. With the invasion of Korea by the prince of the domain of Satsuma (now Kagoshima) during the 1590s, Japan acquired the technology and, by taking craftsmen as prisoners, the personnel needed to commence porcelain manufacturing. From these heroic origins the ceramic industry grew and flourished in Satsuma and throughout southern Japan. Satsuma was again enmeshed in great events during the years leading up to Japan's opening to the West. Increasingly powerful and far removed from the shogun's capital at Edo (now Tokyo), the daimyo of Satsuma became an advocate for Western trade as early as the 1840s. Pottery and silk from Satsuma were exported to Europe in spite of laws forbidding foreign trade. When trade restrictions were lifted during the 1850s, Satsuma was the best prepared to take advantage of opportunities. Quick to embrace industrialization and adept at marketing, the daimyo of Satsuma was the first Japanese to display native products at a world's fair when, in 1867, he participated in the Paris Exposition.[105] Part of the appeal of Satsuma ware was its timing in entering the market (figs. 32, 33, 34).

In addition to Awata and Satsuma wares, more than a dozen distinct types of pottery (fig. 35, 36) were exported from Japan. Prominent among them were Kaga ware, a glazed earthenware like Satsuma, characterized by gold, crimson, and red enamel glaze in geometrical designs; and Arita and Hizen ware, Victorian nomenclature for Imari porcelain, renowned for its export during the eighteenth century. Arita was frequently worked into enormous Western forms, characterized by a deep blue glaze with flowers, geometric panels, and tracery in a rich gilt. Owari was a blue and white porcelain; and crackle ware was reputedly made by subjecting porcelain to a cold blast of air while cooling to achieve the dramatic crazing of the glaze, commonly with a subtle underglaze motif in green or blue on a buff-colored ground (fig. 37 a,b).

Victorian critics observed the changing structure of the ceramic industry in Meiji Japan and frequently found evidence of decline. Japanese trading companies, themselves creatures of this great change, argued the reverse – that greater demand and more sophisticated methods of quality control had actually lifted Japanese art to new heights of glory. Either way, the centralization of marketing and distribution represented a profound change which no doubt altered relations between artisan and market and the familial tradition of apprenticeship.

Christopher Dresser's account of his journey into the mountainous regions of southern Japan and through the maze of small potteries in ceramic centers

Small bowls, such as the three shown here, were relatively inexpensive and allowed a Victorian collector to amass examples of a variety of Japanese porcelains without spending a fortune. Each of these bowls is decorated in a completely different style. The middle bowl, with its swirling bands of flowers on the outside and thousands of tiny butterflies inside, is the work of Yabu Meizan, who used these designs in different combinations on many pieces. The other two bowls, one scattered with a few detailed insects, the other covered with an inner geometric pattern and outer overlapping pictorial scenes, convey opposite approaches to the art of pottery decoration.

(32 left)
Bowl, about 1890
Satsuma ware
Tokyo, Japan
Wadsworth Atheneum

This bowl was part of a collection of Japanese decorative arts and baskets bequeathed to the Atheneum by Constance S. Mead in 1918.

(32 center)
Bowl, about 1885
Kyoto or Satsuma ware
Japan
YABU MEIZAN (1853-1934), decorator
Wadsworth Atheneum

Yabu Meizan is widely recognized among the greatest ceramic decorators of the Meiji Era. This bowl was owned by the Goodwin family of Hartford and may have been part of the bric-a-brac furnishings of the family's 1874 reception room.

(32 right)
Bowl, about 1885
Kutani ware
Japan
Wadsworth Atheneum

(33) Bowl with scalloped rim, 1880s
Earthenware
Japan
Portland Museum of Art
Gift of Margaret E. Jenness in memory of Helen S. Beyer, 1989

Often decorated both inside and out, Japanese decorative arts offered Americans something aesthetically pleasing and unpredictable. The irises decorating the outside of this bowl were quickly recognized in Japan as motifs that appealed to the western eye and identified an object immediately as Japanese.

(34) Pilgrim flask, about 1885
Satsuma ware
Japan
Decorated by KOYAMA
Hall Memorial Library, Ellington, Connecticut

With its label from the New York Japanese art importer A. A. Vantine & Co. still intact, this vase is a good document of the type of Japanese ceramics available in the New York market at the height of the Japan craze. It is a fine example of Satsuma ware, which illustrates the effects of layered blocks of ornament and decoration that imitates cloisonné. The vase was a gift from Yanoshi Iwasaki, a Japanese student who attended the Ellington School in 1864.

(35) Baluster jar, about 1860
Satsuma ware
Japan
George Walter Vincent Smith Art Museum
Springfield, Massachusetts

The carp swimming against the tide, shown here with water chestnuts, was a favorite motif used by American silver and glass manufacturers during the Japan craze. The Japanese quality of balance and decoration that wraps around an entire form is exhibited here in the swirling lines, representing water, that curl around the vase.

(36) Ovoid jar with cover, about 1880
Satsuma ware
Japan
Wadsworth Atheneum

Overlapping fans, bamboo, and irises on a gilt ground are just a few of the Japanesque motifs that decorate this large covered jar. Works like this were ideally suited as bric-a-brac used in room furnishings. This particular jar belonged to the Eldridge family of Hartford during the nineteenth century.

American Taste and the Arts of Japan

(37 a) Covered box, about 1880
Ceramic
Japan
Peabody Museum of Salem, Massachusetts

This box is a type of earthenware known as crackled ware for the intense crazing of its glaze. The crazing or crackling of the glaze was mimicked by American manufacturers and decorators of ceramics, silverplate, and textiles. The bamboo sprig decoration on the cover is accompanied by Japanese characters, which translate poetically to "the wind blows the reeds." It is one of many ceramic forms collected by Edward S. Morse during his travels in Japan.

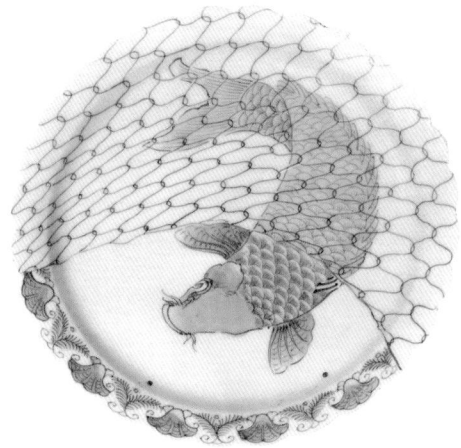

(37 b) Scalloped fish plate, 1879
Porcelain with underglaze blue decoration
Japan
Kyoku-ho-en, maker
Collection of John Quentin Feller

When President and Mrs. Grant visited Japan in 1879, they were given a dinner service of Japanese Arita porcelain as a gift from the emperor. The Grants also returned to the United States with a complementary set of dessert plates, decorated with carp. This plate is part of that set, which was probably also acquired by gift from the emperor. The Grants' interest in Japanese art extended beyond porcelain. Their New York apartment was lavishly furnished with Japanese art objects of all types, many of them acquired during their six-week visit in 1879.

like Kyoto is a portal through which we may view the clash between tradition and modernization. In 1877, fresh from negotiating a buyer's contract with Tiffany & Co. in New York and flushed with acclaim for his widely reported lectures in Philadelphia during the Centennial, Dresser headed west to San Francisco where he boarded a steamer for Japan. During his four-month tour, Dresser visited sixty-eight potteries. Although his interpretations must be viewed in light of his reformist sentiments, his notes and observations are unique.[106]

Anti-giantism, a kind of "small is beautiful" attitude, was a basic ingredient of the art reform movement during the Japan craze. Dresser noted, perhaps apocryphally, that "the largest pottery here would ... in no way be comparable in size with the smallest in Great Britain."[107] Saying "I cannot help feeling that the best productions of Ota, the finest works of Shiba, and the choicest cups of Satsuma, are things unsurpassed in the potter's art," Dresser went on to describe the typical setting in which these treasures were created: "In a lovely room ... dwelt the potter.... One mat being removed from the floor, a potter's wheel is exposed ... a mere circular stone ... on a vertical axis ... [which the potter operated] with the tips of his fingers." Having observed this type of operation repeatedly, Dresser concluded, "I invariably found that where excellent work was produced things were on a very small scale.... Their whole pride lies in the production of meritorious work." Such a picture hardly needed comparison with Western practices to be understood as a call for reform.[108]

Dresser's comments aside, we are still left without an accurate picture of what reformists derisively described as the "meretricious solecisms of the Yokohama School" which "owes its existence primarily to the demand of foreign exporters and tourist amateurs for brightly ornate and decorative specimens ... [in which] profusion of colour and lavishness of labour are set conspicuously above excellencies of technique and chastity of taste." That statement, written in 1893 by Captain Frank Brinkley for the catalog of the Japanese exhibit at the World's Columbian Exposition in Chicago, is a masterpiece of snobbery and condescension which hints at the class conflict that festered among the roots of the Japan craze. Brinkley goes even further:

These things are eagerly acquired by the profanum vulgus

[common public] as Japanese curiosities, and in one sense they certainly merit the term, for it is emphatically curious that there should have sprung into prosperous existence within the past twenty years a large class of objects which are absolutely without prototypes in Japanese art; do open violence to the canons of that art, have their origin solely in the Japanese keramist's deluded conception of foreign taste, and nevertheless pass among foreigners for genuine representatives of Japanese taste.[109]

While acknowledging that Kyoto, the center of Japan's traditional arts and culture, "had become deeply infected with the virus of the commercial fever," Brinkley admitted that work of the Yokohama School, while objectionable on stylistic grounds, "demonstrated... that the technical skill of the old potters and their proficient manipulation of materials were still surviving faculties."[110]

If the Japanese liked it and the vast majority of the buying public liked it and if even the aesthetes recognized its technical virtues, it is hard to imagine what else was bothering them. Clearly ownership of the Japan idea was at stake. If you want to know what people were being told to like, read the reform critics. If you want to know what people actually liked, read Vantine's catalog and enjoy the art illustrated here and on those pages.

The art industry, although decentralized and consisting of thousands of small shops, experienced tremendous growth and change during the Meiji era. Whether or not one approves of these goods on aesthetic grounds, they were the product of a competitive and innovative economy. An analogy with Japan's modern automobile industry is suggested. Japan's success today is not because of government subsidies or unfair trade practices, as one might suppose by reading the accounts in the American press. Japan makes good automobiles because competition among Japanese manufacturers is intense and less subject to restraint. Competition breeds resourcefulness, and this was exactly the quality exhibited by the art industry in Meiji Japan.

In addition to lacquer, ceramics, metals, and cloisonné, Japan exported carved wood (fig. 38) and ivory, basketry, painted folding screens, woven silks and costumes, decorated leather, paper fans and

(38) Carved tray, about 1880
Wood
Japan
Museum of Art, Rhode Island School of Design

Kamakura-bori, the traditional art of woodcarving in the town of Kamakura, south of Tokyo, suffered a loss of interest during the Meiji period and was thus not widely exported to the West. Kamakura-bori is a type of lacquerware produced by carving designs in the wood before starting a long process of lacquering and polishing. This example belonged to Isaac Bates, a prominent collector of Japanese art in Providence, Rhode Island.

(39) Kimono, 1875-1880
Silk
Japan
Peabody Museum of Salem, Massachusetts

Japanese kimonos were favorite choices for fancy dress balls and were made even more popular by Gilbert and Sullivan's musical, The Mikado *(1885). When they visited Japan, American tourists could have their photographs taken in Japanese photo studios, wearing traditional Japanese costume in their choice of settings. Naturalistic motifs, such as spider webs, birds, and flowers, as well as outdoor scenes, were common kimono decorations. This example was collected by Edward S. Morse.*

lanterns, and, by the 1890s, illustrated books, color prints, and painted scrolls (kakemonos). Curiously, the medium most frequently invoked in the study of *japonisme* – the much-vaunted ukiyo-e print – was not widely available at the height of the Japan craze and did not figure significantly in the Japanese exhibits at world's fairs.

For all of this talk about art it is important to remember that Japan was a developing nation. Unlike today, its balance of trade was decidedly tilted toward dependence on foreign goods. Japan's major export was not finished products, but raw silk. Introduced from Korea a millennium before, Japan's silk industry was the world's most vigorous at the time of the Meiji Restoration. American and European silk manufacturers were the first Western industrialists to establish trade in Japan. Between 1880 and 1900, silk exports jumped tenfold from about ten million yen to one hundred million. Until 1890 most of this trade was in raw silk, but in the last decade of the century the export of finished textiles shot up from about five million yen to more than fifty million.[111] This explains why Japanese textiles, so widely regarded in the literature on Japanese art, had such a low profile during the peak years of the Japan craze; there wasn't much to be had.

Dating when specific Japanese art products were introduced into Western markets has proven difficult. Availability was not driven by supply. Although antique goods were a significant factor in the Japan trade, markets revolved around the supply of new products. But domestic demand was far too small to support industrial development independent of international markets. The Japanese appear to have used the international expositions for market research. Manufacturing capacity thus followed the shifting moods of Western taste.

It is most apparent from artists' portraits that silk kimonos (fig. 39) achieved *haute couture* status during the 1890s. The silk-weaving industry, centered in Kyoto, produced the most elaborately embroidered and woven goods the West had ever seen (figs. 40, 41). Kimonos were embroidered with complete landscapes, depicting rocks, waterfalls, flowers, and birds. Silk, woven on traditional draw looms, was worked into satins, brocades, taffetas, velvets, and damasks. These were incorporated into the design of folding screens and sold to the West as upholstery fabric and for use in

(40) Obi, 1885-1880
Silk brocade
Japan
Peabody Museum of Salem, Massachusetts

Once it became available on the American market, Japanese silk brocade was used to upholster the furniture and hang from the curtain rods of America's fashion conscious. Collectors could find many beautiful examples in Japanese sample books, or they could purchase larger examples in the form of fukusa (ceremonial gift wrappers) and obi (worn at the waist of a kimono). This example is richly patterned and woven with metallic threads.

(41) Priest's robe, 19th century
Silk brocade, gold thread
Japan
Private Collection

Along with architectural fragments, bronzes and urns from Japanese temples, American tourists brought home priests' robes made of different patterned swatches of brocade.

American Taste and the Arts of Japan

(42) Stenciled towel (tenugi)
Linen and vegetable dye
Japan
Peabody Museum of Salem, Massachusetts

Tenugi at first seem unlikely candidates for nineteenth-century collections. No gold threads embellish them, no intricate details catch the viewer's eye, and they are not particularly impressive. Yet collections of tenugi appear as very early additions to the Japanese collections at the Peabody Museum in Salem, Massachusetts, and the Museum of Art, Rhode Island School of Design. They are in fact, ideal communicators of Japanese motifs with their uncomplicated and very conventional Japanese subjects. Storks, bamboo, irises, eagles, and carp are some of the themes that appear in many color variations.

making curtains and table covers. Collectors sought out choice specimens of *fukasa*, the decorative and artistic fabrics used for covering and wrapping ceremonial gifts. The textile arts pushed traditional characteristics of Japanese design to new extremes of complexity and elaboration. Pieced woven brocade, among all the arts, best conveyed the effect of overlay patterning that was greeted with such astonishment and excitement by Western collectors and designers.

In addition to woven and embroidered silks Japan's tradition of stencil printing on woven fabric was transmitted in the form of the *tenugi* (figs. 42), the towel-like banners displayed in doorways of shops, still popular throughout Japan. These graphic ideograms provide some of the most dramatic visual images in Japanese art. Large collections assembled before the turn of the century are held by the Rhode Island School of Design, the Peabody Museum, Salem, Massachusetts, and the Boston Museum of Fine Arts. Although rarely mentioned in period literature, stencil-printed towels were acquired by the Boston museum as early as 1877. Examples depicting the spider and web, bold maple leaves, floating faces, and a bamboo forest suggest the range of motifs that adorned these humble works of textile art. Americans also collected the stencils used in textile printing (fig. 43 a,b). How they were used or displayed in Victorian homes remains a mystery.

In the field of carved work, or the glyptic arts, as one Victorian critic described it, Japan developed a significant following. Critics were quick to point out the absence of anything like Western sculpture, painting, and architecture in Japan. Of course, there were houses, but of a character so quiet and unprepossessing that they bore little resemblance to western ideas of architecture. The nearest equivalent to sculpture was carved work which, for technical merit, was unsurpassed by anything produced in America or Europe.

Readers of this book and visitors to its companion exhibition may note the omission of the most renowned of all Japanese carved works – the legendary *netsuke*. Needless to say, Japanese art was not designed with modern museum exhibits in mind. It is almost impossible to display netsuke well for reasons that relate directly to their appeal. Intimacy of scale is an important characteristic in much of the best Japanese decorative art. In keeping with the Buddhist

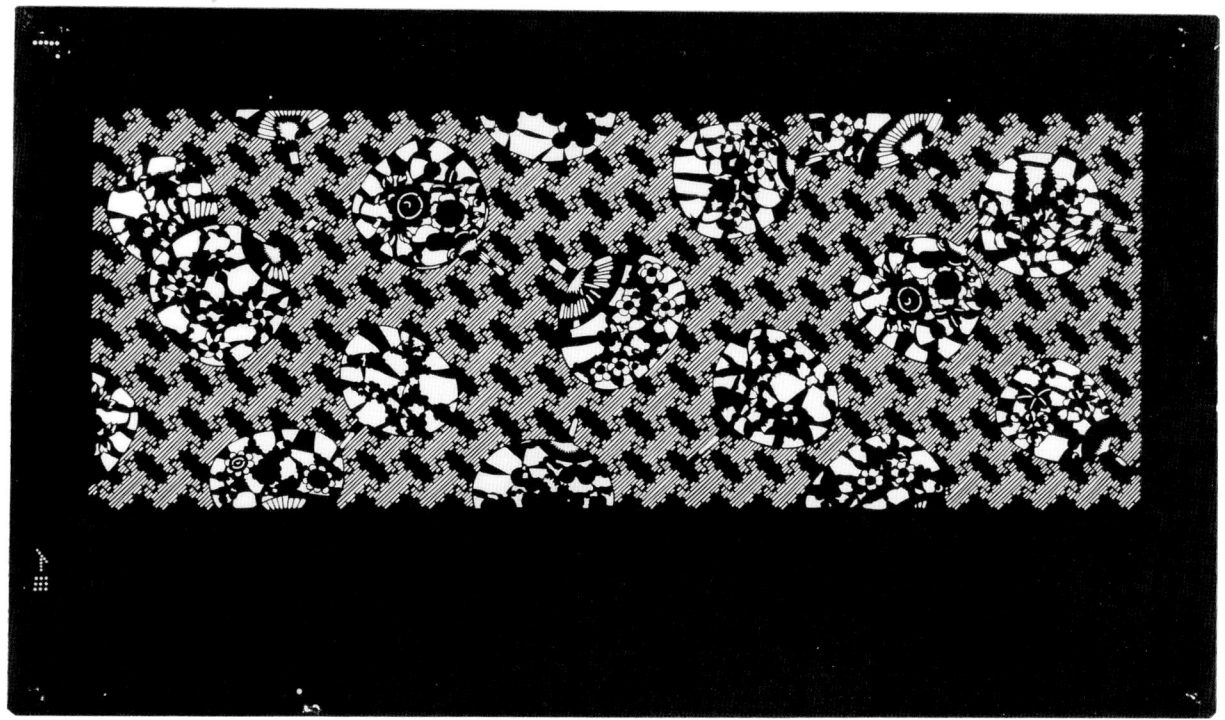

ideal of honesty and purity – even where the effects were not openly revealed – the insides and undersides of many art objects were elaborately finished and decorated. Given the West's overwhelming emphasis on frontality and outer appearances, this quality is most intriguing but almost impossible to convey in photographs or static exhibits. Considering further that the typical *netsuke* is rarely more than two inches square, you can see why we have omitted them. They were, however, widely collected and highly emblematic. More than any other art form, netsuke reveal the Japanese artisan's extraordinary perception of human expression and knowledge of the habits, customs, and folkways of the Japanese people.

Whether American collectors were fascinated by the many steps involved in making and using them, or simply attracted by the repetitive motifs cut into the paper, two collections of Japanese fabric stencils at the Museum of Art, Rhode Island School of Design, given to the museum during the early twentieth century, attest to a late nineteenth-century vogue of collecting these delicately patterned sheets of mulberry paper. After the paper is made and cut, it is rubbed with persimmon juice and reinforced with silk threads, then allowed to age-sometimes for as long as fifteen years! When the stencil is ready, it is placed over the cloth (white cotton) and a rice paste is rolled over it. The stencil is removed and the cloth dipped in indigo dye. The pattern appears when the waxed areas resist the dye, producing bold contrasts of light and dark.

(43 a,b) Patterned fabric stencils (katagami), 19th century
Mulberry bark paper, persimmon juice, silk thread reinforcements
Probably Ise Province, Japan
Museum of Art, Rhode Island School of Design

(44 a) Letter opener, 1880-1890
Ivory
Japan
Wadsworth Atheneum

(44 b) Card case, 19th century
Ivory with gold lacquer, mother of pearl inlay
Japan
Wadsworth Atheneum

(44 c) Card case, 19th century
Ivory with gold lacquer, mother of pearl and coral inlay
Japan
Wadsworth Atheneum

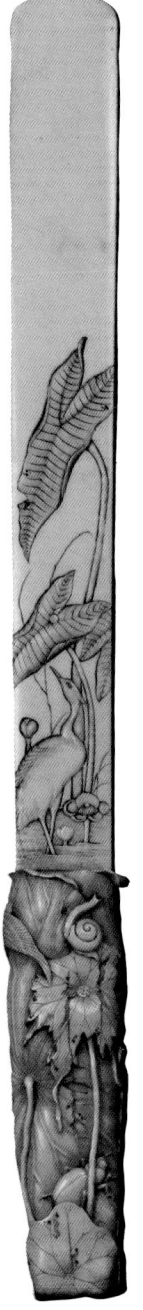

Most *netsuke* were of ivory, which was imported from India. Japan also exported trinkets and bric-a-brac for the Victorian market, such as letter openers and card carriers (fig. 44 a,b,c). Carved and worked bamboo, however, never developed a following in the West like the one it enjoys even today in Japan. Split and woven into baskets and mats and occasionally carved into ornamental vases (fig. 45) and brush holders, bamboo was put to many uses in Japan that had no equivalent in America.

Given the differences, it is not surprising that elements of Japanese architecture were not readily marketable in America. One exception was ornamental architectural fragments, which were exported in abundance. Lattice woodwork panels were custom-made in Osaka for export,[113] while antique temple fragments and *ramma* (fig. 46) – carved and pierced transoms used in doorways – attracted a select following among American architects and collectors. Japanese pressed leather was used as a wall covering (color plate 6) and was imitated by American wall- and-book cover manufacturers. Made by beating leather into an engraved bronze plate and finishing it with paint and gilding, this material was highly prized. Although only fragments of Japanese pressed leather are known in the United States today, entire rooms were covered with it.

The Japanese were regarded as "the best basket makers in the world."[114] Vantine stocked the most banal reed and bamboo woven trays, hampers, picnic baskets, and trash baskets. Yet when Tiffany's chief designer, Edward C. Moore, was building his influential collection of Japanese decorative art, none of the arts attracted him more than basketry (fig. 47). Morse bequeathed more than eighty exquisite basket works to the Metropolitan Museum of Art, where they testify to the achievements in this branch of Japanese art.[115]

Western in form, but Japanese in decoration and execution, the letter opener and card cases shown here were designed for export to America. These items belonged to Charles T. Wells, a Hartford collector who also collected Japanese woodblock prints.

(46) Transom (Ramma), 1875-85
Carved wood
Japan
Peabody Museum of Salem, Massachusetts

Architectural fragments stripped from Japanese temples became popular with Western collectors during the Japan craze. They were used as decorative accents and as transoms over windows and doors of stylish houses. This fragment is carved with a depiction of Mount Fuji.

(45) Carved vase, about 1880
Bamboo
Japan
The Metropolitan Museum of Art
Edward C. Moore Collection
Bequest of Edward C. Moore, 1891

Bamboo, one of Japan's abundant natural resources, was used for fencing and as structural and decorative elements in Japanese architecture. Occasionally bamboo was worked into decorative forms like this vase. The vase was part of a large collection of Japanese art assembled by Edward C. Moore during one of his visits to Japan. Moore was the head of the silver division at Tiffany and Co. His collections of Japanese art inspired some of the ornamentation found in Tiffany silver during the Japan craze.

(plate 6-color reproduction, page 189)
Wallpaper samples, about 1885
Embossed leather with gold leaf and painted decoration
Japan
George Walter Vincent Smith Art Museum
Springfield, Massachusetts

Embossed leather wallpaper from Japan became the wall covering of choice for America's wealthy. Artistic Houses (first published in New York, 1883), which describes the decoration of the homes of the country's then rich and/or famous, lists "Japanese leather wallpaper" at least a dozen times. Its popularity led middle class Americans to seek an affordable imitation. Lincrusta-Walton in Japanesque patterns looked like Japanese leather, but was not nearly as expensive.

The most ubiquitous of the Japanese arts were folding fans, heralded "not only for their cheapness, but for beauty and usefulness." Where else has it ever been possible to acquire a unique art object for seven cents (about two dollars today)?[116] Fans were the least expensive way of acquiring something in the Japanese mode. They were not plain. As the examples illustrated suggest (figs. 48, 49, 50, 51), the best commercial fans were highly evocative of the mood, color, and composition characteristic in Japanese art.

(48) Flat fan, about 1880
Paper on bamboo
Japan
Peabody Museum of Salem, Massachusetts

Flat fans and folding fans flooded into the United States by the thousands once the Japan craze hit. Always considered an art form, both in Japan and in the United States, the Japanese fan enabled everyone to participate in the vogue for Japanese decoration without spending a fortune. Around doorways, and mirrors, on mantles and bookshelves, fans could be found in almost every American home of the eighties and nineties.

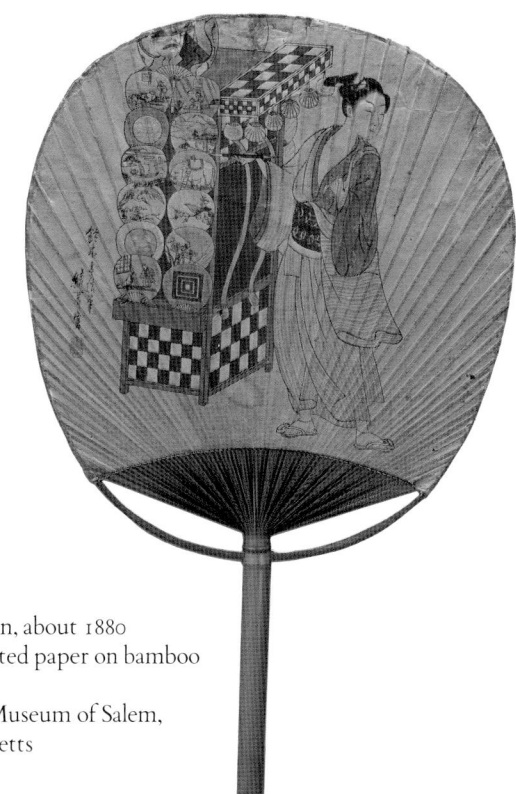

(47) Basket, 19th century
Bamboo
Japan
The Metropolitan Museum of Art
Edward C. Moore Collection
Bequest of Edward C. Moore, 1891

Edward C. Moore, the Tiffany and Co. designer responsible for the company's early experiments with Japanese techniques and designs, amassed a large personal collection of Japanese art. Included in this collection were examples of Japanese basketry. Although never widely marketed in the United States, Japanese basketry was recognized by astute collectors like Moore as one of the most intriguing and important of Japan's traditional arts.

(49) Flat fan, about 1880
Block printed paper on bamboo
Japan
Peabody Museum of Salem, Massachusetts

American Taste and the Arts of Japan 75

(50) Folding fan, about 1880
Paper on bamboo
Japan
Peabody Museum of Salem, Massachusetts

(51) Folding fan, about 1900
Lithograph on Japanese "silk Imperial paper" with hand painted decoration
Lithographed, Boston, Massachusetts
Painted and manufactured in Japan
Concord Museum, Massachusetts

Japanese fan manufacturers filled special orders for custom-made designs for commercial and commemorative purposes. This fan was part of an order commissioned by Miss Edith Buck of Concord, Massachusetts for sale to tourists who arrived in increasing numbers to see the historic sites in Concord. The Old North Bridge of Revolutionary War fame is depicted.

Parasols and paper lanterns (figs. 52, 53) were also exported by the tens of thousands and resold by import firms like Vantine in boxes of a hundred each. At the peak of the Japan craze there were almost as many fans in American homes as people.

Finally, there were folding screens. No other art form better symbolized Japan's connection with Victorian culture. Folding screens speak both to the freer and more open mode of sociability and movement within the Victorian home and to the integration of painting with decorative art and architecture, a cornerstone of art-reform theory. In Japan the folding screen traditionally functioned as an aesthetic focal point and as a useful way of delineating space within homes so open in plan that Western spatial concepts, like formal and informal, public and private, and even indoor and outdoor, appear meaningless.

Screens, so heavily gilded that some were destroyed for the gold on their surface, were described by Edward Morse as "beyond all question, the richest object of household use ... ever devised." Further asserting that there was "no other device in which so many decorative arts are called into play," Morse regarded the combination of the lacquer frame, metallic mounts, and silk brocade borders with the artist's painted work as the supreme demonstration of the integration of fine and decorative art.[117] These qualities, and the fact that folding screens were expensive and conformed with the West's notion of "artists'" work, appealed to collectors and artists.

The export trade in folding screens was big business. More than in the other arts, there was an especially strong market for "antique" folding screens from Japan's "golden (pre-industrial) age," and it may be that Japanese screens reaching America were more often old than new. For the purpose of illustration we chose both a classical antique screen (color plate 7) and a novelty screen (fig. 54) made for export during the Japan craze. The latter, although a type less common than all-paper screens and screens with paint on gold grounds, hint at the form's artistic variety. Screens were made with lacquer and encrusted work, paper and leather, embroidered silk brocade, and, in this case, a remarkable assortment of diapered lattice-and-fretwork panels of the sort made in Osaka.

Liberating Japanese art from the programmatic biases of art history is an enormous enterprise far

(53) Hanging lantern, about 1880
Paper with wood
Japan
Wadsworth Atheneum

(52) Umbrella, about 1880
Paper, bamboo
Japan
Peabody Museum of Salem, Massachusetts

American Taste and the Arts of Japan

(plate 7-color reproduction, page 190)
Folding screen, 1720-1740
A Beauty Playing the Samisen
Painted paper with gold leaf on lacquered wood frame
Japan
Lent by Smith College Museum of Art, Northampton, Massachusetts
Gift of Catherine H. Ayers (Catherine Spicer Hubley '32) in memory of her mother, Nancy Spicer Hubley, and her grandmother, Nancy West Spicer, 1973

Not all of the Japanese art entering the United States during the Japan craze was new. In fact, much to the dismay of Japanophiles, who felt that Japan was being corrupted by her exposure to the West, art of Dai Nippon or old Japan was among the shipments that arrived in American ports weekly. This two-panel folding screen depicts two courtesans and their young attendants under cherry blossoms, symbolic of a brothel interior. This screen was probably owned by Nancy West Spicer, whose granddaughter donated it in her memory to the Smith College Museum of Art.

beyond the scope of this project. Art history is a peculiarly Western construct that imposes hidden and subconscious ideals on its objects of study. It cannot be mistaken as cultural history even though it concerns the major expressions of culture. Its roots are buried deep in the soil of the Judeo-Christian tradition; no comparable discipline exists in Asia or Africa. The history of Japanese art that is taught in the West has been largely written by Westerners and Western-educated Japanese. The history of European and American art that is taught in Japan has also been written by Westerners. Let's just say that art history is something Americans and Europeans do well. It is not, however, the only version of art or history that must be told if we are to truly understand a different culture. Given the apparent unwillingness of American and European critics and reformers to accurately report different sides of the story of art in Meiji Japan, a little skepticism is called for, and it is in that spirit that this study, omissions and simplifications acknowledged, has been written.

This reversible novelty screen is a masterpiece of Japanese latticework. Each panel showcases a technique of design, forming an impressive sampler of wood decorating methods. In a Victorian home, this screen would have been the ideal conversation piece, suitable for a dining room, study, or parlor. Contemporary home decorating magazines strongly advocated the use of screens to hide corners and create privacy.

(54) Folding screen, about 1880
Pine, cedar, ivory, painted rush, and ebonized wood
Probably Osaka, Japan
Private Collection

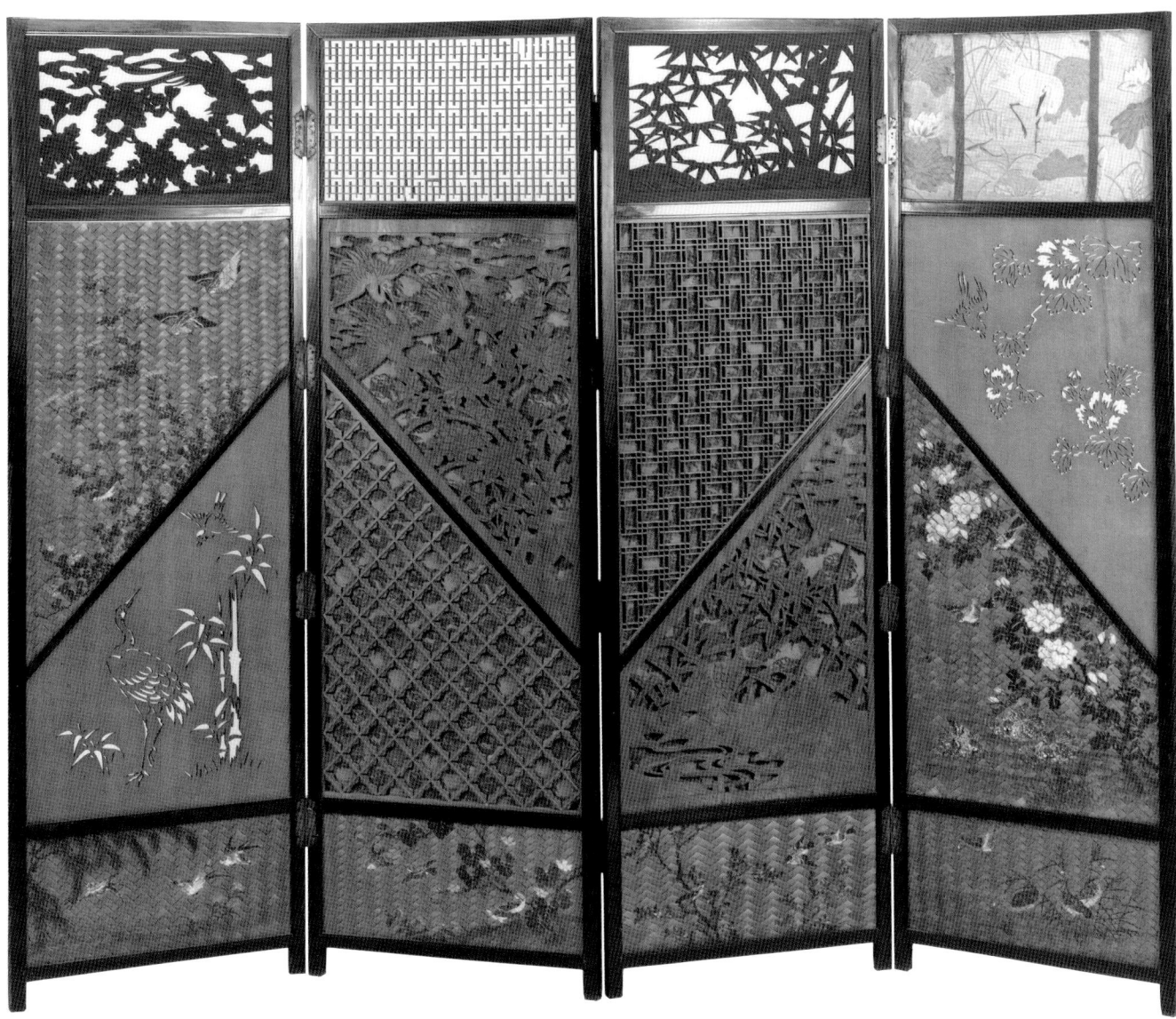

IV. Japan in the Artist's Eye

There is something paradoxical in the fact that the ukiyo-e color print, a form of popular culture suppressed by Japan's elite, was adopted and exalted as an aesthetic triumph by artist elites in the West. One of the most difficult aspects of the Japan idea has been sorting out patterns in taste and recreating the sequence in which different branches of art gained acceptance. The literature on Japanism consistently takes the Japanese art movement into the twentieth century, the time of some of its most refined expressions. Houses by architect Frank Lloyd Wright, the advent of the color print movement, and even the vogue for a kimono cut in women's dress in the 1920s were all late but distinctive expressions of Japanese influence. They were not, however, carried in on the first wave that washed across America during the Centennial.

    The ukiyo-e print gained acceptance in America during the 1890s at the same time that American artists of the first rank – William Merrit Chase, Robert Blum, J. Alden Weir, Mary Cassatt, and John Twachtman – were engrossed in the study and interpretation of Japanese aesthetics. Although American and European artists were among the most voracious collectors of Japanese decorative art, it was Japan's pictorial arts, notably color prints and photography, that they found most inspirational. Before summarizing how Japanese prints and photographs affected American art, let's consider the culture behind them.

    In Buddhism, ukiyo-e, which literally means picture of the world, signified the wretchedness of this life and the spiritual imperfection of man. With the rising prosperity of a new class of artisans, shopkeepers, and traders, the meaning of ukiyo-e shifted from morality to life-style. What religion disdained, the masses loved. Ukiyo-e began to celebrate hedonism, pleasure seeking, and a life of the senses.[118] Just as the art of ukiyo-e was embraced by artists and aesthetes in the West, so was the sensual life-style that ukiyo-e represented. Sight-seeing, drinking, singing, lovemaking, and idle conversation – never before accepted as subject matter suitable for the artist's brush – were now embraced in the name of artistic freedom.

    Japonisme, the French word used to describe Japanese influence in Western art, is at its most lively when tracing the story of France's maverick impressionists and post-impressionists.[119] Paintings like Monet's water lilies and van Gogh's *Irises* overshadow the movement's even more radical effect on portraiture. Of all the Japanese arts, the woodblock

(55) Color woodblock print, dated March 1857
Evening Glow at Seta
From *Eight Views of Lake Biwa* series
Japan
ANDO HIROSHIGE (1797-1858)
Museum of Fine Arts, Springfield, Massachusetts
The Raymond A. Bidwell Collection

Lake Biwa, located at the foot of Mount Fuji, is the subject of a series of eight views by Hiroshige. The zig-zag diagonals formed by the horizon, shore, and bridge are highlighted by the boats in the water. Diagonals inspired by those found in Japanese woodblock prints were used to decorate pottery, silverplate, and advertising cards in the United States.

(56) Color woodblock print, 1857
Plum Trees Flower Garden at Kameido
From *One Hundred Views of Famous Sites in Yedo* series
Japan
ANDO HIROSHIGE (1797-1858)
Museum of Fine Arts, Springfield, Massachusetts
The Raymond A. Bidwell Collection

This plum tree, a traditional Japanese subject, has invaded the foreground and appears to grow out of the borders. Though not as influential as Japanese decorative arts, Japanese prints played a part in familiarizing Americans with common Japanese art motifs such as plum blossoms.

(57) Color woodblock print, 1835-1838
Tonase and Konami Journeying to Yamashina
Japan
KUNIYOSHI (1797-1861)
Museum of Fine Arts, Springfield, Massachusetts
The Raymond A. Bidwell Collection

color prints from ukiyo-e's golden age (1760-1870) are the most remarkable as studies in character and emotion. In spite of its much-criticized flattened perspective and anatomical inaccuracy, no style had ever captured the emotions of sensuality, anger, lust, fear, shyness, arrogance, narcissism, and pride like ukiyo-e. Its impact on western art, then struggling for the liberation of individual expression, was galvanic. Add to this its alluring aesthetic appeal, and the power of ukiyo-e's influence over Western art can be easily understood. Just as Matthew Perry's arrival off the coast of Japan set in motion a sequence of irreversible structural reforms, the discovery of ukiyo-e would alter and shape the course of modern art for more than a century.

With the exception of Utamaro, the color-print artists popular in the West were all working during the first half of the nineteenth century, before the arrival of Matthew Perry. Although a cottage industry now exists among specialists dedicated to separating the work of one artist from the next and delineating the various schools and periods in ukiyo-e's development, the features that most influenced Victorian art are standard throughout: exaggerated perspective; the birds-eye view; the predominance of balance over symmetry; the use of flat unmodulated colors and tones to define shapes, forms, and decorative elements; the use of the diagonal to separate fields of action; the layering of squares, rectangles, circles, and fans, and the picture within a picture. Throughout there is a tendency toward abstraction best represented in the truncated forms and figures that stalk across the foreground of landscape pictures, defining a new psychology of pictorial action that nineteenth-century artists found haunting and alluring. Together these features represented a frontal assault on the conventions of art, and thus opened the way to a new order.

In keeping with our desire to immerse you, the reader, in the visual language of Japanese art *before* exploring its Western ramifications, a selection of color prints and photographs was made. Only a few among the hundreds of Japanese color-print artists became household names in the West. Works by these artists – Hiroshige, Kuniyoshi, Utamaro, Hokusai, and Kunisada being the most prominent – were chosen for their subject matter. Composition, ornament, subject matter, and color also figured in the selection (figs.55, 56, 57)(color plate 8).

Japanese photography has only recently gained recognition as a major factor in the transmission of Japanese images and design principles.[120] Travelers to Japan brought home albums filled with hand-colored photographs of scenic vistas, Japanese folkways, and aesthetic cliches. These images capture the hustle and bustle of the commercial streets of Yokohama, iris viewing, sacred vistas such as Mount Fuji and the bridge at Nikko, Japanese domestic life, cherry and plum blossoms, picnicking, and the inevitable renderings of Japanese beauties (figs. 58, 59, 60, 61, 62, 63, 64, 65, 66, 67).

* * *

(59) Color woodblock print
Woman on Boat in a Snowy Landscape
Japan
KUNISADA
Smith College Museum of Art, Northampton, Massachusetts
Gift of Helen D. LaMonte, '95, 1970

Weather conditions were frequent subjects of Japanese woodblock prints. Here, snowflakes fall in clumps around a woman wrapped in a stunning robe. The contrast of the white snow with the woman's black hair and bright blue robe and the figure's languid pose were qualities unknown in Western art. This print was collected by a nineteenth-century graduate of Smith College, Helen D. LaMonte.

(58) Color woodblock print, 1793
Beauty With Samisen
Japan
EISHI HOSODA (1756-1829)
Wadsworth Atheneum

The woman depicted with a samisen (stringed instrument) in hand was recognizable as a courtesan.

(60) Color woodblock print, 1853
Autumn Rain and Leaves
From *A Selection of Beauties from the Floating World*
Japan
KUNISADA TOYOKUNI III
Smith College Museum of Art, Northampton, Massachusetts
Gift of Margaret Rankin Barker and Isaac Ogden Rankin, 1968

Japan in the Artist's Eye   83

(plate 8-color reproduction, page 191)
Color woodblock print, 1857
Iris At Horikiri
From *One Hundred Views of Famous Sites in Yedo* series
Japan
ANDO HIROSHIGE (1797-1858)
Museum of Fine Arts, Springfield, Massachusetts
The Raymond A. Bidwell Collection

Irises that seem larger than life and miniscule people in the background confuse proportions in this print. American artists were intrigued by the altered perspective found in many Japanese woodblock prints. The people in the background are viewing the iris flowers, a traditional pasttime. The artist has decided to portray the scene from an unrealistic vantage point and has made the people seem much less significant than the bold flowers.

(61, 62) Hand-colored photographs, about 1880
Probably Yokohama, Japan
UNKNOWN STUDIO
Wadsworth Atheneum

One of the most popular souvenirs bought by Americans traveling to Japan were albums filled with hand-colored Japanese photographs. These pictures were sold commercially and illustrate aspects of scenery and traditional folklife that Westerners like to associate with Japan. Scenes of people eating, sleeping, writing letters, serving tea, carrying vegetables, selling brooms, viewing irises, cherry blossoms, and autumn maple leaves were combined with pictures of scenic places like Mount Fuji and Lake Biwa. Although these photographs are not attributed to any one studio, the office of Kimbei Studios, one of the most popular in Yokohama, appears in a streetscape view.

Japan in the Artist's Eye   85

(63-67) Hand-colored photographs, about 1880
Probably Yokohama, Japan
UNKNOWN STUDIO
Wadsworth Atheneum

86   THE JAPAN IDEA

The pictorial arts of Japan were disseminated in the West in the form of colored woodblock prints and illustrated books. Scholars have labored long in searching out and describing the conduit through which Japanese pictorial arts passed from East to West. Unlike the decorative arts, which were adopted, mimicked, and eventually rejected, concepts associated with Japanese prints still exert a powerful influence in contemporary art. The credo of "art for art's sake" that evolved out of the West's encounter with Japanese prints still rears its head today in the defense of artistic freedom.

The European artists who "discovered" Japanese art wrapped their achievement in mythology. Imagine the French artist Felix Bracquemond "finding" an edition of Hokusai's Manga in 1856 and thus laying "the groundwork in Europe for the reception of colored prints." Imagine the Parisian art community's much-celebrated openness to an art form so little regarded in its native country that it was used as "packing material" for export porcelains! These are among the legends surrounding ukiyo-e prints, in which the artist emerges as champion of the true faith, who rescues a great notion from the debris of the Japan idea. The birth of modernism, the movement created by the "art for art's sake" school, claims the heroic individual as its midwife. Its folklore includes a pantheon of saints and sinners. Its leitmotif is the artist as solitary figure struggling against the ignorance and indifference of public opinion, an image encapsulated in stories about the discovery of Japanese prints.[121]

The apostles of Japanese influence in Western art make a good case for Japanese prints as the hinge on which significant events swung. Japanese art, already ennobled by reform critics as the embodiment of a "living medieval culture," was steeped with moral imperative – all the better for waging war against the forces of tradition and commerce that artists believed inhibited freedom of expression. Ukiyo-e prints thus provided direction and the moral imperative needed to move forward into a brave new world where artists declared their independence and asserted control over their work.

Instead of painting history pictures, flattering portraits, dramatizations of the divinity of nature, and morality tales – the serviceable stuff of the mid-nineteenth-century art academy – the apostles of Japanese art created pictures rich in emotion, unorthodox in form, and conspicuous in physicality. They painted pictures in which aesthetic ideas triumphed over representational logic, and form became content. Thus began the long march toward abstraction which ultimately "liberated" – some might argue isolated – artists from their craft, making possible the extremism of conceptual art, which, during the 1960s completed the transformation from artist as artisan to artist as creative spirit.

The effect of Japanese prints on American art has been colored by the role of expatriate artists like James McNeill Whistler and Mary Cassatt. In spite of his tendency to slip in and out of character as "the American artist in Europe," Whistler was too enigmatic, too cosmopolitan, and far too removed from his native land to qualify as its representative Japanist. And yet he epitomized the very American quality of bumptiousness at which Europeans thumbed their nose. Iconoclastic, doctrinaire, free spirited, independent, and litigious, Whistler was ideally suited for a life on the front line of change. He was an undisputed visionary in the aesthetic reforms that stemmed from the West's encounter with Japanese art. Exposure to Japanese prints is reflected in his work by 1863, as early as any artist in Europe. And yet it would be years before the effects of his triumphs were widely felt in his native land.[122] Whistler's story, however, is but a small aspect of American painting's encounter with Japan.

Japanese influence mushroomed with the rise of art education and the allied revival of watercolor painting, printmaking, and etching. It reinforced the mission of America's Pre-Raphaelites, whose way of seeing and depicting nature, first inspired by the art of medieval England, qualifies them as the natural forerunners of Japanism in America. It flourished in the Whistlerian aestheticism practiced by American painters who participated in the British aesthetic movement. It was mirrored in the Victorian era's intense craving for bric-a-brac and collectibles, which was depicted in still lifes that celebrate acquisitiveness and the triumph of decorative art. Finally, Japanese influence in American painting found its voice in the apogee of American impressionism. Along the way were "artists," doubling as commercial illustrators, who traveled to Japan on commission to create new and exotic images for an insatiable home market. Occasionally, Japanese influence took form in the ever

(68) *Manga*, vol. 3, 1814-1819
Bound paper, paper covers
Japan
KATSUSHIKA HOKUSAI (1760-1849)
Private Collection

Of all the Japanese pattern books available to Americans, Hokusai's Manga *was the most frequently cited in the collections of artists and manufacturers. Its small sketches of Japanese folklife, animals, monsters, flora, and fauna were ideally suited as models of decoration on silver, pottery, and textiles.* Manga *was published serially in fifteen volumes between 1814 and 1849. The translation of its title means "the education of beginners by the spirit of things: Hokusai's random sketches."*

more personalized props that individuals assembled as stage sets for their portraits.

Although American painting never achieved the intensity of expression or the depth of commitment to Japanese aesthetic principles exhibited in the work of French artists like van Gogh and Monet, what it did achieve is equally important. Nowhere else than in this nation, shaped by diversity, did the Japan idea take root across more expansive terrain. It is in this variety of expression that the Japan idea shaped the look and ideals of late nineteenth-century American painting.

John La Farge's involvement with Japanese art exceeds that of almost all of his American peers. As a writer, collector, illustrator, painter, interior designer, lecturer, muralist, and stained-glass manufacturer, La Farge applied himself across an astonishing array of media. His professional intersections with Japanism were varied and sophisticated. Murals painted for the Boston dining room of Charles Freeland in 1865, especially a panel depicting hollyhocks and corn (Museum of Fine Arts, Boston) and a contemporary painting titled *The Fish*, are cited as the first evidence of Japanese influence in American art.[123]

La Farge initially encountered Japanese art while studying in France and England in 1856 and 1857. In Paris he mingled in the circle of his cousin, the critic Paul Saint-Victor, which included such trailblazing Japanists as Felix Bracquemond and Philippe Burty. It was there, at the age of twenty-two, that La Farge began building the first of several collections (dispersed in 1865) of Japanese prints, books, and bric-a-brac that he assembled over the next thirty years. Included were editions from Hokusai's "Manga" (fig. 68), the multivolume publication of "random sketches" that figured so prominently in the dissemination of Japanese design in the West.[124] Earlier than any of his peers and a quarter century before they became commercially available in America, La Farge amassed Japanese prints, illustrated pattern books (figs. 69, 70), textile stencil patterns, and assorted bric-a-brac.[125] This was not the standard merchandise of the Japan craze and marked La Farge as a force of enormous individuality and vision.

In 1886 La Farge traveled to Japan with the historian Henry Adams. Although he wrote, painted watercolors, (fig. 71) and sketched constantly during the almost three-month stay, La Farge differed from most American artists in Japan in that he was not

Japanese pattern books were collected and used for reference by American artists and industrial arts manufacturers. This book, which was purchased in 1886 by the artist John La Farge, features stenciled designs on indigo-dyed swatches.

(69) Textile retailers' sample book, early 19th century
Bound paper, paper covers
Japan
Private Collection

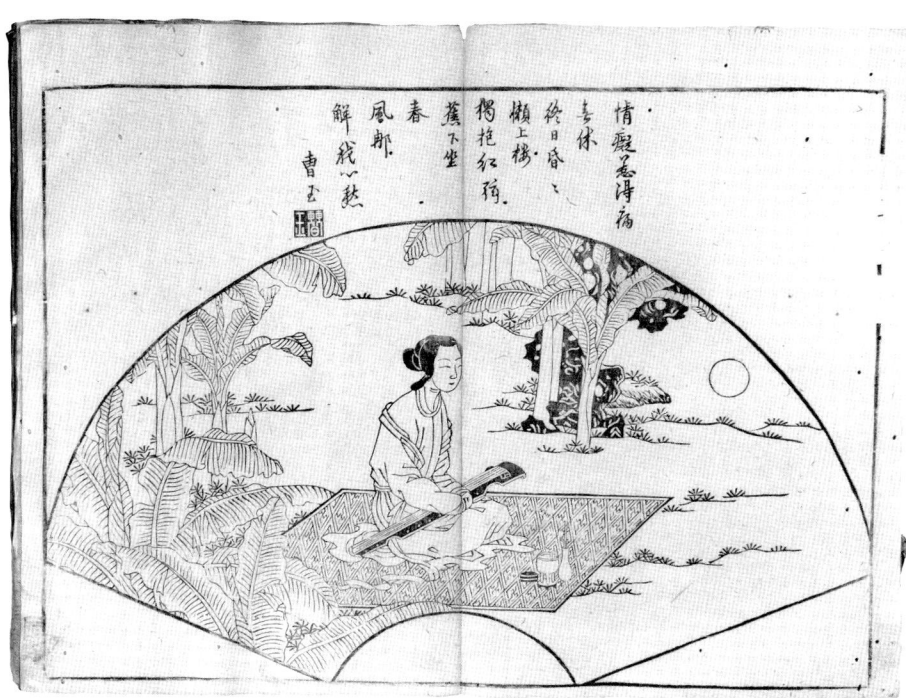

(70) Pattern book, 1775-1800
Fan Paintings (Meiko Senpu)
Album of Fan Designs after Chinese Painters (Hasshu Gafu)
Bound paper, fabric covers
Japan
Private Collection

This book was also part of the collection of John La Farge, listed as lot 426 in the sale of his estate in 1911.

Japan in the Artist's Eye

(71) *Water Lily and Moth*, about 1887
Watercolor on paper
American
JOHN LA FARGE
Wadsworth Atheneum

John La Farge, the premier Japanist among American painters, produced dozens of pictures of Japanese landscapes and Japanese flowers. This watercolor is typical of La Farge's commercial output during the Japan craze and may have been based on sketches taken from direct observation during his visit there in 1886.

there on contract and his sketches of Japan represent only one aspect of his Japanism. La Farge sketched the Great Buddha at Kamakura, the waterfalls and gardens at Nikko, numerous shrines and temples, lush atmospheric mountain vistas, and anthropological renderings of Japanese figure-types. Both he and Henry Adams bought Japanese photographs, and Adams snapped pictures of his own. La Farge used these photographs in preparing hundreds of illustrations and paintings after his return in 1887. These were eventually sold to *Century Magazine* for serialization between 1887 and 1893 and were rebound in book form as *An Artist's Letters from Japan* in 1897.[126]

The notoriety derived from these efforts finally enabled La Farge to command prices for his paintings and watercolors sufficient to support his varied interests and life-style. Between 1885 and 1895 La Farge cranked out hundreds of Japanesque travel views and nature studies which sold at prices that provided an income comparable to half a million dollars per year today.[127] In the study and production of stained glass and decorative arts and by extensive collecting and image making, John La Farge epitomizes how the Japan idea enveloped the world of late nineteenth-century American art. Painters who responded to the mass market for Japanese images flourished while giving form to a new aesthetic that revolutionized the art of picture making in Victorian America.

Japanese influence in the fine arts did not result in a unified taste or style. Two conflicting schools of thought were at war even before the impact of Japanese art was felt. Best represented by the positions of English design theorists, both schools had followers in American art as well. On one side was John Ruskin, the renowned advocate of truthfulness to the forms in nature and honest workmanship. Paintings that accorded with his teachings include the earthy and aggressively anti-modern works of the Pre-Raphaelites and landscape pictures of scrupulous and breathtaking realism that testify to the artist's belief in the divinity of nature. On the other side were Owen Jones, Edward Godwin, Christopher Dresser, and the champions of abstraction. Their philosophy of art was embodied in the teachings of the South Kensington School, and while equally attentive to nature, they regarded the design of leaves and flowers merely as a point of departure toward higher realms of ornament and not something to be slavishly imitated.[128] One side put nature before man, and the other, man before nature.

The similarities between Japanese design and the mid-nineteenth-century interpretations of medieval art by the Pre-Raphaelites are striking. It is therefore not surprising that British apostles of medieval art like the architect William Burges were the first to support the arts of Japan, which they regarded as the product of a living medieval culture. The similarities have, however, made it difficult to separate the sources of influence. Ultimately, the disciples of abstraction carried the day. The side that lost has not greatly concerned students of English or American art who have proven far more interested in proto-modernists like John Singer Sargent and Whistler than relatively obscure painters like John William Hill and Fidelia Bridges.

Bridges is especially interesting as a paradigm of women professionals who poured into the arts during the Japan craze. A New Englander by birth and temperament, Bridges studied art under the noted American Pre-Raphaelite William Tross Richards, with stints in Philadelphia and Rome, before returning to New England where she earned a livelihood as an illustrator for Louis Prang's Boston lithography company. Her airy and naturalistic watercolors of fields and birds and her spare and elegant sketches of flower blossoms and leaves are highly reminiscent of Japanese design (fig. 72 a,b). With her reputation building through the 1860s, Bridges was one of the few women painters in America whose work was exhibited and admired by critics at the Centennial. Two works of unidentified subject matter, shown among the American watercolors, were described as "thoroughly in the Japanese spirit."[129] A survey of her work from the 1870s is unambiguous in revealing her familiarity with Japanese art.

Here then is a relatively minor female artist working with Japanese sources more than a decade before it became commonplace in the ateliers of New York's artist elites. She is known to have owned Japanese scroll paintings and folding screens, but beyond that there is little documentation on her sources.[130] Comparable, but even earlier, is the work of John William Hill, whose watercolors of apple blossoms (The Brooklyn Museum), painted from

(72 a) *Grapevines*, about 1876
Watercolor on paper
American
FIDELIA BRIDGES
Courtesy of May and Frederick Hill

(72 b) *Cherry Twig*, about 1876
Watercolor on paper
American
FIDELIA BRIDGES
Courtesy of Berry-Hill Galleries, Inc.

nature as early as the 1860s, are among the first Japanesque images in American painting. The Japanism of these and other American Pre-Raphaelites is promising ground for future study.

American painters struggled to secure their status as professional artists, independent of the whims of clients and employers. It was not readily granted. Artists' desire for autonomy conflicted with the popular consensus, then developing, to strengthen the industrial arts and design, hardly goals calculated to sustain an artist's independence. Humbled at its Centennial by unfavorable comparisons with the more advanced industrial nations of Europe, the United States was swift to embrace the need for art in the products of industry. This was the age that gave rise to the idea of decorative art and the allied concept of bric-a-brac.

Out of necessity and genuine interest American painters not only responded to the call but occasionally assumed positions of leadership in the retooling of American industrial arts. La Farge founded the La Farge Decorative Art Company, which specialized in interior design and home furnishings, while Louis Comfort Tiffany abandoned painting entirely for a career as a stained-glass designer and decorator. Most artists collected decorative arts and their studios became highly personalized expressions of their tastes and travels. Decorative paintings and paintings of decorative art found a ready market among acquisitive Americans anxious to flaunt their newly rehearsed talents at connoisseurship and art appreciation.

The painters who made still lifes of Japanese decorative art or whose work exhibits a rich vocabulary of ornamentation are a mixed group ranging from highly accomplished, academy-trained masters like Elihu Vedder (fig. 73) and Charles Caryl Coleman (color plate 9), to small-town sign painters and amateurs eager to dabble in fine art. For some it was a sideline adopted as a profitable diversion; for others it was a rite of passage en route to being appreciated as artists.

Although regarded as a minor tributary in the study of Japanese influence, the Japanesque still life was present from the beginning to the end of the Japan craze. As late as 1898 John Haberle, the noted master of American trompe l'oeil, painted what may be the greatest picture of the genre, an enormous six-foot-high room view titled *Japanese Corner*[131] (fig. 74).

(73) *Moths and Blossoms*, 1875
Oil on canvas
American
ELIHU VEDDER
Mr. and Mrs. Jeffrey R. Brown

Elihu Vedder was an American expatriate painter who used decorative art extensively as subject matter in his work. Based in Rome, he explored classical and Japanesque themes. Vedder returned to the United States briefly during the late 1870s, where he participated in the meetings and activities of the Tile Club, a group of New York artists who helped foster an interest in decorative art. This picture, which Vedder painted in Rome, represents classical Japanesque subject matter.

A survey of recent auction catalogs containing nineteenth-century American paintings turns up Japanesque still lifes by little-known artists like Nicholas Alden Brooks of New York and Edward C. Leavitt of Providence, Rhode Island.[132] These are good and interesting pictures, proving that the decorative arts, and Japanese work in particular, had arrived. Dating from as early as the 1870s, the popularity of the Japanesque still life peaked during the 1880s, at the height of the Japan craze. Little studied and rarely preserved in public collections, hundreds of these images were undoubtedly produced by dozens of painters across the country.

Artists' involvement with bric-a-brac and decorative arts became manifest in the making of decorative-art objects. Louis Comfort Tiffany's oft-quoted statement that he was going into "decorative work" as a profession because he believed "there is more in it than in painting pictures" may seem extreme, but many of his most successful peers would have agreed that decorative work offered an abundance of opportunity for artistic expression.[133]

As early as 1877 a group of New York artists banded together to found the Tile Club. Aimed at promoting sociability among New York painters, the

(plate 9-color reproduction, page 191)
Night Owl, 1879
Oil on canvas
American
CHARLES CARYL COLEMAN
Jane Voorhees Zimmerli Art Museum
Rutgers, The State University of New Jersey
In memory of the deceased members of the class of 1954

No American painter explored Japanese decorative effects with greater sensitivity or imagination than Charles Caryl Coleman. Like his contemporary Elihu Vedder, Coleman maintained a studio in Rome where he joined a community of American expatriate painters, many of whom shared his interest in Greek, Roman, and Japanese art. This picture with its exaggerated vertical format owes much to the tradition of Japanese woodblock print.

(74) *Japanese Corner*, 1898
Oil on canvas
New Haven, Connecticut
JOHN HABERLE
Museum of Fine Arts, Springfield, Massachusetts

club included, among others, Winslow Homer, J. Alden Weir, William Merritt Chase, Elihu Vedder, John Twachtman, and Stanford White. Meetings were held in one or another of the members' studios where food and entertainment were provided and the work of tile decorating commenced. In 1879 the Club chartered a canal boat to go up the Hudson River to Lake Champlain. Decorated with Japanese lanterns and outfitted with the props and equipment necessary to sketch from nature, this and subsequent excursions helped promote the club's activities and enhance the prestige and popularity of tile painting.[134] The Tile Club's summer excursions were also an important prelude to the culture of camaraderie and pursuit of picturesque settings that culminated in the founding of artists' colonies by many Tile Club alumni during the 1890s. In the years that followed prominent painters would paint folding screens and fans, design picture frames and furniture, dabble in architectural painting, and generally remain open to the unlimited potential for artistic expression in the decorative arts.

John La Farge was neither the first nor the most renowned American artist to visit Japan. As an illustrative genre, pictures of Japanese life gained favor with collectors and popular magazines hungry for an image that would attract their readers' interest. The majority of painters who visited Japan, arrived with a commission from one of several popular illustrated magazines. Albert Parson traveled with a commission from *Harpers,* and Robert Blum with one from *Scribners.* The first American artist to travel to Japan was a lesser-known New England landscape painter named Winckworth Allan Gay. Assisted by a commission for "a picture of Japanese landscape" for Boston's Somerset Club, Gay spent the years 1876 through 1881 in Japan, a period longer than any other American painter. He filled sketchbooks and produced finished landscapes and genre scenes while living in Yokohama and Kamakura. Like La Farge and Robert Blum, Gay returned to his sketchbooks as a source for new paintings and illustrations years after his return to America.[135]

American artists who traveled to Japan during the Japan craze include Theodore Wores (1885-1887 and 1892-1894), Charles Dater Weldon (1892), Albert Herter (1893), Frank Alfred Bicknell (ca. 1894), and H. Humphrey Moore (1890s). But the most influential of all, the American painter best remembered for his work in Japan, was Robert Blum, whose trip to Japan (1890-1892) became the consummating experience of his career and the source for some of the period's most powerful images of Japan. Having trained as a lithographer in Cincinnati during the 1870s, Blum became associated with an emerging network of Cincinnati artists such as Kenyon Cox, John Twachtman, and Frank Duveneck. As a muralist, illustrator, and pastel painter, Blum adapted to the need for diverse skills and approaches and was thus well qualified for the assignment that took him to Japan in 1890. Traveling with the British poet Sir Edwin Arnold, Blum's assignment for Scribners involved illustrating a series of articles for Arnold's *Japonica* (fig. 75), which was serialized and later reissued in book form. Blum's own account of his travels was serialized as "An Artist in Japan." While in Japan, Blum assembled a large collection of Japanese photographs (Cincinnati Art Museum), which together with his sketches formed the basis for the dozens of oil and pastel paintings that he exhibited and sold after returning to New York in 1893. Blum's

(75) *Japonica*, 1891
Bound paper with embossed hard covers
Written by Sir Edwin Arnold
Illustrated by Robert Blum
New York
Charles Scribner's Sons
Hartford Public Library

subject matter included quick impressionistic pastels of Japanese figures, quasi-aesthetic seascapes and street scenes, and genre pictures illustrating daily life in Japan. The most monumental and acclaimed of Blum's genre pictures is "The Ameya" (color plate 10), a picturesque composition that captures the details of the traditional candy maker's stall amidst the commotion of a busy street. The qualities of color, expression, and detail mark this as a masterpiece of genre painting, all the more startling and impressive for being undertaken in so foreign a land.[136]

Looming across the main stage of nineteenth-century American art is the long shadow of an elect group of predominantly male painters who worked or studied abroad and in whose studios a vigorous and distinctive new art was born. Not all of the painters from the 1880s and 1890s now regarded as American masters developed an explicitly Japanesque style and none of those who did worked only in that style. But the influence of Japanese art on some of the major

(plate 10-color reproduction, page 191)
The Ameya, 1893
Oil on canvas
ROBERT F. BLUM
The Metropolitan Museum of Art
Gift of the Estate of Alfred Corning Clark, 1904

The Ameya *(candy vendor) is the most monumental and important work produced by the New York painter Robert Blum following his tour of Japan in 1892 and 1893. The picture was first illustrated to accompany the text of Sir Edwin Arnold's* Japonica *(1892) with a caption that compared the work of the candy maker to the art of glass-blowing as "certainly as artistic and finished as regards workmanship."*

painters of the late nineteenth century is striking and has left us with some of the most engaging works of the period.

Japanese influence is best revealed in work by the disciples of British aestheticism and French impressionism. Both movements gained force in America around 1885. Among the American impressionists, J. Alden Weir, Childe Hassam, William Merritt Chase, and John Twachtman produced works most striking in the assimilation of Japanese compositional effects and details. But the influence of Japan was deeper. Japanese art opened a new chapter in the artist's timeless preoccupation with nature. One of the great transformations brought about by the encounter with Japanese art was abandoning the quest for realism in the depiction of nature. A shift from the kind of botanical accuracy and picturesque settings characteristic of the monumental landscapes of the 1870s is revealed in the move toward more intimate and atmospheric qualities found in the work of the American impressionists beginning in the mid-1880s. Continued interest in painting outdoors and seeking out ideal settings where the qualities of light, color, and atmosphere could be evoked led from the excursions of the Tile Club to a search for aesthetic locations where groups of artists could luxuriate in nature while enjoying the companionship of their peers.

American painters were among the early advocates of country life. Although New York had become the hub for exhibiting and marketing fine art, painters like Twachtman, Weir, and Hassam increasingly drew inspiration from their summers spent in the country at shared retreats in Greenwich and Old Lyme, Connecticut, Cornish and Dublin, New Hampshire, Shinnecock, Long Island, and on the coast north of Boston and in Maine. In 1889, when John Twachtman began exploring southwestern Connecticut for a country place so he could "live in an environment he wished to paint," he was fulfilling the Japanese-inspired fantasy of achieving a total personal and professional engagement with an aesthetic landscape.

One of Twachtman's great achievements was perfecting a style of winter landscape that was soft, ethereal, shadowless, and atmospheric – much like Japanese prints. A similar effect is revealed in "Japanese Winter Landscape" (fig. 76), a work from 1879 that is one of the earliest images in American painting that renders the atmosphere and colors of nature in a manner that is unmistakably Japanesque. Its strong horizon line and the diagonals of the snow-covered path beg a further investigation into the timing and sources of Twachtman's involvement with Japanese art.

William Merritt Chase, best known for his impressionist portrait studies and domestic interiors, painted "The Blue Kimono" (fig. 77), one of the earliest depictions of a kimono-clad woman surrounded by tokens of Japanese aestheticism: the folding screen, a bronze vase, and a bamboo and paper fan. The qualities of Japanese art incorporated in the work of the American impressionists are subtle: a prominent diagonal within a landscape, the mimicking of Japanese cliches like the sacred bridge, and the pure color of a flattened portrait on a gold or mica ground. Most of all, these artists used Japanese art as a way of reinforcing their ideals and building a bridge toward the liberation of their work and their conscience from the constant demand for the functional and literal in art. These pictures, whether taken to the compositional extremes of Twachtman's low-tone, nearly monochromatic winterscapes or the rich shimmering textures of Weir's sun-drenched rural landscapes (color plate 11), assert the artist's freedom of expression. By avoiding the sentimental and picturesque, the artist resisted the demands for theatrical performance. In moving to the country and simply painting what was before them, the American impressionists affirmed the dignity of human experience and observation.[137] What could be a more essentially Japanese approach to nature, than to share the blessings of its surrounding presence?

The impressionists were not the first or only celebrated American artists to process the message of Japanese art. Having already discussed the impact of decorative art and decorative detail in trompe l'oeil and still-life pictures, it is worth retracing familiar ground by considering the artist Americans liked best. Winslow Homer is in many respects the most American of late nineteenth-century American painters. He is one of the only major figures in the New York art world during the Japan craze who did not study or tour Europe extensively. Having risen up through the ranks of magazine illustrators, his attraction to watercolor painting was due partly to its portability. His earliest on-site painting was not in the

This is one of the earliest paintings by a major figure in American art to incorporate elements of Japanese composition. Twachtman's fascination with the atmosphere, light, and texture of the winter landscape signals the growing interest in seasonal variation among American painters.

(76) *Japanese Winter Landscape*, 1879
Oil on canvas
American
JOHN TWACHTMAN
Philadelphia Museum of Art

(77) *The Blue Kimono*, 1888
Oil on canvas
American
William Merritt Chase
The Parrish Art Museum, Southampton, New York
Littlejohn Collection

William Merritt Chase produced the most evocative Japanesque portraits of any American artist. Sensitive to the Japanese qualities of color, posture, expression, and texture, pictures like this also reveal the artist's interest in collecting Japanese art and bric-a-brac. Chase's New York studio was a veritable gallery of art and antiques, which he occasionally used as props for portraits like this one. The emphasis on aesthetic consideration is reflected in the portrait's title.

Japan in the Artist's Eye

realm of plein air impressionism but in recording prison life on the front during the Civil War. Homer's response to the tremendous developments in aesthetic theory during his lifetime might best be described as pragmatic rather than idealistic. In spite of his reputation for formal composition and as a brilliant colorist, Homer never abandoned the well-worn path of representation. Whether they are views of the White Mountains, the Adirondacks, or the Maine coast, or the timeless depictions of everyday life, Homer's images were always narrative. None of his contemporaries can better claim the honor of having captured and defined the national experience.

Homer lacked the affectations usually associated with japanists of the aesthetic and impressionist schools. Unlike William Merritt Chase whose New York studio was draped in fabrics and brimming with bric-a-brac,[138] Homer was not a collector, and his studio appeared sparse and functional. And yet his membership in the Tile Club and his close association with John La Farge points to an unmistakable familiarity with Japanese art. Homer escapes being pigeonholed with the aesthetes mostly because his subject matter, yeoman's credentials, and unaffected airs do not fit the usual description. That is the great beauty of Homer's work. Evidence of exposure to Japanese prints is apparent almost immediately following his trip to Paris in 1867. Look again, and you cannot help but see many of the well-seasoned conventions of Japanese color prints in Homer's pictures: the use of extraordinary angles of vision, the low horizon lines, the predominance of balance over

(plate 11-color reproduction, page 192)
The Laundry, Branchville, about 1894
Oil on canvas
American
J. ALDEN WEIR
Private Collection

During the early 1890s J. Alden Weir became deeply absorbed in the study and collection of Japanese prints. The Laundry, *a view depicting the scene outside his country home in Branchville, Connecticut, is one of his earliest works to incorporate features of Japanese composition. The unusual vantage point, raised horizon line, and the dominant field of color in the foreground are recognizable features of Japanese art.*

symmetry, flat unmodulated colors and tones used to define shapes, the prominence of the diagonal as a compositional device to separate fields of action, and the haunting presence of truncated forms and figures. Add to this Homer's startling use of bold, graphic colors, and his japanism appears unmistakable. In "Breezing Up" (1876, National Gallery of Art), a sea story that has become one of the most famous images in American art, Homer's use of the truncated form of a sail boat passing out of the picture frame has no likely precedent outside of Japanese art. Albert Gardner, one of the first to assess the influence of Japanese art in Homer's work, concluded, "Once the idea of Japanese influence on the art of Winslow Homer is accepted, it becomes easy to find evidence of it in all his work after 1867."[139]

"Wild Geese in Flight" (fig. 78), painted in 1897, is one of Homer's most Japanesque pictures. The qualities of atmosphere and unmodulated color, the prominence of strong diagonals, the appearance of frozen motion, the unusual angle of vision, and, most obviously, the use of waterfowl as subject matter convey a rich involvement with Japanese design and an eerie psychology of pictorial action that is the hallmark of Homer's greatest work.

Given the focus of this book on the American context for the Japan craze, a movement that peaks during the 1880s and peters out during the 1890s, the inclusion or exclusion of Mary Cassatt, the great American expatriate and impressionist, is bound to elicit howls of protest. Those who regard her as the avatar of American impressionism will believe not enough is made of her importance here, while those who see her as a remote figure absorbed in the currents of French japonisme, could interpret her influence as superfluous. Both are, to some degree, correct. As an advisor to American collectors and a pioneer in the color-print movement of the 1890s and early 1900s, Cassatt's influence is significant. The series of ten woodblock color prints that she made in 1891 after visiting an exhibition of Japanese art in Paris with her friend Edgar Degas stands as one of the monuments of the Japanese influence (fig. 79). They were exhibited and sold in America and their influence was felt, most notably through the work of Arthur Wesley Dow of Boston and Ipswich, Massachusetts.

As a leader in the development of the color-print movement, the artist and art educator Dow

(78) *Wild Geese in Flight*, 1897
Oil on canvas
American
WINSLOW HOMER
The Portland Museum of Art
Gift of Charles Shipman Payson

This picture is one of Winslow Homer's grandest and most successful Japanesque paintings.

(79) *The Fitting*, 1891
Color print with drypoint and aquatint
American
MARY CASSATT
Smith College Museum of Art, Northampton, Massachusetts

The Fitting *is one of the famous series of ten color prints inspired by Mary Cassatt's 1890 visit to an exhibition of Japanese woodblock prints at the École des Beaux Arts. The next year the Paris gallery of Durand-Ruel exhibited the series to wide acclaim. Although Cassatt was an expatriate, she advised American collectors and developed a following for her work in America. The Worcester Art Museum purchased a set of these prints shortly after they were made. Cassatt was one of the first artists to experiment with Japanese printing methods; the flattening of forms, emphasis on pattern and line, and use of bright colors reveal the influence of Japanese prints.*

In 1891, Arthur Wesley Dow came to appreciate Japanese color prints through an association with Ernest Fenollosa, the curator of Japanese art at the Museum of Fine Arts in Boston. As a teacher, painter, printer, and art education theorist, Dow emerged as a leader of the color print movement that flourished during the early years of the twentieth century. He later visited Japan and witnessed traditional block-printing firsthand. Both in technique and subject matter, these prints mark an important chapter in the Japanism of American artists during the late years of the Japan craze.

(80) *The Lily*, about 1895
Color woodblock print
Ipswich, Massachusetts
American
ARTHUR WESLEY DOW
Ipswich Historical Society

(fig. 80) is an important, albeit late, exponent of the Japan idea. Helen Hyde, one of the early proponents of color woodblock prints, actually moved to Japan in 1899, where she employed Japanese printmakers to assist in the production of pictures that were sold in the United States. When Dow visited Japan in 1905, he was introduced to her printmaker and thereby gained a firsthand knowledge of the technique of block printing which he helped popularize back in Boston.

The resonant influence of the Japan idea in American art was fragmented and diffused over the next half a century. With the growth of art photography, especially in the work of early pictorialists like Edward Steichen and Alfred Steiglitz, the continuing influence of Japanese art is deeply felt. At the turn of the century society painters of the Boston school – notably William Paxton, Robert Reid, and Edmund Tarbell – painted languid interiors in which Japanese screens, fabrics, and bric-a-brac often appear. Clay Lancaster in his pioneering study *Japanese Influence in America* (1963) observed the lingering impact and continuing power of Japanese design in the work of Franz Kline, whose compositions in abstrac-

(81) Bust of Japanese maiden, "Okamoto," 1886
Bronze
New York City
LOUIS AMATEIS
Robert Bahssin-Post Road Gallery

This is one of the few known examples of American sculpture in the Japanese style. Louis Amateis was raised and trained in Turin, Italy. Having established a reputation in Europe, Amateis settled in the United States in 1884 where he helped found the School of Architecture and Fine Arts at Columbian University in Washington, D.C. His portrait busts are exhibited in the United States Capitol. This bust of "Okamoto" was exhibited at the National Academy of Design in 1886 and may have been sculpted from life of a Japanese woman whose biography is currently unknown.

tion resemble nothing so much as the calligraphy on kakemonos, Japan's classical scroll paintings. But as painting moved toward a deeper involvement with abstraction it becomes nearly impossible to isolate specific intersections with the art of Japan.

The schism between the fine arts and popular culture emerged full-force among the late Victorian painters who were, in fact, the first generation to liberate themselves from the popular tastes of their age. Perhaps in doing so they shaped the tastes of the future. But until the art of painting is seen from the vantage point of its surrounding context, the complete story of Japanese influence in American art cannot be fully told.

Clearly, the story of American "art" and painting has been too narrowly told. The impact of Japan on American sculpture has received almost no attention. Yet a bust by Louis Amateis (fig. 81) and the work of anonymous sculptors employed in the terra cotta and bronze casting industries suggest an area ripe for further study. Further outside the mainstream are the myriad Japanesque folding screens, many decorated by amateurs, but some – like those illustrated here (fig. 82 and color plate 12) – were almost certainly the work of highly accomplished professionals. By allowing this to be shown alongside the work of recognized "masters," we perhaps gain a richer perspective on what the Japan idea meant to the culture at large.

(82) Folding screen, about 1887
Painted maple
United States or Great Britain
Wadsworth Atheneum

This screen illustrates the convergence of Japanism with the work of British Pre-Raphaelite painters like Edward Burne-Jones, whose design for a set of stained glass windows it closely resembles. The screen is made of American maple and is decorated on both sides—perfectly suitable for use in a formal reception or dining room. It was presumably made in the United States but is unrelated to any presently known genre of American painting. More technically proficient than the work usually associated with amateur and women artists, it is most likely the work of a professional ornamental painter or an interior design studio like Associated Artists. Regardless of who painted the screen, its vocabulary of Japanese, classical, and medieval ornament is astonishing. The screen is included to illustrate a genre of Japanesque decorative art that merits further study.

(plate 12-color reproduction, page 192)
Folding screen, about 1885
Wooden lattice core covered with paper under watercolor and metallic painted silk front panels, silk brocade backing
San Francisco, California
Painted by FORAKECHI YATA for the ICHI BAN STUDIOS
Essex Institute

This screen represents the ultimate in Japanesque portraiture. It was commissioned by Josiah Brodhead, a major in the United States Army, stationed in San Francisco and Arizona during the late 1870s and early 1880s. The screen depicts Brodhead's three daughters, Eleanor, Carolyn, and Rebecca, each outfitted in a Japanese kimono and surrounded by props that suggest they might have been painted while visiting Japan. The screen was produced by a Japanese artist employed at Horace Fletcher's "Ichi Ban" Japanese art goods emporium. The artist probably worked up the images from photographic portraits of the women supplied by Brodhead.

V. Architecture and the Japanesque Interior

American architecture on the eve of the Japan craze was poised for sweeping change. The interpretations of classical and neoclassical design had become increasingly stiff, formal, and academic, climaxing during the 1860s and 1870s with mansions built in the Italianate and French Second Empire styles. Based on Renaissance and baroque schemes of ornament, these styles were baronial and ostentatious without being especially inviting or comfortable. The American mansion of 1870 was more of a statement than a family retreat. Impossible to operate without servants and highly structured as to room use and the flow of interior space, these dwellings were the antithesis of what Americans came to admire and understand about architecture in Japan.

More than one critic suggested that the Japanese architecture was not architecture at all, at least not by Western standards.[140] The relative poverty of the vast majority of Japanese and a tradition of impermanent housing in a country notorious for earthquakes were two reasons frequently cited. More importantly, Japanese housing was what today might be called vernacular or folk architecture. Houses were designed by builders working in centuries-old traditions, using local materials and adapting to local environmental conditions. It may seem unusual that a culture that regarded potters and weavers as artists had no architects. As a consequence, Japanese architecture proved unsuitable for emulation, and its impact in America was more subtle than in the other arts.

The analysis of Japanese houses by the legendary Japanophile Edward Morse suggests that values that shaped American architecture during the 1880s were apparent in Japan's traditional housing. Even if Japanese features were not translated literally, the spirit of Japanese architecture permeated and reinforced the direction of American architecture during the post-Centennial era.

The contrast between Japanese housing and the housing popular in the United States in 1870 leads to the conclusion that these two distant cultures had their priorities exactly reversed. And yet many of the ideas encapsulated in Japanese housing were embraced by American architects and their clients during the 1880s and 1890s. If not translated directly, Japanese architecture provided symbols used to promote architectural reform.

Morse's study of Japanese houses is filled with testy anecdotes aimed at amplifying and reinforcing reforms already underway when his book was released in 1886. Anticipating the growth of landscape architecture and gardening and the integration of housing and environment, epitomized in the work of Frank Lloyd Wright, Morse marveled at the way Japanese houses communicated with their settings: "In the cities nothing is more surprising to a foreigner than to go from the dust and turmoil of a busy street directly into a rustic yard and the felicity of quiet country life."[141] Inside, exposed framework and construction created an earthen, rustic effect opposite that sought by American classicists bent on artifice, slick finish, and excessive ornament. "On entering a Japanese house," Morse continued, "one notices ... the constructive features everywhere ... stout wooden posts, supports and cross-ties.... The absence of all paint, varnish, oil, or filling, which too often defaces our rooms at home, is at once remarked.... Wood is left in just the condition in which it leaves the cabinetmaker's plane."[142]

Equally startling to the Western eye was the absence of furniture. Hinting at impending reforms, Morse wrote scathingly of the "monstrous bills for carpets, curtains, furniture, silver, dishes, etc., often entailed upon young housekeepers at home," which he regarded as "social miseries that the Japanese happily know but little about."[143] He was less convinced of Japan's advantage in doing without modern heating, concluding implausibly that the "Japanese do not suffer from the cold as we do."[144] His description of "winter-parties" in which rooms were "entirely open to the garden ... glistening with a fresh snowfall" are confirmed by a genre of ukiyo-e print that documents just such entertainment. Images like this further reinforced Japan's reputation as a nation that put art and beauty above all else, even human comfort!

The most radical feature of the Japanese interior was its open plan. Sliding and folding screens were used as permanent and impermanent partitions to separate spaces within spaces and indoors from the outdoors. Light and flimsy, screens shared none of the overpowering quality of walls and doors in mid-nineteenth-century American mansions. In the traditional Japanese house the front door and stairway leading to the upper floor were quietly hidden, while the roof, with its ornamental ridgelines and shingles, was lofty and conspicuous.

Two styles of architecture became popular in England and America during the 1870s and 1880s: modern Gothic and Queen Anne. Architectural historians debate the origins of these styles while recognizing types and variants of each. In one of the earliest and most influential works on American Victorian housing, Vincent Scully identified two important variants which he named the stick style and the shingle style.[145] Although they occurred sequentially, both have roots in the reforms associated with the British aesthetic movement, a sweeping cultural phenomenon that combined Japanism with medieval revivalism as the way Britain could establish its world eminence in the industrial arts. Whether the source was John Ruskin proselytizing about honest workmanship and English Gothic ornament or the reform styles emanating from the South Kensington School, American architecture during the Japan craze was British in descent, even as it found inspiration in the architecture of Japan.

Japanese influence in Victorian American architecture is demonstrated in the content of specific styles and in subordinate ornament, both inside and out. Most of all it was communicated through moveable furnishings and wall and window treatments, without which the architecture appears barren and confusing. One of the most intriguing arguments in favor of Japanese influence in American architecture is Scully's stick style, the most radical, modern, and explicitly American of the reform styles.

The stick style, a product of the 1870s, is characterized by the conspicuous display of exposed framing. It is a style that glories in the elements of craft, turning the frame inside out and rendering its exterior ornament as a window through which the angles and lines of construction are handsomely revealed. The style flourished in the construction of the most modern of all architectural forms, the country and suburban railroad station. Well into the 1880s, small towns along the eastern seaboard discovered an affordable response to the cutting-edge monumentality of big city railroad stations. Together with libraries, town halls, opera houses, and museums, the railroad station stood at the head of the development of a national architecture expressive of America's growing industrial might. Nothing spoke more clearly or inexpensively to the need for a modern look than the stick style.

The antecedent of the stick style is found in the imitations of Swiss chalets, popularized by American-pattern book authors during the 1850s. As early as the 1860s the style was fully developed in the summer cottages designed for Newport, Rhode Island clients by the architect Richard Morris Hunt. It reached its apogee in the exhibit buildings erected by New Jersey and Michigan at the Centennial Exhibition. These towering confections of latticework, with their steep pitched roofs, and projecting eaves, are as close as nineteenth-century American architecture gets to a Japanese look. And yet the style would appear to have developed independent of Japanese sources. Lack of documentation aside, the relationship between the stick style and Japanese design is unambiguous.

An intriguing example is furnished by a train

station built in Strafford, Pennsylvania (on the National Register of Historic Places) out of the remains of the Japanese dwelling from the Centennial. The builders produced a gem of stick style design that demonstrates the compatibility of this most American of Victorian architectural styles with the traditional architecture of Japan.[144] The Underwood house, in Tolland, Connecticut (fig. 83), designed by George and Charles Palliser and illustrated in *Palliser's Model Homes* (1878), is a classic expression of the style designed and built just as the Japan craze was sweeping the nation.

The style of architecture dubbed Queen Anne was Japanesque in a different way. Here the move away from the traditional rectangular box, a standard of Western housing for centuries, was finally taken to its logical extreme. The Queen Anne style was the first in America to treat interior space as a primary variable and also the first to make a conspicuous display of stylistic variety. The style was intentionally difficult to characterize. It was an eclectic mix of classical, American colonial, Japanesque, English Gothic, and Elizabethan ornament that also assumed an endless, seemingly random variety of forms and shapes. Think of the controlled-accident effect in the design of Japanese ceramics or the conspicuous avoidance of repetition in most Japanese arts, and you can see how the Japan idea relates to American Queen Anne architecture. It is especially apparent in the work of the architects Stanford White and the firm of Peabody and Stearns.[145] Japanesque ornament is not present in all Queen Anne structures and is not easily recognized. The Opera House built in Norfolk, Connecticut (fig. 84), in 1883 and the Goodwin Building (fig. 85), a mixed-use office and apartment complex built for Francis and James Goodwin in Hartford, Connecticut, in 1881 are two exceptions that epitomize both urban and country versions of the Queen Anne style. Both are rich in Japanesque detail.

The Queen Anne style, with its interminable verandas and open interiors, was ideally suited to the construction of summer homes where considerations of heating economy and mixed usage could be tossed to the winds. Only in the late 1890s would anyone in America adopt Japanese architectural forms literally, and then, as custom prevailed, such whimsy was restricted to the summer home where it would not interfere with the demands of urban propriety.

(83) Frank H. Underwood House, 1878
Tolland, Connecticut
Designed by GEORGE AND CHARLES PALLISER
Bridgeport, Connecticut

The Underwood house is a classic example of stick style architecture. The gridwork of mock post-and-beam construction that decorates the exterior of the house suggests a fascination with the Japanesque quality of construction. Although the house now lacks its original slate roof and most of the stained glass panels that provided colorful accents in the Japanese taste, its open plan construction and the presence of decorative fans under the eaves suggest the spirit of the style. The architects are best remembered today for the architectural guidebooks they published. The Underwood house was featured in the 1878 version of their book Palliser's Model Homes.

(84) Opera house or village hall, 1883
Norfolk, Connecticut

The Japan craze affected the look of rural villages throughout New England through the growing popularity of new architectural forms, such as libraries, opera houses, and town halls. The opera house, providing a secular meeting space, housed an auditorium where dances, lectures, and theatrical performances were staged. In short, the opera house became the cultural center of village life and, as such, needed to affect a stylish and modern air. The Norfolk Opera House conveys the qualities of Japanese design through the laying of its variegated bands of shingles, picturesque and asymmetrical arrangement of windows, and the inclusion of ornamental details like quarter-fans, mons, and the crescent moon. The building's architect is unknown.

(85) Goodwin Building, 1881
Designed by KIMBALL & WISEDELL of New York
Hartford, Connecticut

The Japanesque terra cotta details on this brick Queen Anne style commercial building demonstrate that the Japan craze was not limited to vacation retreats or suburban homes, but also influenced urban architecture. The growth of the ornamental terra cotta industry was one of the defining influences in American architecture during the 1880s. Terra cotta details for the Goodwin Building were supplied by the Boston Terra Cotta Company, which later used the building as a model in its advertising.

Designed and built by Japanese craftsmen involved with the Japanese exhibits at the World's Columbian Exposition held in Chicago in 1893, Pine Tree Point on Upper St. Regis Lake in the Adirondacks (fig. 86) is one of the greatest artistic achievements of the Japan craze.

Japanism in American architecture is usually confined to ornament and accessories, especially painted decoration, wallpaper, fireplace tiles, fixed woodwork, decorative glass and hardware – features often removed or destroyed and thus difficult to document. The movables will be discussed later in a section on industrial art. Among the fixtures, however, is an important but little studied tributary in Victorian architecture. In buildings that may otherwise appear devoid of Japanesque ornament the work of the fresco painter warrants a close look.

The ceiling has a long history as a decorated surface. Plain, light, monochromatic ceilings have been so dominant a fashion during the twentieth century

(86) Pine Tree Point Camp, 1894
Upper St. Regis, New York
Private estate

Pine Tree Point is one of the few instances in America where Japanese architecture was adopted literally. The collection of buildings—in addition to the main house there was a pagoda, guest house, tea pavilion, and boat house, all in the Japanese style—was conceived by Frederick W. Vanderbilt and his wife following a visit to the 1893 World's Columbian Exposition in Chicago. Hiring the workmen who built the Japanese tea house and Ho-o-den in Chicago, Vanderbilt arranged for a complete make-over of the family's Adirondack "camp," situated at the edge of Upper St. Regis Lake, overlooking a mountain vista. Details throughout demonstrate a faithful observance of the sources and methods of Japanese design and construction. Nowhere in America is the effect of Japanese architecture carried out with greater splendor.

that we forget the extent to which ceiling ornament flourished during the century before. Indeed, throughout the history of American architecture, from the molded, carved, and painted beams and joists of the seventeenth-century to the elaborate plaster medallions found in neoclassical and Greek revival mansions, ceiling ornament has been common.

The practice of decorating a ceiling with painted designs and patterns began during the 1850s, but it was not until the 1870s and 1880s that painted (and the less expensive papered) ceilings became standard in the better houses. To accommodate this growing demand, a new trade, that of the fresco painter, was born. By 1880 even modest-sized cities like Hartford, Connecticut, and Worcester, Massachusetts, supported more than one fresco painter, while New York and Philadelphia supported dozens.[148] Fresco painters worked from elaborate ceiling plans using the methods of stencil and freehand painting on a prepared ground. A client would typically commission the decoration of several rooms, each in a different style. As in the S.S. Kimball house (color plate 13), a modern Gothic mansion built in Concord, New Hampshire, in 1876 from the designs of Cutting and Holman, architects of Worcester, Massachusetts, the Japanese style was usually reserved for the flash and dazzle of the quasi-public reception room, a space located just off the main entrance where a family could flaunt its artistic pretensions.

Interior woodwork in the Japanese style included spool-and-ball transoms, carved and molded chimney pieces, and carved and painted door panels and trim. Since the building trade was more decentralized than furniture making and glass manufacturing, architectural millwork companies tended to develop regional rather than national markets. Consequently, they advertised less frequently in the national periodicals and rarely issued trade

(plate 13-color reproduction, page 193)
Ceiling fresco, about 1880
Samuel Sparhawk Kimball House, 1876-1882
Possibly painted by WILLIAM HENAY & SON
Concord, New Hampshire
Courtesy of the Kimball-Jenkins Estate

This remarkably well-preserved fresco-painted ceiling was part of the original furnishing plan of the sitting room in the brick modern Gothic style mansion designed for a Concord, New Hampshire industrialist by the Worcester architectural firm of Cutting-Homan in 1876. The sitting room, or reception room, was a quasi-public space where the family exhibited its most modern affectations and stylish decor. Although several other rooms in the house are fresco painted, this was the only room that adopted the Japanesque. Its delicate figures set inside gilt-ground medallions are suggestive of Japanese folding screens. The work may have been executed by William Henay and Son, the only fresco painter in Concord at the time the house was being completed.

catalogs, the sources most frequently cited in the study of related Victorian industries.

Exceptions gleaned from the pages of art magazines, city directories, and the rare trade catalog hint at the output of this large but poorly documented industry. Manufacturing Japanesque fixtures, custom- and ready-made, for the building trade was big business (fig 87). S. Huet of Philadelphia illustrated Japanese-style "artistic wood mantles" with asymmetrical shelving and Japanesque ornament. Cutting and Delaney of Buffalo, New York, developed a national market for Japanese-style fretwork and lattice transoms and spool-and-ball doorway surrounds. The Porter Manufacturing Company in Montpelier, Vermont, made fan-and diagonal-paneled screen doors using spool-and-ball ornament.[149] Allen and Leonard and R. Hanger & Co., both of Fair Haven, Vermont, manufactured flamboyantly Japanesque marbleized-slate chimney pieces.[150]

The renaissance in the art of stained, opalescent, and mosaic glass, which coincided with the Japan craze, is but the tip of an iceberg that includes a great many technical and stylistic innovations in the production and use of glass as architectural ornament. Glass panels that had been wheel engraved, stencilled, and sandblasted, and pressed into molds in the Japanese style found their way into houses and public buildings across the country. Very little has been written about these industries, and their products are rarely preserved in public collections. The fact is, until fairly recently only a few dealers and collectors paid any attention to it.[151] But a growing collection of trade catalogs preserved at the Corning Museum of Glass in Corning, New York, hints at a field of study ripe for further research.

Manufacturers like the R.S. Groves Company in Philadelphia marketed some of the wildest and most colorful American decorative art produced during this

This carved panel was removed from a house designed by the Worcester, Massachusetts architect, Stephen C. Earle. As a champion of the modern Gothic and Queen Anne styles, Earle would have been attuned to the applications of Japanese decoration, both as interior ornament and exterior sheathing.

(87) Architectural fragment, about 1885
Carved wood
United States
Designed by STEPHEN C. EARLE
Worcester Historical Society, Worcester, Massachusetts

(88) Window pane
about 1885
Transparent amber glass
New York
Wadsworth Atheneum

Pressed glass patterns in the Japanese style were made by several American manufacturers. Although this pane cannot be precisely documented, an identical pattern is illustrated in an advertisement for R.S. Groves's art glass company in Philadelphia.

(89) Door panel, about 1885
Cut glass
American
Wadsworth Atheneum

At the height of the Japan craze, glass panels decorated by pressing, sand blasting, wheel engraving, staining, and etching found their way into stylish houses across America. This example testifies to the use of Japanesque decoration. It was probably one of a pair installed as panels on massive walnut doors, separating the entry foyer from the interior of the house.

period. Groves sold glass panels installed as windows (fig. 88), sidelights, and doors (fig. 89) for use in "churches, dwellings, steamboats and cars." Mixing pressed, blown, and stained glass framed in lead, these panels draw from a rich vocabulary of Japanesque ornament which included brocades, cracked ice, storks, owls in the moonlight, and flower blossoms rendered as a rich mixture of squares, circles, and diagonals.[152]

Dubuque, Iowa, a boomtown in the 1890s, furnished a market for the products of Carr, Ryder & Adams Co., wholesalers and manufacturers of glass and interior woodwork. A catalog of its products included Japanese-style cut glass and sandblasted window panes of remarkable sophistication and complexity. Modeled, perhaps, after stenciled *tenugis*, the stenciled towels which they closely resemble, the patterns include airborne birds, pine branches, bamboo groves, and brocadelike diaper work.[153] A wider assortment of decorative sand-blasted glass was offered by John Matthews of New York City, whose 1886 catalog of decorative glass featured more than two dozen of the most ambitious designs yet documented, including zigzag compositions of brocadelike patterning and the most elegant aquatic scenes and spiders with webs.[154]

* * *

The passion for layers of decoration – columns and rows of patterned color, the alternation of controlled and random design, and the artistic placement of carefully chosen things – was part of a move aimed at the personalization of interior space. What caused people to crave these qualities in the industrial America of the 1880s is a study unto itself. Rising affluence, declining autonomy, the growth of a national culture, and the corresponding erosion of traditional communities – these are some of reasons frequently cited.

Domestic life during the Japan craze was about the pursuit of repose and the multiplication of outlets for creativity and individual expression. If one could flaunt one's wealth at the same time, all the better. My things, in my room, in my house – an attitude that would have seemed unconscionably self-centered a generation before – was now a means of survival and self-definition in an increasingly complex and centerless world. The structure of family, town, church, and shared traditions that bonded Americans during the colonial period collapsed during the industrial revolution. Cut loose from traditional anchors, Americans of 1880 were further disrupted by new forces designed to suppress the individual and shoehorn each citizen into communities based on class, occupation, and gender. Home and work were now separate spheres for a majority of Americans. More than ever, the home functioned as a refuge and retreat where the individual found sustenance and comfort. It was a temporary escape, valued all the more because for most Americans, complete escape was only achieved during a week's or month's vacation at a resort hotel or cottage on some mountain lake. That which was separate from the throbbing core of urban life provided more and greater opportunities for comfort, frivolity, and self-expression. From an architectural perspective, the porch was freer than the reception room, which was freer than the parlor, which was freer than the spirit-crushing rituals of etiquette associated with the dining room. But nothing compared with getting out of the city altogether and finding some quiet place where one could be oneself. Where freedom of conscience was found, where the individual was released from the aching demands of Victorian society, that is where the Japan idea flourished.[155]

Of all the works made by man and machine, from the vaunted sensibility of the impressionist canvas to the studied workmanship of the handcrafted chair, the Japan idea resounds most clearly in the artifice of the Japanesque interior. Almost past the point of restoration – the best example I know is a rustic "camp" restored on the grounds of the Adirondack Museum – the Japanesque interior is something we can only know today through photographs. If an example remained intact up to the Second World War, it has long since been swept away. And yet, what marvelous photographs they made. Fashionable, not accidentally, at the same time, the room portrait became popular as a photographic genre. There are undoubtedly hundreds of images of Japanesque interiors scattered in family albums and historical society archives around the country. We have selected a few of the best so that you might see the Japan idea in its full glory.

By 1880 America had become a society of collectors. Everything, from coins and butterflies to exotic porcelains and colonial American furniture was eagerly sought. The Japanesque interior was ideally suited to showcasing the individual collector's trophies. Even when its components were not Japanese-made or Japanese in inspiration, a room filled with carefully chosen and placed bric-a-brac is unmistakably Japanesque and must be recognized as *the* look sought after at the height of the Japan craze. Cluttered corners, mantlepieces groaning with the weight of decorative accessories, and cabinets – little museums – filled with odd bits of china and glass, that is what the Japanesque interior was all about. Its studied and self-conscious frivolity is one of the most memorable and evocative images of Victorian life.

The concept of bric-a-brac was one of the engines that powered this new approach to interior design. Writing about the phenomenon in 1878, (Appleton's) *Art Journal* noted that the phrase bric-a-brac, although not found in any dictionary, was of rising interest and that the "fashion of forming collections of bric-a-brac is rapidly increasing in this country." Establishing that the word bric meant a fragment, the author defined the term as meaning "literally 'odds and ends,' broken fragments, rubbish & etc." The article further suggested that the phrase originated with "wealthy dilettanti rather than... men of learning, or the general public" and was associated with an antiquarian mode of collecting that gave equal weight to aesthetics, historical context, and rarity. "Old china" was cited as an example "once ... valuable as heirlooms, but not otherwise" that was "now bought out and sold at fabulous prices to bric-a-bracquers."[156]

Even in their collecting habits Americans turned to Japan for inspiration. Edward Morse was the first to describe the strong tradition of bric-a-brac collecting among the Japanese. Once again, an idea that was gaining favor in America was legitimized by association with the art-loving society of Japan.

The accompanying illustrations were selected to show a broad range of domestic contexts. They date from 1880 to 1895 – the peak years of the Japan craze – and include a boy's room at Harvard College (fig. 90) and a girl's room at Mount Holyoke College (fig. 91), a White Mountain hotel lobby (fig. 92), a rustic "camp" in the Adirondacks (fig. 93), and typical middle-class interiors (figs. 94, 95). Rooms furnished by noted

(90) Dormitory room of John G. Coolidge, about 1884
Harvard University
Cambridge, Massachusetts
Courtesy of the Stevens-Coolidge Place, North Andover, Massachusetts

For John Coolidge, a lifelong interest in Japan was suggested as early as his college days at Harvard where he furnished his dormitory room with Japanese printed fabrics and bric-a-brac arranged in the Japanesque manner. Although the furnishing of Japanesque interiors was usually undertaken by women, a discrete accent was perfectly compatible with the more masculine artifacts of team sports and military ephemera associated with boys. Through his aunt, the legendary collector Isabella Gardner, Coolidge was introduced to Edward S. Morse. Following graduation from Harvard in 1886, Coolidge taught school in Tokyo, where he continued to collect and study Japanese art and culture.

(91) Dormitory room, about 1890
Mount Holyoke College
Williston Memorial Library Archives
Mount Holyoke College, South Hadley, Massachusetts

Teenagers revelled in the Japan craze, developing their own personalized expressions by furnishing rooms with inexpensive collectibles and art goods of their own make. This was room was furnished by Mary Hadsell Castle '91 and Jean Grant '92, students at Mount Holyoke College.

(92) Fabyan House office, about 1885
Franconia Notch, New Hampshire
Courtesy of the New Hampshire Historical Society

The Fabyan House, although torn down long ago, was one of the premier mountain resorts in New England at the height of the Japan craze. With easy access to railroads, the Fabyan House affected a casual and artistic manner. At dinner, visitors studied the menu from a printed card illustrating Japanese vases and tureens, and were presumably served from Japanesque platters and tureens. Although this picture probably represents furnishings arranged for a special occasion, a more emphatic expression of the Japanese taste can hardly be imagined. Japanese fan and paper lantern decor was taken to new extremes in this remarkable hotel lobby.

(93) Interior, Camp Cedars, about 1885
Forked Lake, New York
Photograph by EDWARD BIERSTADT
Courtesy of the Adirondack Museum

The rustic and the Japanesque were compatible styles. Nowhere was this more apparent than in the furnishings of the great camps (summer homes) of the Adirondacks. A carefully placed fan, a table covered with Japanesque art needlework, or, as shown here, a paper lantern chandelier; these were the decorative accents that gave camp life artistic flavor. During the Japan craze, more than one hundred camps were built on lakeshores, hillsides, and islands in the Adirondacks. Camp Cedars (1880) was one of the earliest and most famous. It was built for Frederick Clark Durant by Alvah Dunning and Seth Pierce, Adirondack guides who made their living by trapping, fishing, and making rustic furniture and woodwork.

Architecture and the Japanesque Interior   113

(94) Parlor interior, about 1884
Concord, New Hampshire
Courtesy of New Hampshire Historical Society

Most middle class families embraced the Japan craze on a scale that was modest and affordable. Instead of building houses with specialized reception rooms, they remodelled the old parlor to create an eclectic mix of patterns and forms. This room from a Concord, New Hampshire house is bursting with Japanesque references and the accoutrements of the middle class aesthetic culture. Hand-painted pottery, art needlework, and macrame reveal the artistic skill of the woman in the home, while a mixture of folding fans, ostrich plumes, and framed pictures—all set against an extraordinary commercially printed Japanesque wallpaper—suggest an aesthetic in which display took precedence over comfort.

(95) Erving House parlor, about 1885
821 Prospect Avenue
Hartford, Connecticut
Courtesy of C. Erving

William Agustas Erving and his wife Lucille Erving sat for this self-portrait a few years after they occupied the house designed for them in 1879. The Ervings were avid collectors of decorative arts. Henry later emerged as one of the pioneer collectors of early American furniture. Japanese pottery on the mantle and Japanesque art needlework on the mantle and door suggest the subtle ways in which Japanese art was incorporated into the furnishing plan of artistic interiors during the Japan craze.

collectors, an ex-president, and a legendary robber baron are also illustrated (figs. 96, 97, 98 a,b). In these rooms you will see fans, ceramics, Japanese prints, cloisonné vases, split-bamboo wall covering, everything imaginable packed into gridworks of asymmetrical shelving in the style of the Japanese *chigoi-dana*. All of it, of course, is layered and overlapped with studied casualness.

(96) Dr. William A. Hammond's Japanese bedroom, about 1883
Philadelphia, Pennsylvania
From *Artistic Houses* (1883)
Wadsworth Atheneum

Following its publication in 1883, the bedroom of the noted Philadelphia collector Dr. William Hammond was cited as one of the most radical and dramatic Japanesque interiors in America. The description in Artistic Houses *noted that "the walls are converted into brilliant but never noisy schemes of color, by the aid of variegated fans, porcelains, [and] matting." The use of Japanese woodblock prints was a novel innovation.*

(97) General Grant's parlor, about 1883
New York City
From *Artistic Houses* (1883)
Wadsworth Atheneum

Following their much publicized tour of Japan in 1879, the retired President Ulysses S. and Julia D. Grant began refurnishing their New York townhouse on 73rd Street to incorporate some of the extraordinary gifts and purchases acquired along the way. Among those illustrated, the fringed curtains were worked up from Japanese embroidery. To the left of the mantlepiece was a Japanese embroidered screen, with representations of a cock and a hen. The teakwood cabinets in the far corners were Japanese-made, as were the fans and most of the porcelains exhibited in this room.

(98 a) Mr. W. H. Vanderbilt's
Japanese room,
about 1881
New York City
From *Artistic Houses* (1883)
Wadsworth Atheneum

The William H. Vanderbilt house on Fifth Avenue in New York was arguably the most ostentatious interior in America during the 1880s. Widely noted in the art journals and gossip columns of the period, the house was one of the few that devoted an entire room to Japanese art. Vanderbilt's "Japanese parlor" was more a museum than a sitting room. Even though the room was crammed with Japanese bronze, pottery, textiles, and fans, the author of Artistic Houses *noted that "while the general effect is Japanese, nothing has been copied directly. . . . The furniture and woodwork are of cherry stained and enameled to look like red lacquer"—a reference to the growing capabilities of American craftsmen and manufacturers to supply sophisticated goods in the Japanese taste.*

(98b) Emily W. Vanderpoel parlor
about 1900
New York City
Courtesy of Slater Memorial
Museum, Norwich, Connecticut

Serious collectors of Japanese art were rare compared with the hundreds of thousands of Americans for whom a few Japanese trinkets were just part of a larger program of acquiring bric-a-brac for the home. Mrs. Emily Vanderpoel was an artist who built an enormous collection of Japanese art by patronizing New York import houses. Several rooms in the house were plastered and stuffed full of Japanese bronze, carved architectural fragments, porcelain, and textiles. These were juxtaposed with collections of shells embedded in plaster. Although this photograph was taken during the 1920s, Mrs. Vanderpoel began assembling the collection during the Japan craze.

VI. American Industry Responds

In the autumn of 1876 American industry limped home from the exhibit fields of Philadelphia, bruised but determined. While second to none in machinery, agriculture, and invention, Americans did not delude themselves about their inferiority in the fine and industrial arts. Art goods, home furnishings, and decorative accessories had become one of the fastest-growing sectors of the economy and the one sector where national pride was most at stake. England, France, and Germany had cleaned America's clock long enough. The time to act was now.

As the Centennial Exhibition came to a close, Philadelphia newspapers bewailed the dismal state of American industrial arts while campaigning outspokenly for the "new Pennsylvania museum and school of industrial art" (Philadelphia Museum of Art) then being built. One article noted, "It has been wisely suggested that the exposition will render the new school more necessary than ever by elevating the standard of public taste and making consumers crave a liberal admixture of the beautiful and the useful.... It is a mere question of time when the city will be *forced* in self-protection to teach its rising youth arts by which they can earn a living."[157]

A Bostonian named Charles Wyllys Elliot, in issuing an unprecedented call for state support of the arts, bemoaned the nation's inability to compete with England or Japan, where the arts achieved a "wonderful perfection" due to "the fact that the government gave direct, persistent, and liberal pecuniary aid to the industry." The Kensington Museum School, in London (now called the Victoria & Albert Museum), widely credited as the major impetus behind the rise of the industrial arts in Victorian England, was, Elliot noted, a "creation of the state."[158]

American art critics like James Jackson Jarves were quick to go on the attack. In a scathing indictment of American artists, manufacturers, and consumers Jackson wrote condescendingly:

As a people, we Americans have some slight experience and cleverness in the mechanical direction; but are destitute of sound aesthetic taste.... [The] majority of artists ... have little or no aesthetic feeling.... Outside of their dry studio work, they neither cared for nor enjoyed art ... [being a] mercenary, egotistical class, largely ignorant of culture ... whose highest ambition is to get rich and famous by shamming a feeling and knowledge it does not possess.... [Their] works are soulless and mechanical.

The common taste follows the grooves of trade ... [with] fashions invented to fill covetous tradesfolk's pockets.... All this might be endurable ... if workmen were free artists as in Japan. But to make art more unspeakably sordid and mechanical, we manufacture ... objects ... palmed off as artistic ... by workmen each of whom is a slave to a fraction of the whole of a soulless, mechanically conceived, and machine-executed object.... It is utterly impossible that such objects should be either artistic or aesthetic.... They not only stultify the workman, but they debase invention and demoralize taste.... Anything less ... than art for art's sake ... is certain to vitiate the whole system.[159]

And this from the expatriate son of a Massachusetts glass manufacturer!

Leave it to Cincinnati to have restored balance in the debate. In one of the great instances of an American social movement rising up in more distant fields, Cincinnati did indeed emerge as *the* voice of the industrial-arts renaissance in America. It was Cincinnati that supplied expertise and leadership in the industrial arts at the Centennial: Major Alfred T. Goshorn, the Centennial's director-general, qualified for the job by managing a series of ever more extravagant industrial-arts expositions that earned Cincinnati a national reputation before 1870. It was work produced by students of Benn Pitman at the University of Cincinnati's School of Design that attracted some of the most favorable reviews at the Centennial. It was a rivalry between two society women that contributed to Cincinnati's emergence as the first center of art-pottery manufacturing in America and a leader in women's art education. And, finally, it was Cincinnati where some of American painting's most avid Japanists – John Twachtman, Robert Blum, and Kenyon Cox, to name three – began their careers.

Cincinnati's position in the emerging debate was presented best by a local advocate of the arts and education, George Ward Nichols. A former art critic for the *New York Tribune* and an awards judge at the Centennial, Nichols is best remembered as the husband of Maria Longworth Nichols, founder of the Rookwood Pottery, and as the author of *Art Education Applied to Industry* (1877), in which he outlined a convincing plan for addressing the inadequacies of the industrial arts in America:

The American mechanic has heretofore been more ingenious than artistic. His inventive faculty exceeds that of any other people, but he has not had the advantages of artistic training. He has filled the world with useful labor-saving machines, without adding much to the sum of grace and beauty. We have attempted to put the machine in the place of the man. It has been the tendency of our industries to save labor by making the laborer almost as automatic as the machine itself. The idea that art has any necessary relation to industry rarely enters into the mind of those most interested in the matter. Our mechanics are too often workmen, and not artisans. If this condition of things is not changed, we shall go on in our subserviency to European art products, and will never be able to gain any independence or individuality. Art is not simply an amusement, an indulgence which delights the fancy of the idle and rich. It is decidedly practical, and concerns the well-being, the advancement, the pleasure, of the laborer and the poor. Whenever art is applied to the simplest, commonest product of labor, there will come order, intelligence, grace, and increased value. Art is not the privilege of a class; it is essentially human, and is both individual and universal.

How can it be developed? . . . The experience of other nations teaches us what we have to do, and how it is to be done. It is by technical education in public and special schools; by the study of great works of art; by the establishment of museums which shall be open to the public; . . . [and] by expositions of pictures, statuary, objects of ancient art, and of all products into whose composition art may enter.[160]

The book continues by outlining a detailed program of art education with comments on how trades such as cabinetmaking, weaving, fresco painting, and potting can acquire the expertise needed to invest their goods with the quality of art.

Even as art critics and leaders of industry in America were possessed by a sense of national failure, Japan was being regaled as the world's great art nation. One critic noted that the since Japan had joined "the family of nations, nearly every department of decorative art has felt in some degree the influence of Japanese suggestiveness."[161] It was only a matter of time before American industry discovered the equation that would solve its problem: Japan = Art.

The story of American industry's role in the Japan craze may be told from hundreds of case studies of businesses, small and large, from Philadelphia to San Francisco and from Meriden, Connecticut to Dubuque, Iowa. Whether it was an organ manufacturer in Brattleboro, Vermont, a silk weaver in Manchester, Connecticut, or book publishers in Boston, one sector after the next of American industry discovered that the formula Japan = Art equalled profit.

Ceramics

In the traditional luxury-goods sectors – silversmithing, furniture making, and ceramics – the response was swift and overwhelming. Even more interesting is the way industries not formerly associated with art or decorative work jumped on the bandwagon. Manufacturers of hardware, carpets, printed cottons, cast iron, and granite tombstones all found good fortune in the Japan craze. A paper factory even sold toilet paper marketed as "Japanese Crepe."[162]

Pottery manufacturing in America reached a turning point in the 1870s. With the exception of factories in Trenton, New Jersey, the Ohio River Valley, and Bennington, Vermont, the ceramic industry in nineteenth century America was unable to compete in the luxury-goods market dominated by England since the eighteenth century. This changed during the Japan craze as American manufacturers jockeyed for position in the booming art-goods market. Some of the firms launched at that time eventually became industry giants.

Pottery manufacturing on a large scale was capital intensive, and business failures were common. Small specialty shops faced the problem of developing a market. With large and small potteries squeezed by continued British dominance, it is small wonder that American art pottery before 1890 is rare. Nonetheless more than a dozen American firms produced ceramic goods in the Japanese style during the Japan craze. A few, like Hugh Robertson's Chelsea Keramic Art Works in Massachusetts (fig. 99), produced work of great subtlety and elegance. For others, like Goodwin Brothers Pottery Co. in West Hartford, Connecticut (fig. 100), Japanesque vases were a mere sideline to the

(100) Pottery decoration pattern, about 1880
Oil on canvas
West Hartford, Connecticut
GOODWIN BROTHERS POTTERY CO.
The Connecticut Historical Society

Goodwin Brothers was a regional pottery manufacturer with roots in the eighteenth century. During the Japan craze, they expanded into the production of art goods in the Japanese style, which were marketed through a salesroom in New York City. Although none of their Japanesque work is presently known, this painted design pattern is part of a collection that was used as models by the company's staff decorators.

(99) Vase, about 1875
Tin glazed stoneware
Chelsea, Massachusetts
CHELSEA KERAMIC ART WORKS
Designed by HUGH C. ROBERTSON
Wadsworth Atheneum

Attracted by the availability of iron-rich clay along the Snake River in Chelsea, Massachusetts, Hugh Robertson founded New England's earliest and one of its most successful art potteries. Despite several restructurings, the business was active from 1872 until its founder's death in 1908, when it was reorganized as the Dedham Pottery. During the peak years of the Japan craze, Robertson was responsible for several important and enduring innovations. This vase imitates the qualities of Japanese red earthenware from the Suma precinct and is one of Robertson's earliest works in the Japanese style.

(101) Plate, 1883
Transfer-printed earthenware
Trenton, New Jersey
THE WILLETS MANUFACTURING COMPANY
Robert Tuggle and Paul Jeromack

Willets was the most successful of New Jersey's leading art pottery manufacturers at imitating popular British imports such as Royal Worcester and Beleek. In June 1883 Willets patented a transfer-printed pattern in the Japanese taste that is marketed under the name "Tropics." This was the most successful American transfer pattern.

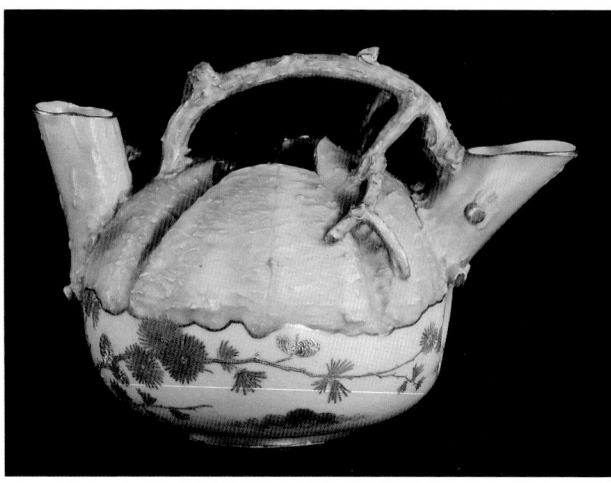

(102) Pitcher, about 1884
Enameled porcelain
Trenton, New Jersey
OTT AND BREWER
Wadsworth Atheneum

During the 1880s, William Bloor's Etruria Pottery—named Ott and Brewer after the two men who backed it financially—experimented with and finally perfected the imitation of Irish Belleek porcelain. This example, with its rustic appearance, is also imitative of rustic Japanese pottery, which sought to duplicate forms and textures found in nature. During the 1880s, Ott and Brewer became America's most innovative porcelain manufacturer. Several lines of Japanesque porcelain were developed. At its height during the late 1880s, the factory employed 250 workers.

routine of producing utilitarian goods. In Trenton, New Jersey, the Mercer China Co., the Willets Manufacturing Co., and Prospect Hill Pottery all entered the highly competitive market for transfer-printed earthenwares.[163] In 1883 Willets patented a line of Japanesque tablewares dubbed the *Tropics* (fig. 101), composed of diagonals, fractured and oblique patterning, airborne birds, and bamboo leaves.

In the manufacture of porcelain Ott and Brewer's Etruria Pottery in Trenton (fig. 102) and Edward Lycett's Faience Manufacturing Co. in Greenpoint, New York, both entered the high-prestige business dominated by Britain's Royal Worcester Porcelain Co. Having apprenticed in the Staffordshire district in England, Lycett was one of many technical and artistic advisers who immigrated to America during the Japan craze. He was an accomplished painter and innovative designer who taught china painting on Greene Street in New York. Through his travels and correspondence with critics and art educators in Cincinnati, St. Louis, and New York, Lycett emerged as a pivotal figure in the early development of American art pottery. With a staff of more than two dozen decorators, his Greenpoint factory turned out exquisite Japanesque porcelain (fig. 103) decorated with gilt and enamel on a deep midnight blue ground.[164] Ott and Brewer's great achievement was developing a thin ivory-colored porcelain body that resembled Irish Belleek and Royal Worcester. Its experiments with Japanese forms and ornament established its Etruria Pottery in the vanguard of the art-pottery movement in America.

An American entry in the booming art tile industry was the J. & J.G. Low Art Tile Works in Chelsea, Massachusetts. The company's founder was John Gardner Low, a painter turned decorative art designer and veteran of Hugh Robertson's innovative Chelsea Keramic Art Works. Low was among the first American manufacturers to recruit skilled designers from the South Kensington School in England. With the arrival of British-trained designer Arthur Osborne in 1879 Low began building what soon became one of the most successful industrial arts enterprises in America. Low's trade catalogs of 1881 and 1884, bound in printed covers rich in Japanesque ornament, identify retail outlets in cities across the country, including Chicago, Minneapolis, Baltimore, and San Francisco, while boasting of awards won at expositions in England, Cincinnati, and New York. Osborne is credited with developing a process of making pattern molds using leaves and natural grasses. These elegant compositions of overlapping fragments of pattern and ornament are some of the simplest and most memorable artistic accomplishments of the Japan craze. With patented trade names like *Cobweb Frieze, Apple Blossom, Bamboo,* and *Japanese Quince,* Low was able to capture the lion's share of the American tile market and in so doing testified to America's growing competitiveness in the industrial arts (color plate 14).[165]

The big story in art pottery unfolds in Cincinnati where a web of ambitious and competitive women and men raced with single-minded determination to master and improve the technique of underglaze slip decoration they had seen in the Haviland faience exhibit at the Centennial. With an intensity that rivaled that of the 1960s space race, three separate camps, led by Louise McLaughlin, Thomas J. Wheatley, and Maria Longworth Nichols, mobilized resources and technology for a battle that lasted from 1875 to 1880. This being decorated pottery, the stakes were perhaps not so large. Although there were accusations, insults, and lawsuits, the war was never formally declared or resolved. By all accounts the victor, Louise McLaughlin, appears to have retreated to her tent in 1880, satisfied with her accomplishments and moderate in her response to the success of rival Maria Longworth Nichols's much-acclaimed Rookwood Pottery. Rookwood was, in fact, the outcome of a race so fierce that Cincinnati was easily first in the nation in the development of art pottery.

The story begins in 1873, when the British arts impresario Benn Pitman founded a department of wood carving at the University of Cincinnati's School of Design. Expanding the curriculum in 1874 to include the nation's first course in china painting, Pitman's students were mostly women from Cincinnati's prosperous middle class. Louise McLaughlin was among his first students. Several others went on to become leaders or active participants in Cincinnati's industrial-arts boom.

McLaughlin's drive and intellect were unmatched. Voracious and acquisitive, she studied art and ceramic technology and before the end of 1875 had perfected a method of underglaze slip decoration that led eventually to the imitation of Haviland faience. As McLaughlin's reputation grew, experimentation and posturing intensified. By late 1877 she had perfected a method of ceramic decoration using white slip mixed with mineral paints applied while the clay body was still moist. This work was shown and acclaimed in New York and Paris in 1878 and 1879, earning McLaughlin a national reputation. She documented her progress and laid claim to her "discovery" in the 1877 publication *China Painting: A Practical Manual for the Use of Amateurs in the Decoration of Hard Porcelain,* one of the earliest self-instruction books in the industrial arts. In 1879 McLaughlin founded the Cincinnati Pottery Club, which promoted china painting and women's employment in the ceramic-decorating industry. Recollections and examples of work in the collections of the Cincinnati Art Museum and the Cincinnati Historical Society document this group's efforts to replicate English and French art

(103) Vase, about 1884–1885
White earthenware, overglaze painted and gilt decoration
Brooklyn, New York
FAIENCE MANUFACTURING COMPANY, decoration attributed to
EDWARD LYCETT
Newark Museum
Louis Bamberger Bequest Fund

(plate 14-color reproduction, page 193)
Art tiles, about 1881
Glazed earthenware
Chelsea, Massachusetts
J. AND J. G. LOW ART TILES
Private Collection

J. and J. G. Low produced Japanese style art tiles in an astonishing array of patterns. The group illustrated here was selected to suggest the range.

pottery such as Longwy, Crown Darby, and Royal Dresden.

McLaughlin never commercialized her achievements. After 1880 she concentrated on writing and experimenting with decorative cast bronze. Her rival, Maria Longworth Nichols, on the other hand, founded the Rookwood Pottery, which eventually dominated the pottery industry in America and remained significant until the 1960s. Nichols's achievements were many, and although initially overshadowed by McLaughlin, she ultimately had far greater influence.

Maria Nichols studied china painting as early as 1873, and like McLaughlin, she experimented with underglaze slip decoration in the mode of Haviland faience, which had impressed her at the Centennial. Nichols is noted as one of the first industrial-art advocates in America to acquire Hokusai's *Manga* (fig. 104). Japanese decoration figured prominently in her early experimental work and in subsequent phases of Rookwood's production (color plate 15). Although overshadowed by the fame of its matte-glaze products in the arts-and-crafts style of the 1890s and early 1900s, Rookwood's earliest underglaze slip-decorated wares are the most Japanesque work (fig. 105) they produced and best illustrate the art-pottery industry's roots in the china-painting phenomenon, discussed further on. Perhaps to compete with McLaughlin's Cincinnati Pottery Club, Nichols opened the Rookwood School for Pottery Decoration in 1881, scoring another triumph by recruiting as an instructor Ichidsuka

(105) Vase, 1885
Enameled earthenware
Cincinnati, Ohio
ROOKWOOD POTTERY
Wadsworth Atheneum

The layering of picture planes and the absence of a dominant pictorial center—Japanese compositional features exhibited by this vase—fascinated the West. Superimposing opposites—a framed picture amid unframed ornament, rectangles-on-circles, and the integration of applied and structural decoration—provided a dissonant quality opposite those found in traditional Western art. The rectangular streamscape, applied to a Japanese-style "moon-vase," decorated with a plum-blossom branch weaving its way over the top and through the picture, with a flock of sparrows bursting out across the horizon below, epitomize the Japanesque qualities inherent in the best early work of Rookwood Pottery.

(104) Plate, 1878
White earthenware with blue underglaze decoration
Cincinnati, Ohio
ROOKWOOD POTTERY
Philadelphia Museum of Art: Gift of Mrs. James Cameron Bleloch

Hokusai's Manga *was the source for the decoration on this early example of Rookwood pottery. Maria Longworth Nichols, Rookwood's founder and artistic director, began collecting Japanese art and pattern books during the mid-1870s and was one of the first American ceramic artists to incorporate Japanese motifs in her work. This plate represents a short-lived experiment with transfer printing undertaken to support operations at Rookwood.*

The decoration of these vases is attributed to Albert Valentien, who came to work at Rookwood in 1881, just one year after the pottery's founding. Valentien, a graduate of the University of Cincinnati's School of Design, played a key role in perfecting a commercial line based on Maria Longworth Nichols's experiments with underglaze slip-decorated earthenware. With thick daubs of glaze, this early type of Rookwood pottery achieved the most Japanesque effects of any subsequent line. Its roots in the tradition of china painting are immediately apparent, while an emphasis on varied decoration assured that each vase would be a unique work of art.

(plate 15-color reproduction, page 194)
Monumental vases, 1883
Enameled earthenware
Cincinnati, Ohio
ROOKWOOD POTTERY, decoration attributed to ALBERT VALENTIEN
Collection of Everson Museum of Art (left)
Wadsworth Atheneum (right)

124 THE JAPAN IDEA

Kenzoa, a Satsuma potter from Japan. Six years later Rookwood became one of the first companies in America to employ a Japanese decorator, Kataro Shirayamadani. He arrived in Cincinnati in 1887 and remained with the company for many years, playing an important role in developing its award-winning lines during the 1890s.[166]

Anywhere else in America Thomas J. Wheatley and the products of T. J. Wheatley & Company would have represented a unique success. A graduate of Cincinnati's School of Design, Wheatley also experimented with underglaze slip during the 1870s and actually filed a patent for his Limoges method, which he claimed to have discovered in New York in 1877. With a distribution contract from Tiffany & Co. and several awards of his own, Wheatley was another major player in Cincinnati in 1880. Unfortunately, he either lacked the deep pockets or the business acumen of his female competitors, for T. J. Wheatley & Company would never exert as much influence as Rookwood or McLaughlin. Inspired by the arts of Japan, Wheatley's work has great merit and further testifies to Cincinnati's leadership role in the industrial arts during the Japan craze (fig. 106).[167]

Rookwood was not the only American art pottery to employ Japanese artists. James Taft's Hampshire Pottery in Keene, New Hampshire, added a Japanese decorator to its staff in the 1890s. Taft's pottery started out like many others, in the business of making utilitarian earthenware – jugs, pots, churns, kegs, and spittoons – but, recognizing the tremendous growth potential in the market for art goods, the firm hired an English designer named Thomas Stanley in 1879. Under Stanley's direction Hampshire entered the art-pottery market with a line of decorative majolica-type wares. Examples in the Japanese taste were popular, and the company's reputation grew so that after 1900, during the arts-and-crafts movement, Hampshire was one of New England's most successful art potteries (fig. 107).[168]

Metals

The mantle of Japanese art was donned by one industry after the next in the battle for a share of the rapidly growing art-goods market. Where American industry was most competitive, the specter of Japan loomed large and reassuring. Identifying with Japan established a company's membership in the fraternity of the artistic elite. Varied and novel interpretations of Japanese ornament and innovative methods of fabrication improved a company's chance of garnering medals at the many regional and national expositions. High medal counts and effusive critical acclaim almost guaranteed sales and profits. The combination of intense competition, rapidly developing technology, and the world's richest source of raw material positioned the American silver and silver-plating industries on the front line of innovation. In no other American industry did the Japan idea shine with greater brilliance.

Once again we have a story rich in human initiative that involves technological breakthroughs, corporate espionage, international competition, and a rivalry between the middle class and the elite. It is

(106) Vase, 1880
Earthenware
Cincinnati, Ohio
T. J. WHEATLEY AND COMPANY
The Saint Louis Art Museum
Purchase: Funds given by the Decorative Arts Society in honor of Lynn E. Springer

(107) Teapot and two creamers, about 1885
White earthenware with painted decoration
Keene, New Hampshire
J. S. Taft Company, Hampshire Pottery
Collection of The Historical Society of Cheshire County, Keene, New Hampshire

Delicate irises and a lily pad hint at a Japanese influence behind the decoration of these examples of Hampshire Pottery. Under the direction of Wallace King, Hampshire Pottery operated a pottery decorating studio staffed by local women. Although not as sophisticated as the firm's work in the Arts and Crafts style, it was one of the few art pottery manufacturers in New England during the Japan craze.

ironic that Japan, with no native silversmithing tradition, would play so large a role in the development of artistic silverware in America. In one corner, servicing the carriage trade of the Gilded Age, stood two champions, the Gorham Manufacturing Co. and Tiffany & Co. In another corner, servicing the middle class, stood a battery of manufacturers, mostly based in Connecticut, that would eventually dominate the market for plated wares throughout the world. Both sides produced work of towering aesthetic power, and their triumph is one of the great chapters in the history of American industry.

Much has been written about Tiffany & Co. Still thriving today after almost a century and a half, Tiffany has become synonymous with artistic excellence and fine craftsmanship. No American company of the period managed its reputation with greater aplomb nor plotted a path to distinction more assuredly. A model of corporate vision and foresight, Tiffany was America's most successful art-goods manufacturer and one of the few whose work was bought and praised throughout Europe and Japan. Not surprisingly, Tiffany was also the first to adopt and the most adept at interpreting the arts of Japan.

The man behind Tiffany's success was Edward C. Moore. In a career that spanned forty years, Moore rose up through the ranks, beginning as a silversmith and ending as head of the entire silver manufacturing division. A pioneer collector of Japanese decorative art (bequeathed to the Metropolitan Museum of Art), Moore built Tiffany's renowned study collection and library. Moore also very likely contracted Christopher Dresser to assemble a collection of "objects . . . calculated to aid in the development of their silversmith business" during his historic tour of Japan in 1877.[169] As one source described it, Dresser was given "carte blanche to pick up for them whatever he found characteristic and likely to transmit a vital influence from the arts of Japan to the arts of America."[170] After Dresser returned, Tiffany unpacked 160 crates containing almost 2,000 works of Japanese art, including carved jades, pottery, bronze, textile fabrics, wood, basketwork, iron, and lacquers.

In the years that followed Morse developed another study collection of Japanese art for Tiffany. A newspaper account of Tiffany's workrooms described "bookshelves well stocked with works of art . . . drawers filled with photographs . . . a glass case filled with fine Japanese lacquer work" and an aquarium filled with frogs and fishes.[172] An "inventory of the objects and books . . . bought for patterns" taken during the 1880s cited 296 items, everything from a fan valued at fifty cents to a "carved lacquer box with daisies" valued at thirty dollars. Highlights of the collection included a "Japanese plate with a curved over edge," a "fan shaped lacquer tray," a "stork vase," a Japanese "crazy quilt, [with] red patch," and "4 pcs of inlaid work." Among the books were "3 volumes of *Manga*" and a variety of related "Japanese books," appraised at a wopping $110. There were several volumes of Japanese wallpaper, a collection of drawings by Japanese artists, and works by French and English art critics like Aime Humbert, Thomas Cutler, Owen Jones, and Dresser.[173]

Tiffany's achievements were widely reported by a national press anxious for a field victory in the battle of the art markets. An 1884 newspaper account, beaming with national pride, cited Tiffany's achievements at making silverware "to send to Japan" and "sending decorative art . . . over to England, where the renaissance of the industry occurred . . . ten or so years ago."[174] Following Tiffany's surprise triumph at the Paris Exposition in 1878, demand for their work in the Japanese style exploded throughout Europe, one English commentator describing it as "some of the most striking Japanese silver work to be seen in Paris and other Continental shops."[175]

Japan's response to the Japan craze mostly involved shifting resources into the production and export of art goods. Initially the trade was one-sided and even after Western manufacturers developed Japanese-style products, real Japanese art retained a lustrous aura of superiority. With Tiffany, however, the Japanese encountered an adversary eager and able to outmaneuver them at their own game, a game that involved wistfully fresh and innovative design, ostentatious workmanship, and inscrutable methods of fabrication.

After the Paris Exposition it became a matter of hyperbole and pride to cite Tiffany as proof that American art "could be even more Japanese than the Japanese themselves."[176] It was not long before a Japanese delegation arrived at Tiffany & Co. to inspect its workshops. Their response, translated from reports in the Japanese press, was a mixture of self-congratulation and suspicion. While admiring Tiffany's "Japanese American silverware," they were skeptical about claims that its interpretations of "our 'mokume' metal" were the "fruit of their hard study and work of many years." If the Japanese suspected Tiffany of pirating their unique but unpatented alloy formulas, they were correct. Both Tiffany and Gorham conducted metallurgical analyses of Japanese metalwork with the intent of cracking and subsequently duplicating their formulas. With their "art so much imitated and admired," the Japanese delegation concluded that "it is to be sure very pleasing to see, but at the same time to be feared."[177]

Tiffany was one of the first American manufacturers to adopt Japanese-style decoration. It began importing Japanese work in 1869, long before it became fashionable. Two years later Tiffany introduced its first Japanese-style flatware pattern (fig. 108) under the tradename "Japanese."[178] This and subsequent lines were popular, but it was in the production of hollowware forms that Tiffany earned its reputation (fig. 109). Its mastery of exotic forms and decoration and its pioneering efforts at reproducing legendary Japanese alloys like *Mokume* (fig. 110)(red copper, silver, and gold laminated to imitate wood grain), *Shaku-do* (purplish alloy of copper with gold and silver), and *Shibu-ichi* (silvery-gray alloy of copper with silver) were unprecedented in the West.[179] Tiffany had become the undisputed world leader in the production of artistic silverware in the Japanese style (color plate 16).

Tiffany, however, was not without competition, and no doubt its rivalry with the Gorham Manufacturing Co. in Providence, Rhode Island, accounts for its aggressively innovative disposition. Gorham was a family silversmithing operation that expanded from humble origins in 1831 to become

(108) "Japanese" pattern flatware set, 1888
Sterling silver
New York
TIFFANY AND COMPANY
Loan of Mrs. Horace Bushnell Learned and Mrs. H. C. L. Colt

Of the several Japanesque flatware patterns designed by Tiffany and Company, the "Japanese," also known as the "Audubon," was its first (patented 1871) and best-seller. In keeping with the Japanese emphasis on variety, each hand-chased piece has a slightly different combination of delicate birds, cherry blossoms, and foliage. This set belonged to Mary Bushnell Cheney, whose husband Frank Woodbridge Cheney was director of Manchester, Connecticut's, Cheney Brothers silk mill and one of the first American industrialists to open trade with Japan.

New England's premier fine metalwork establishment. John Gorham and his chief designer, George Wilkinson, ran close behind Tiffany in adopting Japanese principles in the development of artistic silver. As early as 1851 John Gorham reputedly displayed examples of Japanese metalwork at the Rhode Island State Fair, and the firm preceded Tiffany by introducing a Japanesque kettle and stand as early as 1869.[180] Like Tiffany, Gorham maintained a remarkable art library that included works by Hokusai and British and French design theorists.[181] In 1881, Gorham became the first American manufacturer to perfect and market Japanese-style objects of red copper with silver appliques, hand wrought, hammered, and engraved by their silversmiths (fig. 111).[182]

(109) Coffee pot, 1879
Sterling silver, copper, brass, and niello
New York
TIFFANY AND COMPANY
Detroit Institute of Arts
Founders Society Purchase with funds from Mr. and Mrs. Charles Theron Van Dusen and Beatrice W. Rogers Fund

By the time this mokume banded coffee pot was made, Tiffany and Company had already made headlines for its exhibit at the Paris Exposition the previous year. Most notable was Tiffany's mastery of Japanese metals, using formulas and techniques perfected after careful analysis of the many examples of Japanese metalwork Christopher Dresser had gathered in 1877 for Tiffany's designers to work from. Although the coffee pot is a western form, the use of the dragonfly as its principal motif was an unmistakable reference to the arts of Japan.

(110) Tea caddy, 1880
Sterling silver, red copper, shakudo, and ivory
New York
TIFFANY AND COMPANY
New York Historical Society
Gift of Mr. Robert G. Goelet

After much experimentation and many failed attempts, Tiffany silversmiths finally found a way to duplicate a type of Japanese metalwork called mokume. Mokume was made from a combination of copper, gold, silver, and bronze. The metals were rolled in sheets, soldered together, and then hammered and rolled to create swirling patterns that imitate Japanesque woodgrain. Although most frequently used as an accent and embellishment, a few objects like this tea caddy were made entirely of Tiffany's mokume metal.

(plate 16-color reproduction, page 194)
Vase, about 1878-1880
Sterling silver with mixed metal and patinated alloy decoration
New York
TIFFANY AND COMPANY
From a friend of the Wadsworth Atheneum

Under the artistic guidance of Edward C. Moore, Tiffany and Company produced masterpieces like this vase, made with a combination of metals including imitations of such prized Japanese alloys as shakudo, mokume, and shibuichi. These alloys were set in panels like little jewels and combined with hand-hammered and cast copper and brass ornament. Few works of American silver produced during the Japan craze better testify to Tiffany's mastery of technique and artistic ingenuity.

American Industry Responds

(111) Tray, 1882
Patinated copper and sterling silver
Providence, Rhode Island
Wadsworth Atheneum

Gorham's shortlived (1880-1885) experiment with Japanesque hammered copper resulted in the production of a range of widely acclaimed colorful alloys, from the deep red of this tray to mellow brown tones. Made at the height of the Japan craze, this tray is distinguished by a hammered "woodgrain" surface, naturalistic curled edges, and a random juxtaposition of insect and wildlife in applied silver. This tray was acquired in Europe where Gorham developed a strong market for its Japanesque work.

Gorham was more adventuresome than Tiffany in its experiments with mixed media; it made table knives out of cannibalized kodzukas (sword ornament), worked ivory and silver into exotic confections, and utilized a wide range of mixed-metal alloys which were combined with electroplated base metals. In 1880 George Wilkinson traveled to Japan, and throughout the seventies and eighties, Gorham was outstanding in its commitment to Japanese-style work (fig. 112).

The Tiffany-Gorham rivalry was intense. A fascinating document in the corporate archives, now at Brown University's John Hay Library, is a manuscript titled "Notebook on Gorham's History of Techniques before 1877."[183] The notebook contains dozens of formulas for metal alloys, including red metal, yellow metal, *Shibu-ichi, Shaku-do,* and *Mokume.* In the margins are extensive notes on Tiffany's progress along similar lines, so detailed and specific that it is entirely possible that Gorham had conducted corporate espionage to secure the information.[184] Gorham and Tiffany were not the only sterling silver manufacturers at the time. Firms like the Whiting Manufacturing Company in North Attleboro, Massachusetts also produced Japanesque silver (fig. 113). But the two leaders defined the upper limits of what was possible and set a standard gained America its first international market in the industrial arts.

Of all the arts in Victorian America, silver had the richest associations with class. It was the original status marker, used to distinguish families of title and influence from everyone else. In colonial America the custom of engraving family crests on tankards, which passed from one generation to the next as heirlooms, gave silver a symbolic power even greater than its monetary value. The vast majority of colonial Americans owned no silver at all, not even a simple spoon. This changed overnight with the discovery and

(112) Vase, 1880
Sterling silver, copper, and bronze
Providence, Rhode Island
GORHAM MANUFACTURING COMPANY
Historical Design Collection, Inc., New York City

Gorham's experimentation with textured silver and mixed metals is handsomely illustrated in this vase. The main body of the vase imitates woven basketry to which are applied Japanesque bronze medallions featuring the ever popular airborne swallow and moon and owl motifs. The reverse side has an applied rooster and butterfly placed randomly in the Japanese manner.

development of the technology of electroplating, by which relatively inexpensive base metals like pewter acquired a silver skin. Suddenly silver, the great demarcator of status, had lost one of its most cherished qualities. As the new kid on the block, electroplated wares, or silver plate, had to try hard to be convincing. What it lacked in the value of its base material, it made up for in sheer exuberance of design and expression. It is this author's opinion that silver plate, even more than its aristocratic cousin sterling, epitomized the spirit of technological experimentation and aesthetic innovation that flourished within the Japan idea.

How this came about is Connecticut's story. As one of the primary crucibles of American industrialization, Connecticut had deep roots in industries like pewtersmithing, brass and iron founding, and blacksmithing – the perfect base for a new industry that demanded breadth and depth of experience at working metal. Connecticut's resourceful work force, excellent system of railroads, and access to large urban markets gave it an edge over domestic and foreign competition during the formative decade of the 1850s. Thirty years later, at the height of the Japan craze, Connecticut's silver-plate manufacturers ruled over an enormous industrial empire with international markets and a reputation for excellence.

Inside Connecticut, competition between silver-plate manufacturers was intense. Unlike sterling silver, which had only two major competitors at the top, the electroplating industry was one of the most competitive in America. At the height of the Japan craze almost a dozen companies based in Connecticut were slugging it out for market share. Smaller players like Holmes and Edwards of Bridgeport, the Derby Company in Birmingham (fig. 114 a,b), and the

(114 a) Pitcher, about 1885
Silverplate
Derby, Connecticut
DERBY SILVER COMPANY
Collection of Helen Hersh and Charles Sporn

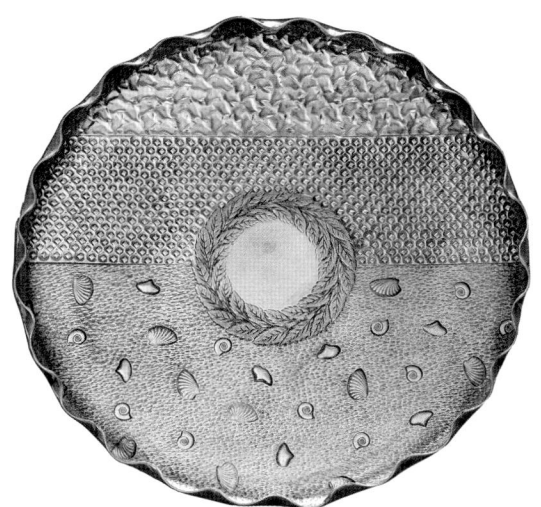

(114 b) Tray, about 1885
Silverplate
Derby, Connecticut
DERBY SILVER COMPANY
Collection of Helen Hersh and Charles Sporn

In the search for new ways of replicating the effects of Japanese art, American silverplate designers latched on to the importance of surface texture. By tradition, silversmiths sought a smooth, unvariegated surface relieved only intermittently by applied, chased, and engraved details. In Japanese decorative art, hand-worked surfaces assumed an astonishing array of textures, to the point where smoothness almost ceased to exist, even in details. This pitcher and the matching tray epitomize the search for new textures based on Japanese sources. The whimsical frog near the handle of the pitcher alludes to another Japanese convention—the seemingly haphazard placement of decoration.

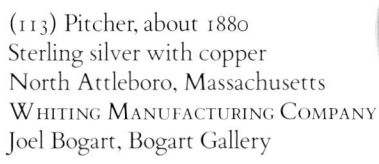

(113) Pitcher, about 1880
Sterling silver with copper
North Attleboro, Massachusetts
WHITING MANUFACTURING COMPANY
Joel Bogart, Bogart Gallery

The Whiting Manufacturing Company was one of a small group of manufacturers that competed with Gorham and Tiffany, the two industry leaders. This pitcher, with its hand hammered finish and swimming carp, is similar in form and decoration to work produced by both Tiffany and Gorham around 1880.

American Industry Responds 131

(115) Tea set, about 1880
Silverplate
Boston, Massachusetts
James W. Tufts Company
Wadsworth Atheneum

This squared off tête-a-tête tea set has "bamboo" handles and is covered with diagonal bands of decoration. A closer look at the surface reveals a mixture of Japanese motifs including fans and birds. James W. Tufts made a huge impression by erecting an entire building to present his company's wares at the Centennial.

(116) A selection of hollowware forms, about 1885
Silverplate
New Bedford, Massachusetts
Pairpoint Manufacturing Company
Sugar bowl (left) and Kerosene lamp (center)
Robert Tuggle and Paul Jeromack
Demitasse (right)
Collection of Helen Hersh and Charles Sporn

This group has been assembled to illustrate the way one die-rolled pattern of Japanese lanterns, fans, diapers, and bamboo was used to make an assortment of hollowware forms. As was often the case, Japanese details were combined with features influenced by other eastern cultures, notably the Turkish form of the demitasse and cast Chinese figures on the handles of the lamp base.

Wilcox Silver Plate Company in Meriden battled it out with the industry giants like Simpson, Hall and Miller in Wallingford and Meriden Britannia in West Meriden. As if this was not enough, there were the Massachusetts companies of Reed and Barton in Taunton, James Tufts in Boston (fig.115), and Pairpoint Manufacturing in New Bedford (fig. 116). Whether in Connecticut or Massachusetts, they all produced silver plate; they all advertised aggressively; they all developed diverse product lines; and they all embraced the Japan idea.

The case of Meriden Britannia is interesting because it has the longest roots and its descendant, the International Silver Co. (INSILCO), is still with us today. The Meriden Britannia Co. grew out of the 1852 merger between a Meriden-based partnership in the Britannia-ware trade and a consortium of four competing manufacturers, one of whom – Curtis and Lyman of Meriden – traced its roots back to the Danforths of Middletown, the founders of Connecticut's eighteenth-century pewtersmithing industry.[185] For those who suppose that hostile takeovers and mergers and acquisitions are unique to our time, Connecticut's electroplating industry makes a good study. Meriden Britannia was not only the creation of a merger, but it swallowed up the parent company of the entire industry, Rogers Brothers of Hartford. Meriden Britannia continued to swallow up its competition so that by the turn of the century it was far and away the industry leader.

What is left of Meriden Britannia's nineteenth-century corporate archives is now in the care of the Meriden Historical Society, where it has yet to be thoroughly mined for information that might help identify some of the anonymous designers responsible for the extraordinary works the company produced. Unlike with Tiffany and Gorham, whose design departments were managed by individuals of great artistic vision, it is not now known how Connecticut's electroplating manufacturers developed designs or who led them in new artistic directions.

It is doubtful that any of Connecticut's manufacturers had a jump on Gorham's experiments with Japanesque ornament in the early 1870s. But between the Centennial and 1882, when Meriden Britannia made over its marketing image in the Japanese style, all of Connecticut's electroplating companies jumped on the bandwagon. That year Meriden published the first of several trade catalogs (color plate 17) that were works of art unto themselves. This deluxe volume, printed in a bold black and gilt on red, must have delighted small-town dry-goods and crockery merchants anxious to appear up-to-date by stocking artistic merchandise in the modern styles. Between the covers were hundreds of silver-plated forms and patterns, including some of the jazziest work in the Japanese taste. There was a "hammered gold inlaid tea set" with flying storks and brocade patterned borders. There was a "waiter" with a boldly Japanesque aquatic scene; and as if the idea that Japan equaled art was not apparent enough, there was a card receiver featuring an artist's palette,

(plate 17-color reproduction, page 195)
Trade catalog, Meriden Britannia Co., 1882
Hartford, Connecticut
Printed by CASE, LOCKWOOD AND BRAINARD
Meriden Historical Society, Inc.

Diagonals, stylized florals and birds, geometric medallions, and cobweb encrusted arabesques stamped in gilt form the wrapper designed to promote the new product lines of the Meriden Britannia Co. in 1882. Because Meriden offered a wide range of products, deluxe catalogs provided sales representatives with an effective means of showing customers what was available at a glance. As stylish and Japanesque as the products themselves, this book is the work of Connecticut's then-sophisticated book publishing industry.

(plate 18 a-color reproduction, page 195)
Wall plaque, 1885
Copper enamel and silverplate
Meriden, Connecticut
MERIDEN BRITANNIA CO.
Collection of Helen Hersh and Charles Sporn

(plate 18 b-color reproduction, page 195)
Clock, about 1885
Copper enamel with silverplate applied decoration, brass and enamel face
Taunton, Massachusetts
Attributed to REED AND BARTON
Collection of Helen Hersh and Charles Sporn

The brilliant red of these two mixed-metal pieces was inspired by the colorful metalwork from Japan that mystified American metalsmiths. Made of copper that has been treated to turn a deep red, and decorated with hammered designs and silverplate appliqué in the Japanese style, these objects provide some idea of the level of skill and variety of wares offered as the silverplate business flourished. The extremely competitive market forced the various companies to constantly improve upon old techniques and invent new ones. If one manufacturer offered something like patinated copper in the Japanese style, it can safely be assumed that most of them did.

brushes, and easel and engraved with Japanesque waterfowl and swamp grass.

Electroplated wares may look like silver, but the methods used in fabrication were different. By combining gold and silver plate and by blocking out borders and details to expose the Britannia – a copper and tin alloy like pewter – underneath, electroplate manufacturers were able to mimic the effects of gilding, chasing, and metallic inlay associated with sterling silver. Persistently resourceful in finding inexpensive ways to achieve expensive-looking results, the industry explored the idea of mixed metals by electroplating silver, gold, and copper on the same object. Cast and plated appliques were occasionally fastened to copper-, gold-, or silver-plated forms. Meriden Britannia was one of several New England firms to experiment with copper enameling (color plate 18 a,b) in an attempt to replicate the look of rare Japanese alloys like *Shakudo*. They also manufactured kerosene lamps with wells made of hammered copper and decorated with cast bronze frogs and swamp foliage (fig. 117).

Figuring that the buying public did not understand silversmithing methods, manufacturers tossed around choice terms of the trade like "chasing," "hammering," and "hand burnished" to give their products cachet and associations with handcrafted silver. This is not to say that silver plate lacked qualities of design and workmanship or that it was inexpensive. With tea sets and water sets selling in the range of twenty-five to fifty Victorian dollars and prized presentation pieces for as much as one hundred and twenty-five, high-end electroplated ware was not cheap. But it definitely delivered more bang for the buck than sterling. One of its virtues is that the money saved in raw material and hand workmanship could be rechanneled into elaboration and design. Whether or not one prefers the ostentatious, almost hyper-ornamental look silver plate occasionally achieved, the vigor of its design cannot be denied. These are some of the most evocative and uniquely American works of art produced during the Japan craze.

The process of adopting Japanesque ornament and the span of its popularity with the buying public are documented by the case of the Simpson, Hall, Miller Company of Wallingford, Connecticut. Here was a firm that boasted a place among the "three largest manufacturers in the United States of fine

Electro Plated Goods," had salesrooms in New York, San Francisco, Chicago, Canada, and Australia, and had beaten forty-four domestic and foreign competitors for the highest awards at international expositions. A look at its trade catalogs from 1878, 1879, 1881, and 1891 reveals a decisive pattern of increasing involvement with Japanesque design.[186] In 1878 the closest suggestion of Japanese influence in any of Simpson's products is in the use of diagonal banding. A year later the firm introduced a few more explicitly Japanesque designs, including a tea set described as "chased Japanese" and a waiter decorated with Japanese fans and diagonals. Each year Simpson added more products in the Japanese style (fig. 118). By 1891 the company manufactured more than a dozen Japanesque patterns, including a water set with bamboo handles and engraved birds and flowers.

The manufacture of artistic metalwork expanded prolifically during the 1880s, to the point that it is difficult keeping track of all the different companies. Although the production of sterling and plated silver and artistic brass and hardware tended to remain segregated, a few companies like Gorham were involved in almost everything. But that is an exception. Most of the electroplate manufacturers marketed a few forms that employed glass or ceramic parts. These were usually acquired by contract with glass manufacturers. Meriden Britannia acquired glass from the Meriden Glass Company and the New England Glass Company in East Cambridge, Massachusetts. The Pairpoint Manufacturing Company and Mt. Washington Glass Co., both of New Bedford, Massachusetts, developed a collaborative relationship that put them at the head of the market for electroplated forms like epergnes, fruit bowls, pickle casters, and cracker jars that combined decorated glass with silver plate.[187]

A distinct branch of the metals industry specialized in the production of artistic brass and copper. The Palmer Manufacturing Company in New York made Japanesque umbrella stands, clocks, and looking glasses with hammered and die-rolled copper frames and ornament.[188] Also in New York was F. H. Lovell & Co., which specialized in artistic glass with a sideline in making hammered brass wells for its kerosene lamps.[189] Hammered copper and brass is one of the more innovative interpretations of Japanese art found in American metalwork of the 1880s. During

(117) Kerosene lamp
about 1885
Copper, silverplate, gilt, oxidized plate
Meriden, Connecticut
MERIDEN BRITANNIA CO.
Collection of Helen Hersh and Charles Sporn

Honeycomb-shaped hammered copper was one of the most innovative products developed by the electroplating industry.

(118)
Nut bowl
about 1887
Silverplate
Wallingford, Connecticut
SIMPSON, HALL AND MILLER COMPANY
Meriden Historical Society, Inc.

Cracked ice, hand-hammered texturing, and an applied dragonfly and cherry branch embellish what was advertised as a "Venetian" style Nut Bowl by Simpson, Hall and Miller. The firm's Japanese inspired line, which commenced with a few entries designed in 1879, was distinguished by an attention to detail that rivaled that of the art lines produced at the same time by the leading silver manufacturers.

(119) Door handle and escutcheon, about 1886
Bronze
Nashua, New Hampshire
NASHUA LOCK COMPANY
Wadsworth Atheneum

the height of the arts-and-crafts style at the turn of the century hammered metal developed a vast following, as it epitomized the quality of hand workmanship deemed sacrosanct. During the 1880s when these two companies introduced hammered work, it was novel.

In the mid-1880s the biggest name in artistic bronze and brass plating was that of the Charles Parker Company of Meriden, Connecticut. Like most of his neighbors in the electroplating industry, Parker did not commence manufacturing Japanesque and artistic metal products until after 1880. In 1879 Parker was the proprietor of a conglomerate of metal manufacturers with branch operations in five locations and product lines ranging from cast iron coffee mills and bench vises, to machine tools, shot guns, and door latches and hinges – hardly artistic work. Around 1882 he expanded into the production of "artistic bronze" and "fine art goods," including parlor lamps and chandeliers, hammered-bronze umbrella stands, and cast-brass tables, easels, and looking glasses. Parker imported imitation cloisonné ceramic tiles and cylinders from Longwy in France. Much of the company's best work, and that most frequently featured in its advertisements, has a decidedly Japanese feeling.[190]

The most surprising entry in the field of Japanese-style metalwork is the lock and hardware industry. In an age that seemed almost obsessed with decorative details it is perhaps understandable that, having finished everything else, doorknobs, latches, and escutcheons could not be overlooked. Among those companies that can be documented as having manufactured Japanesque products are the Peck, Stow and Wilcox Co. of Southington, Connecticut, the Russell and Erwin Manufacturing Co. and P.F. Corbin, both of New Britain, Connecticut, and the Nashua Lock Co. of Nashua, New Hampshire. In each case the Japanese line represented a small segment of the artistic hardware output. But as the products from the Nashua Lock Co. (fig. 119) and Russell and Erwin (fig. 120) suggest, this work could be novel and exciting. In addition to latches and doorknobs, these firms manufactured Japanesque bronze shelf brackets, bird-cage hooks, door hinges, and fireplace sets comprising matched shovels, tongs, and pokers.[191]

The prominence of Japanese influence in the fine and base metals owes much to the fact that the industry was booming at the same time as the Japan craze. As the industrial history of nineteenth-century America attracts new and deeper scholarship, the role of art in stimulating demand for manufactured goods is bound to be told. The decorative arts field's bias against plated silver and near total neglect of the more utilitarian branches of the metals trade have kept us from learning about one of the great moments in American business history – when industry and art embraced. It is perhaps most of all along the margins, among the hardware and oil-lamp manufacturers, that this story needs to be told.

Furniture

For most periods furniture reigns supreme in the decorative and industrial arts. Allied with architecture and offering endless possibilities for ornamentation and design, chairs, tables, night stands, and bureaus are the most common components of a home's furnishings. Furniture is so central to the purpose of furnishing that the word has taken on associations with the entire process of outfitting interior space. And yet the furniture made in America during the Japan craze is surprisingly devoid of Japanese influence. With the exception of Herter Bros. in New York, Mitchell and Rammelsburg in Cincinnati, A. and H. Lejambre in Philadelphia, the occasional piece by Kimball and Cabus, and a small branch of the industry that specialized in imitation bamboo, very few manufacturers produced patterns or lines of furniture in the Japanese taste. The reason, in part, traces back to the concept of bric-a-brac and the fact that the Japan idea was an image and not a complete life-style. It was most frequently incorporated as an accent, not the dominant motif for an entire room. Furniture was usually too important a component of a room's furnishings to sustain the frivolity associated with Japanesque design. The Japanese style was a nice embellishment, but most people didn't want it to dominate their lives.

Herter Bros. was the first and most prominent advocate of Japanesque design in the American furniture industry. With a high-society following, Herter attracted commissions for handmade, one-of-a-kind designs. Custom work enabled Herter to develop the Japanesque masterpieces for which the company is now best remembered. But Herter also designed for

(120) Doorknobs, 1879
Brass
New Britain, Connecticut
RUSSELL AND ERWIN COMPANY
top:
Design patented by H.E. RUSSELL, JR., May 13, 1879
Mugnier Higgins Antiques, New Castle, Delaware
bottom:
Design patented by R. CHRISTENSEN, June 3, 1879
Robert Tuggle and Paul Jeromack

The manufacture of Japanesque doorknobs less than three years after the Centennial suggests how rapidly Connecticut hardware manufacturers responded to the demand for art products in the Japanese taste. These are two among several Japanese patterns developed by Russell and Erwin.

(121) Side chair, about 1880
Ebonized cherry and oak
New York City
HERTER BROTHERS, attributed to CHRISTIAN HERTER
The Currier Gallery of Art, Manchester, New Hampshire
Currier Funds and Gift in memory of Dr. and Mrs. Daniel Capron from Dr. and Mrs. Russell C. Norton

retail a number of limited-production patterns in the Japanese taste that count among the earliest and most intriguing examples of the style produced in America.

Herter Bros. was founded in 1865 as the partnership of two German cabinetmakers, Gustave and Christian Herter. The latter, educated in Germany and Paris, where he studied at the École des Beaux-Arts, was the most cosmopolitan figure in the furnishings industry in America. With his European training, worldly airs, and natural aptitude, he made Herter Bros. the most progressive force in the New York furnishings and decorating business during the 1880s. Far more than just furniture makers, Herter Bros. were among the first to include interior-design services so that clients could commission an entire room. Herter's client list reads like a who's who of the Gilded Age: it included J. Pierpont Morgan, William H. Vanderbilt, Jay Gould, James Goodwin, and Ulysses Grant's White House.[192]

Christian Herter made the rounds of architects' offices and design studios in London around 1871, just as the British aesthetic movement was cresting. It was probably then that he first encountered the furniture designs of Edward Godwin, who incorporated Japanesque elements into his work as early as 1867. Herter's most influential designs have been compared with Godwin's. Both achieve a super delicacy of line, a Japanesque quality of rectilinearity and patterning, and an emphatic use of traditional Japanese motifs. Herter's work features stylized chrysanthemums floating on black panels, stained and inlaid bamboo leaves, carved airborne swallows (fig. 121), inlaid sprays of flowers, panels painted with willowy naturalism on a gilt ground, and pie-shaped panel inserts painted with Japanesque flowers and insects.[193]

By drinking deep at the well of British aestheticism, Herter was among the first American designers to absorb the movement's meaning. Its reverence for traditional craftsmanship and emphasis on sleek lines and hard-edged patterning became defining characteristics of interior design. Herter was not alone among Americans in this pursuit, and it may have been around 1871 that he first met his future client, the Reverend Francis Goodwin of Hartford, also in London at that time, meeting architects and furnishings designers to prepare for his work designing the enormous Ruskinian Gothic-style mansion that his parents built between 1871 and 1874. Herter supplied a

(124) Étagère, about 1880
Ebonized cherry, poplar, glass, and painted tin
Philadelphia, Pennsylvania
Attributed to A. AND H. LEJAMBRE
Wadsworth Atheneum

Best known as manufacturers of furniture in the French taste, the firm managed by Anna and Henri Lejambre also produced several documented works in the Anglo-Japanese style. Elements of the construction of this remarkable étagère and its use of American woods suggest that this may have been a limited production item manufactured by Lejambre. Japanesque étagères were ideally suited to the display of "bric-a-brac" in the parlor or reception room. While the velvet and gold accents and oriental fretwork ensure that, even empty, it would attract attention, once crowded with glass and ceramics the ensemble becomes irresistible.

American Industry Responds

(125) Desk, about 1877
Mahogany with cherry paneled drawers, brass hardware
American
Strong Museum, Rochester, New York

The carved fretwork, incised bamboo, and Mount Fuji decoration leave no doubt as to the Japanese influence on the unknown maker of this desk.

Although most of work traced to Mitchell and Rammelsberg during the late 1870s and early 1880s is in the modern Gothic and Renaissance revival styles, a few examples of Japanesque design have been identified. An unpublished suite of parlor furniture, labeled and dated 1878, by Mitchell and Rammelsberg (Cincinnati Art Museum) is one of the few documented instances where imported Japanese silk brocade was used as an upholstery fabric. The bedstead here illustrated (fig. 126) is a hybrid design featuring elements of modern Gothic and the Japanesque. Most notable are the panels painted with bamboo and butterflies on a gilt ground. Painting on gilt is a sophisticated detail that became a hallmark of some of the best Japanesque design.

The furniture industry's most direct response to the Japan craze was the emergence of a network of imitation-bamboo manufacturers. The reform critic Clarence Cook advocated the use of Japanese bamboo furniture for country houses as early as the late 1870s, citing A.A. Vantine & Co. in New York as an importer. The earliest reference to its imitation in maple is by J. Lavezzo and Bros. in New York, which began advertising bamboo furniture in 1883. By the end of the decade half a dozen manufacturers had commenced production, including J.E. Wall and the American Bamboo Co., both in Boston. The American Bamboo Co.'s illustrated advertisement from 1887 depicts an entire room furnished in imitation bamboo, including doors, mantles, stair rails, chairs, easels,

(126) Bedstead, about 1880
Ebonized wood with gilt and painted decoration
Cincinnati, Ohio
Mitchell and Rammelsberg Furniture Company
Strong Museum, Rochester, New York

The gilt-ground floral panel on the headboard of this bedstead was Mitchell and Rammelsberg's way of incorporating the Japanesque in its product line.

picture frames, and cornice moldings (fig. 127). No one lived in such a space, but it suggests the possibilities

(127) Advertisement, 1887
AMERICAN BAMBOO COMPANY
Boston, Massachusetts
From *The Decorator and Furnisher* (October 1887)

inherent in the style.[197] Bedroom sets, tables, and desks (fig. 128) turn up most frequently on the antique market today, suggesting that imitation bamboo was not thought proper for public or more formal settings. The majority of what survives dates from the early 1890s when demand for imitation bamboo surged.

Furniture is one of the few products of the Japan craze that grew in popularity during the early twentieth century when it was assimilated into the arts-and-crafts movement. In fact, it was not until the qualities of hand-craftsmanship were glorified by the movement that Japanese influence became a major factor in furniture design. The furniture designed by Frank Lloyd Wright and Greene and Greene in California, the rustic handcrafted Adirondack furniture made with birch bark and split twigs, and the extraordinary carved tables (fig. 129) modeled after Japanese jin-di-sugi – traditional raised wood carving – by John Scott Bradstreet of Minneapolis are some of the most striking work in the Japanese taste ever produced in America.[198]

(128) Lady's desk, about 1890
Birdseye and curly maple
Probably New York City
Wadsworth Atheneum

Encouraged by the popularity of expensive, imported bamboo furniture, American manufacturers were soon fashioning their own. While some used imported bamboo, others, such as R. J. Horner in New York and The American Bamboo Co. in Boston, produced what they called "imitation bamboo," made of plain and birdseye maple. Desks like this one were used in parlors and bedrooms. New York and Boston were the leading manufacturing centers.

(129) "Lotus" center table, about 1905
Carved cypress wood
Minneapolis, Minnesota
Designed by JOHN S. BRADSTREET
Manufactured by
JOHN S. BRADSTREET AND COMPANY
Mr. and Mrs. David W. Dangremond

Inspired by his interest in Japanese art and his many trips to Japan, this "jin-di-sugi" Lotus table was one of J. S. Bradstreet's most successful designs. Bradstreet was largely responsible for promoting Japanese art in Minneapolis, where he established John S. Bradstreet and Company in 1876. The Bradstreet Craftshouse was a combination showroom and self proclaimed "institute of decorative art." On display there were examples of Bradstreet's "jin-di-sugi" furniture, the finish of which is modeled after the Japanese technique from which it takes its name. Also available were Japanese objects, many gathered by Bradstreet on his biennial trips to Japan, beginning in 1886.

American Industry Responds 143

(130) "Crown Milano" vase, about 1890
Blown opaque glass, with painted decoration
New Bedford, Massachusetts
MOUNT WASHINGTON GLASS COMPANY
Collection of Mr. and Mrs. Morris Greenberg

Soaring waterfowl in various postures was a popular Japanesque motif and one of the few to find its way into the decorative repertoire of American art glass manufacturers. The decoration on this vase is one of several patterns marketed under the trade name of Crown Milano. Patented in 1886, Crown Milano was one of the most successful products of the art glass industry.

(131) "Lava" vase, about 1880
Blown flint glass mixed with
potash and volcanic slag
New Bedford, Massachusetts
MOUNT WASHINGTON GLASS COMPANY
The Jones Museum of Glass and Ceramics

A process patented by Frederick Shirley's Mount Washington Glass Company in 1878 produced a black glass marketed as "Lava." This is the earliest type of American art glass in the Japanese taste. This example is decorated with a flying crane and randomly placed incrustation of color along the rim.

Glass

American glass manufacturers were not as quick to adopt elements of Japanese design as their peers in the metal and ceramic industries. With the exception of stained glass the qualities of color and hand decoration were not as readily applied in glass as in other media. And except for Charles Comfort Tiffany (son of the founder of Tiffany & Co.), who worked in a highly Japanesque manner at the turn of the century, no American glass manufacturers developed extensive product lines. Like with furniture, the Japanese taste was a sideline, and only a few names are currently associated with it.

The most interesting and prolific American art-glass manufacturer during the Japan craze was Frederick Shirley's Mt. Washington Glass Co. in New Bedford, Massachusetts. Product lines marketed under the trade names of *Burmese, Lava, Amber Craquelle, Peach Blow, Coralene,* and *Crown Milano* testify to the firm's technical and artistic inventiveness. Although none of these lines was exclusively Japanesque, individual objects were frequently decorated with Japanese motifs. *Amber Craquelle* emphasized the quality of crazing or cracked ice, introduced by way of Japanese pottery. *Burmese* and *Peach Blow,* which Shirley patented in the mid-1880s, were types of shaded glass, the former bleeding from yellow to pink, and the latter, gray-blue to a bluish pink tint. The most expensive examples were enameled with Japanesque flowers and insects with an occasional epigram painted in Gothic script.

About 1890 Mt. Washington introduced *Crown Milano,* a type of opal glass frequently blown into patterned molds before receiving enamel decoration. An example attributed to Mt. Washington (fig. 130) is decorated with airborne water fowl possibly based on details taken from Hokusai's sketchbooks. Shirley's earliest patent for art glass decorated with Japanese ornament was dubbed *Lava,* which Mt. Washington began manufacturing in 1878. *Lava* is a black glass actually made from a formula including volcanic slag. Although rare today and presumably not produced in great quantities, this was Mt. Washington's earliest and most emphatically Japanesque line. The example illustrated (fig. 131) is enamelled with Japanese pictographs that also may have been taken from Hokusai.[199] *Albertine,* another Mt. Washington product (fig. 132) also incorporated Japanesque details.

In 1894 the Mt. Washington Glass Co. was acquired by the Pairpoint Manufacturing Company, whose electroplating operations had been combined with its glass operations some years earlier. Mt. Washington remained largely intact, but its goods were now marked with the Pairpoint name. About the time of the merger Pairpoint came out with a line named *Verona,* a type of clear pattern-molded glass decorated with enamel. An example with a strong Japanese-style aquatic scene is illustrated here (color plate 20).

New Bedford's most famous glass decorators, the brothers Alfred and Harry Smith, were raised and trained in England before joining the decorating department at Mt. Washington Glass in the early 1871. Prior to that, the Smiths had worked with their father, who founded the first glass-decorating department in the United States while employed by the Boston and Sandwich Glass Company. The Smiths essentially founded the glass decorating industry in America and remained its most acclaimed practitioners. In 1874 Alfred and Harry left Mt. Washington to found Smith Brothers, which specialized in the production of "Fine Decorated Glass Ware," especially glass lamp shades and vases. The glass decorating industry flourished in

(132) "Albertine" vase, about 1887
Enamel decorated, free-blown white opal glass
New Bedford, Massachusetts
MOUNT WASHINGTON GLASS COMPANY
The Jones Museum of Glass and Ceramics

(plate 20-color reproduction, page 196)
"Verona Ware" pitcher, about 1895
Blown glass with enamel decoration
New Bedford, Massachusetts
PAIRPOINT MANUFACTURING COMPANY
Collection of The New Bedford Glass Museum
New Bedford, Massachusetts

Aquatic scenes like this, which illustrates a carp swimming in the sea grass, were widely adopted by American industrial arts manufacturers. "Verona ware" was one of the first lines of art glass introduced following the merger of the Mt. Washington Glass Company with the Pairpoint Manufacturing Company.

American Industry Responds

(133) Kerosene lamp, 1878-1882
Mold-blown enameled glass, brass mountings
New Bedford, Massachusetts
S. R. BOWIE AND COMPANY DECORATORS
Collection of The New Bedford Glass Museum
New Bedford, Massachusetts

Samuel R. Bowie was a prominent figure in New Bedford's thriving glass industry. Working his way up as a pattern maker at Mt. Washington Glass, his success at developing patentable innovations enabled him to branch out on his own. In 1876, he founded the Samuel R. Bowie Co., which specialized in decorating art glass, like this Japanesque lamp. Bowie was influenced by the work of the Smith Brothers in New Bedford, and the decoration on this lamp is almost indistinguishable from their work. The cherry blossom, tied with small squares of paper in the branches, is an unusual Japanesque motif that refers to the Japanese custom of fastening poems to the tree as part of the courting rituals of spring.

New Bedford so that during the peak years of the Japan craze several independent companies were in business there. Among them was the firm of Samuel R. Bowie (fig. 133), whose work is so similar to Smith Brothers' that it can be mistaken for it. Smith Brothers produced picturesque Japanese-style compositions of overlapping circles and squares intertwined with flower blossoms and birds.[200] The lamp is interesting as one of the only examples in American decorative art that illustrates the Japanese custom of tonzaku, tying poems on the branches of trees at blossom time.

The most overlooked body of glass in the Japanese taste is the less expensive work of pressed, engraved, and sandblasted glass. Firms like Bryce Brothers and George Duncan & Sons, both in Pittsburgh, and the Columbia Glass Company in Findlay, Ohio, patented pressed glass patterns with names like *Mikado Fan, Fish Scale, Japanese,* and *Bamboo Beauty* as early as 1880.[201] The LaBelle Glass Co. in Bridgeport, Ohio, produced several Japanesque patterns in pressed glass as early as 1883, including *Bamboo* (fig. 134) and *Oriental*.[202]

Having already discussed the extraordinary Japanesque designs in pressed, sandblasted, engraved, and etched architectural glass, it is perhaps sufficient to end by noting that the same methods were employed in decorating glass shades for chandeliers, lamps, and torcheres. Because these items were found in the most public rooms in the house, they can be tremendously stylish. The etched-glass shade here illustrated (fig. 135) combines brocade and floral patterns with airborne swallows, cracked ice, and pie-shaped medallions similar to the types advertised by the Asa G. Neville Glass Company in Blairsville, Pennsylvania.[203] If there were two manufacturers of this type of work, there could as easily be twenty. Little work has been done to preserve the memory of this fascinating chapter of the industrial arts and its intersection with the Japan idea.

* * *

(134) Creamer and covered butter dish, about 1883
"Bamboo"
Pressed clear glass
Bridgeport, Ohio
LA BELLE GLASS COMPANY
The Arkansas Arts Center Decorative Arts Museum

Japanese-inspired pressed glass existed primarily in the form of window panes, but some companies did offer lines of tableware in response to the Japan craze. The La Belle Glass Company produced one of the most overtly Japanesque patterns. Two pieces of their "Bamboo" line shown here are decorated with fan-like patterns and simulated bamboo borders.

(135) Lamp globe, about 1880-1885
Sand blasted glass
American
Mark Twain Memorial, Hartford, Connecticut

Decorated globes like this one were advertised in trade journals for use in chandeliers, wall sconces, and lamps. Plain and frosted globes were more common than decorated examples. This globe is loaded with Japanesque references including cracked ice, fish scales, airborne swallows, and flower blossoms.

American Industry Responds

By now I suspect the point has been made: the Japan idea's infiltration of the industrial arts was complete. Not only did it affect manufacturers of ceramics, furniture, metalworks, and glass, but it left its imprint on manufacturers of textiles, wallpapers, jewelry, and countless other products. At least two of New England's dozens of textile mills produced printed cottons influenced by Japanese art: Cocheco in Dover, New Hampshire (fig. 136), and Hamilton in Lowell, Massachusetts (fig. 137). Cheney Brothers silk mills in Manchester, Connecticut, sent a member of the family to Japan in 1859 to buy silks[204] and during the 1880s became America's leading manufacturer of silk damask patterns (color plate 21) in the Japanese style. As the silk manufacturer of choice for the prestigious decorating house of Associated Artists, Cheney Brothers was in the vanguard in producing artist-designed woven goods. Warren, Fuller and Lange in New York advertised artistic wallpapers designed by Louis Comfort Tiffany, Candace Wheeler, and their partners in Associated Artists. Japanesque wallpapers furnish some of the best examples of the overlapping and layering of pattern (fig. 138, color plates 22, 23). Few of the growing number of documented papers in the Japanese taste can be associated with a manufacturer, however. Clocks (fig. 139), thermometers, table lamps, woven tapestries (fig. 140), tin cracker boxes, fans (color plate 24) and jewelry (fig. 141) round out a survey of American manufactured goods in the Japanese taste that leaves little doubt that the Japan craze left its impression on every facet of domestic life in America.

(136) Engraver's sheet, 1886
Dover, New Hampshire
COCHECO MANUFACTURING COMPANY
Museum of American Textile History

At the height of the public flurry over the touring version of Gilbert and Sullivan's The Mikado, *Cocheco issued a printed dress fabric illustrating scenes from the opera superimposed on a crazy quilt ground. Cocheco was one of New England's most prolific manufacturers of printed cottons. At the height of the Japan craze it employed 500 men and 70 women who produced 50,000,000 yards of printed fabric annually. During the 1880s, Cocheco's print works were managed by Washington Anderton, a British printer hired in England and brought to the United States. Prints like this one were first designed on paper and then transferred to a copper roller for printing.*

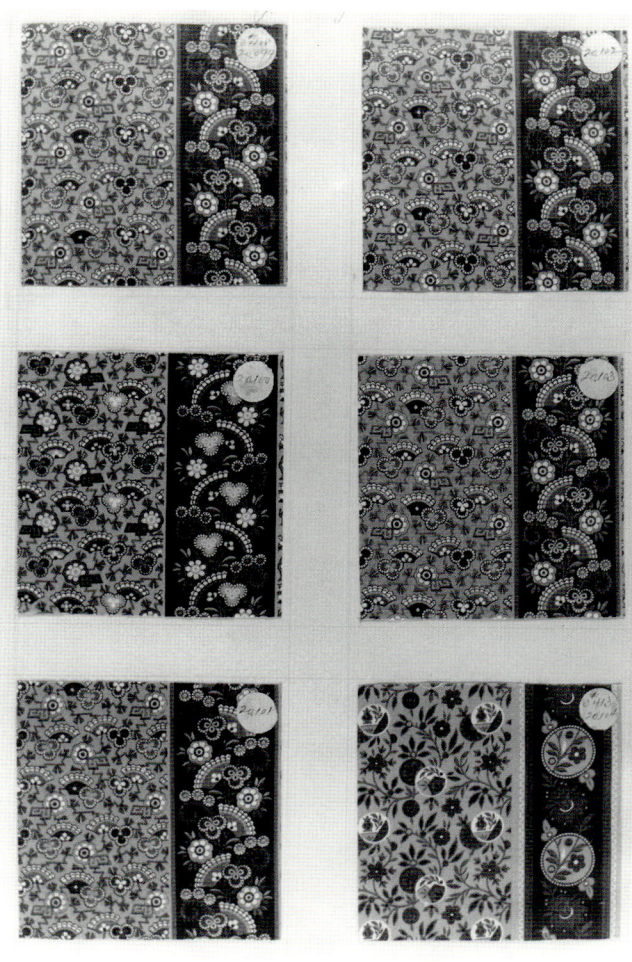

(137) Pattern book, 1881
Lowell, Massachusetts
HAMILTON MANUFACTURING CO.
Museum of American Textile History

The Hamilton Manufacturing Co. began printing cotton fabric in 1828. At the height of the Japan craze companies like Hamilton produced up to one thousand new prints a year, mostly dress and furnishing fabrics of a plain weave. Most of their products were checks, plaids, and floral patterns devoid of Japanesque qualities. Around 1880 the firm began experimenting with Japanese inspired patterns, turning out several dozen in the years that followed. A page from a pattern book, dated January 1881, illustrates how Japanese details like fans and overlapping circles were adopted. Five of the six patterns illustrated differ only in the combination of colors used.

(138) Wallpaper sample, about 1885
American
Henry Ford Museum, Greenfield Village

American Industry Responds 149

(plate 21-color reproduction, page 196)
Textile fragment, about 1882
Silk damask
Manchester, Connecticut
CANDACE WHEELER
Cheney Brothers
Mark Twain Memorial, Hartford, Connecticut
Gift of Mrs. Horace B. Learned

This gold toned quince pattern silk damask represents one of the earliest and most successful experiments with high-end textile manufacturing in the Japanese taste. It was probably designed by Candace Wheeler while she was directing the textile division of Associated Artists.

(plate 22-color reproduction, page 197)
Wallpaper, about 1884
Composition material, embossed and colored
Stamford, Connecticut
Possibly manufactured by FREDERICK BECK & CO.
Cooper-Hewitt Museum

Lincrusta Walton, the trade name associated with a type of relief-decorated wallpaper invented by Frederick Walton in England, was ideally suited to the imitation of traditional Japanese embossed leathers. It was made from composition material treated with oxidized linseed oil mixed with wood pulp, which was passed under rollers that impressed a pattern. Lincrusta Walton was one of the breakaway success stories in the home furnishings industry during the 1880s. Beginning in 1883, it was produced in America by Frederick Beck & Company, a New York firm with a factory and design studio in Stamford, Connecticut. This sample was removed from the dining room of the John D. Rockefeller house on West 54th Street.

(plate 23-color reproduction, page 197)
Wallpaper sample, about 1885
American
Henry Ford Museum, Greenfield Village

Machine-printed wallpapers aimed at the middle market are some of the boldest and most evocative designs produced during the Japan craze. Although little is presently known about the industry that produced these papers, several dozen Japanesque patterns can be documented in situ and from period photographs. Two types predominated—the composite overlay and the Japanese trailing vine. Both emphasized muted colors with gilt accents, complex patterning, and Japanesque motifs. The composite overlay was favored in public buildings or rooms in houses where a flamboyant effect was desired. Artful and eclectic, the composite overlay involved seemingly random juxtapositions of fragments of different designs. The shapes included circles, squares, and odd-shaped polygons that served as windows allowing the viewer to see a variety of scenes or patterns simultaneously.

(139) Mantle clock, about 1888
Brass and copper case
New Haven, Connecticut
NEW HAVEN CLOCK COMPANY
Wadsworth Atheneum

The New Haven Clock Company was one of the most successful and innovative manufacturers in Connecticut at a time when the industry enjoyed international markets and prestige. At the height of the Japan craze, the New Haven Clock Company operated retail outlets throughout the United States and in England and Japan. This clock shares features in common with models marketed under the trade names "Hilda" and "Albatross." The "Albatross," the firm's best known design in the Japanese taste, incorporated ceramic tiles manufactured by J. & J.G. Low. This example combines the cast brass casing and mechanism of the "Albatross" with the more expensive chased and molded copper panels of the "Hilda."

American Industry Responds 151

(140) Woven tapestry, about 1885
Cotton
Probably New England
Robert Tuggle and Paul Jeromack

Jacquard loom-woven cotton tapestries like this were used as wall hangings and table coverings. Although several New England based textile mills were capable of producing work like this, the industry is poorly documented. This tapestry resembles carpet design of the period, especially in the use of a heavily patterned border design. The ground design resembles Japanesque crazy patchwork. The range of patterns and motifs is remarkable, calling attention to the textile industry's embrace of art and Japanese design as a marketing tactic during the 1880s.

(plate 24-color reproduction, page 197)
Folding fan, about 1890
Painted satin on wood ribs
East Braintree, Massachusetts
Attributed to the ALLEN FAN COMPANY
New Hampshire Historical Society

The manufacture of Japanese style fans was a small industry in the United States. The Allen Fan Company, established in East Braintree, Massachusetts, in 1880, is one of the only large scale manufacturers known. At the peak of its success during the late 1880s, the Allen Fan Company was producing almost one thousand fans per day in a wide range of styles and sizes, including one almost six feet in diameter that sold for fifty dollars.

(141) Necklace, 1880–1890
Sterling silver
Probably American
Marked "H.M."
Private Collection

Hat pins, brooches, bracelets, and necklaces like this were among the accessories worn by fashionable women during the Japan craze. This necklace, by an unidentified silversmith, is composed of sixteen linked fans cast in Japanese patterns of birds, flowers, and fish.

American Industry Responds 153

VII. British Pottery Invades America

The story of Victorian America's response to Japan is incomplete without reference to the British industrial arts movement and the overwhelming dominance of British pottery on the American market. Of all the industrial arts, British pottery held the strongest position in the American market. By the mid-eighteenth century British pottery was stocked by merchants in every city and small town in America. Anticipating shifts in taste and through the relentless pursuit of efficient methods of production, Britain maintained its grip on the American market while expanding exports throughout the world. But it was more than economics and trade at work in the startling ascendancy of British industrial arts in America. There is something extraordinary about the image of the United States and Great Britain celebrating *together* the Centennial of America's struggle to be free of British oppression and rule. Clearly much water had passed over the dam in a century, so that by 1876 mutual admiration prevailed in British-American relations. In an increasingly competitive world economy the bond of shared values, language, and ethnicity counted far more than the dry facts of history. For Britain, the United States represented a vast and rapidly growing market. For the United States, still striving for acceptance among the family of nations, an alliance with Great Britain was an alliance with a winner.

The triumph of British over French ideas was one of the most important transformations in the cultural life of the late nineteenth century. As one critic wrote at the time of Oscar Wilde's lecture tour in America: "to be English today is to be in good form. ... Not long ago the New York swell had a French tailor, a French bootmaker, and cultivated French manners."[205] Nowhere was the triumph of British ideas more pronounced than in its lead in the industrial arts. At the Centennial, British exhibits of electo-plated wares, art needlework, and—most of all—pottery, testified to its growing dominance in those markets and in all branches of consumer goods manufacturing. The French may have made great art and the Germans great music and weapons, but it was the British who lead the world in producing things for the home. Manufacturers like Elkington & Co. were among the first to employ major artists as decorators and designers of mass-produced art goods. Elkington's pathbreaking imitations of Japanese cloisonné (fig. 142) were widely admired by Centennial-goers who increasingly recognized how far America had fallen behind in the race for market share in the booming consumer goods industries.

The story of British pottery during the Japan craze parallels that of the fine metals in America. At the top were a few industry giants that specialized in high-end goods on the cutting edge of taste and of the most exquisite workmanship. Josiah Wedgwood and Sons, Ltd.—the legendary firm that revolutionized the production and marketing of pottery during the eighteenth century—was joined by the Worcester Royal Porcelain Company, Doulton & Company, and Minton and Company, nineteenth century firms whose reputations became synonymous with excellence and artistic innovation. Alongside these leaders was a vast network of earthenware manufacturers—mostly based in the Staffordshire region—that catered to the middle market through aggressive stylistic and technological innovation that kept costs down and fashion high. Like silverplate in America, the story of Britain's middle-market art-pottery industry—especially wares decorated by transfer printing—is largely unrecognized in the literature on the arts. But also like silverplate, it is apparent that the literature has overlooked a magnificent phenomenon. Far from being an aesthetic backwater, transfer printers created some of the most complex and intriguing designs produced during the Japan craze. British transfer-printed earthenwares saturated the American market to such an extent that crockery merchants in New York and Boston adopted it as an advertising gimmick to tell the public they were in style.

As of this writing the literature on English transfer printing in the Japanese taste is virtually non-existent and significant public collections in America or Britain are unknown. Yet demand for Japanesque pottery is growing among private collectors and has become an increasingly ubiquitous commodity in the antiques trade[206]. Fortunately, English transfer-printed earthenware is frequently marked with the name and date of its manufacture, making it possible to introduce some of the key players and assess the aesthetic impulse behind their most popular patterns.

The invention of transfer printing during the eighteenth century revolutionized the art of pottery decoration. It made possible for the first time the standardization of complex painted patterns while eliminating the need for expensive hand work. Prior to that time the decoration of standard production British earthenwares was achieved by molding and through the use of colored glazes. Transfer printing was ideal for mass producing pictures and patterns, thus shifting a larger share of the cost of manufacturing to the important work of pattern design. Once a pattern was developed tens of thousands of objects in dozens of forms could be made consistent in style and color. Everything from dinner plates and tea pots to brush holders and soap dishes were fair game. It became a mark of status to own large sets in one pattern, a possibility available only at the extreme fringes of wealth and privilege a few generations before.

(142) Vase, about 1875
Cloisonné enamel with gilt base and handles
England
ELKINGTON AND COMPANY
Wadsworth Atheneum

By 1876, the Japanese art movement in Great Britain was already in full swing. The British were the only Western participants to include significant examples of Japanesque industrial art at the Centennial Exhibition. Elkington and Company, the inventor of electroplating, perfected an imitation of Japanese cloisonné that was widely acclaimed as a technological breakthrough. This vase was purchased at the Centennial by Elizabeth Colt, widow of the legendary arms manufacturer.

British Pottery Invades America

(143)
Platter, 1881
Transfer-printed earthenware
Burslem, Staffordshire, England
GILDEA & WALKER
Wadsworth Atheneum

The pattern Gildea & Walker marketed under the trade name of "Melbourne" was the most popular transfer-printed design in the Japanese taste in America. For vigorous design and eclectic Japanesque references, the Melbourne pattern was unmatched. Diagonals, seascapes and horizon lines, airborne sparrows, bamboo, apple blossoms, and the owl in the moonlight—Melbourne was a veritable encyclopedia of Japanesque decoration arranged in a way that was pure Victorian. This platter is printed in five colors, which was just one of more than a dozen colorways in which the pattern was offered.

(144) Platter, 1883
Transfer-printed earthenware
Turnstall, Staffordshire, England
BROWNHILLS POTTERY CO.
Robert Tuggle and Paul Jeromack

This platter is an example of the Brownhills Pottery Co.'s "Kioto" pattern, designed in 1883 to compete with the hugely successful "Melbourne" pattern introduced two years before by Gildea & Walker.

At the height of the Japan craze there were crockery merchants in every fair sized town in America. All of them stocked or could order English transfer-printed earthenware. No statistics are presently available but it is likely that the quantities exported to America numbered over one million units. Diversity and eclecticism being everything, only a fraction of the goods were in the Japanese taste. But from a look at their advertisements during the 1880s, the Japanese was the style chosen when a merchant wanted the public to think he was in fashion. Among the leading crockery merchants in America were George F. Bassett & Co. and Burgess & Goddard in New York, and Jones, McDuffee & Stratton, Richard Briggs, and Davis, Collamore & Co., all of Boston.[207] Bassett's frequent advertisements in the *Crockery and Glass Journal* document a brisk wholesale trade in Japanesque transfer designs. Promoted as good sellers at "a low price," Bassett promoted Japanesque transfer-printed wares manufactured by Wedgwood; Henry Alcock & Co.; and—"the bestseller ever placed on the market"—Gildea & Walker's legendary "Melbourne" pattern (fig. 143), a pattern available in more than a dozen different color combinations printed on "ivory" brand, lead-glazed earthenware.[208] Advertising in *The Decorator and Furnisher* in 1883, Jones, McDuffee & Stratton illustrated the main showroom in their six-story crockery warehouse in Boston, filled floor-to-rafters with Japanesque designs.[209] Brown, Westhead, Moore & Co.'s "Depose" and Minton and Company's "Bombay" are two among a small number of Japanesque patterns issued before or during the Centennial Exhibition. The development of new designs increased dramatically during the peak years between 1879 and 1883. Popular among them were Edge, Malkin & Co.'s "Tonquin" and the Brownhills Pottery Co.'s "Kioto" (fig. 144)— both similar to and issued following the success of "Melbourne;" a group of circle-and-rectangle overlay patterns like J. Dimmock & Co.'s "Warwick;" and Old Hall Earthenware Co.'s remarkable and colorful pattern "Excelsior".[210] These are bold and visceral designs untainted by academic pretense and aesthetic snobbery. Even though designers remain anonymous, their work demonstrates a wide familiarity with the vocabulary of Japanese ornament and an extraordinary ability to adapt and transform several aesthetic tendencies in effect at the same time. Transfer-printed wares and the companies that produced them are begging for serious study, not only as decorative art but as a primary agent in the dissemination of the Japan idea throughout the West.

Having opened the discussion of British pottery with material traditionally regarded as commercial and artistically inferior, it is especially important that the achievement and true eminence of firms like R.W. Binns's Worcester Royal Porcelain Company (hereafter referred to as Royal Worcester) be acknowledged. As one of the premier Japanists in the industrial arts and a renowned scholar of British pottery in his own right, Binns's role in promoting Japan and the Japanesque was unsurpassed among his Victorian contemporaries. Binns founded Royal Worcester in 1862, the year of Sir Rutherford Alcock's landmark exhibition of Japanese art at the London Exhibition of 1862. Although not immediately adapted for work in the Japanese taste, the ivory colored porcelain Binns perfected in 1862 was eventually recognized as one of the most important contributions to Japanism in the ceramic arts. Royal Worcester began manufacturing Japanesque pottery in 1866, earlier than any other known industrial arts manufacturer and only a couple years after James McNeill Whistler's much-touted experiments with Japanese design principles and motifs.[211] By the time of the Centennial Exhibition, R.W. Binns was being lionized as one of the few champions in the industrial arts that could match the Japanese at their own game.[212] Royal Worcester's Japanesque work dominated its production throughout the Japan craze. Characterized by delicate enamel and gold on molded forms, this work has a jewel-like quality perfect for cabinet pieces and for display in the best Japanesque interiors (fig. 145).

(145) Group of works by the Worcester Royal Porcelain Company

The plate on the right belonged to Elizabeth Colt of Hartford, Connecticut, who probably purchased it at the Centennial Exposition, which she visited during the first week in July 1876.

Plate, about 1880 (left)
Gilt on underglaze painted porcelain
Worcester, England
THE WORCESTER ROYAL
PORCELAIN COMPANY
Mark Twain Memorial,
Hartford, Connecticut
*Manufactured for
Tiffany and Co. in New York*

Pitcher, 1889 (center)
Enameled porcelain
Worcester, England
THE WORCESTER ROYAL
PORCELAIN COMPANY
Wadsworth Atheneum

Plate, 1876 (right)
Enameled porcelain
Worcester, England
THE WORCESTER ROYAL
PORCELAIN COMPANY
Wadsworth Atheneum

Royal Worcester was not stocked by common crockery merchants, but it was widely available in America. Tiffany and Co. in New York contracted with Royal Worcester for the production of specialty wares in the Japanese taste and exotic forms could be custom-ordered. Although best known for its ivory colored porcelain, Royal Worcester also developed lines that imitated Japanese Satsuma ware (color plate 25) and the deep cobalt blue ground of Arita ware.

Minton and Company and Josiah Wedgwood and Sons were both eighteenth-century firms that flourished with the advent of art pottery during the Japan craze. Although best known as a manufacturer of architectural tiles, Minton was a fully diversified pottery manufacturer that employed artists of the stature of Christopher Dresser and Walter Crane as designers. Unlike Royal Worcester, which never dabbled in middle-market goods, Minton spanned the range from the inexpensive transfer-printed earthenwares to hand decorated porcelain to monumental limited edition designs that count among the most extravagant ceramic productions of the age (fig. 146). Similarly, Josiah Wedgwood and Sons branched out into new areas, one

(plate 25-color reproduction, page 198)
Tea set, 1878
Gilt and enameled earthenware
Worcester, England
THE WORCESTER ROYAL PORCELAIN COMPANY
Robert Tuggle and Paul Jeromack

This tea set represents a style of Japanesque art pottery that was Royal Worcester's attempt at imitating Japanese Satsuma pottery. Gilt and enameled fans, mons, and sprigs of flowers are placed randomly over a yellow glazed body similar in color and decoration to Satsuma.

of the most intriguing being a line of printed earthenwares decorated with pictographs from Hokusai and graphic representations of ukiyo-e prints by Hiroshige (fig. 147).

The British pottery invasion was not unique to the era of the Japan craze, but its assault was more intense than Americans had experienced ever before. The British were not the only foreign manufacturers to export Japanesque ceramics art to America—the French firms Haviland, Longwy, and Galle each gained a position in the American market as did Irish Beleek (fig. 148)—and Britain's industrial art export trade with America was not limited to pottery. But the impact of British pottery overshadowed other industries at a time when pottery was regarded with greater reverence than at any time since. British pottery was thus an important instrument for conveying the Japan idea and was one of the thickest links in a chain that bound the cultures of Britain and America during the late Victorian era.

(146) A selection of Minton Pottery

Minton was one of the most prolific of the Staffordshire region's art pottery manufacturers. Although best known for the production of encaustic architectural tiles, the firm experimented in almost every branch of pottery production. In 1875, Minton became the first in the industry to develop transfer-print designs in the Japanese taste (left). At the top of its line was porcelain decorated in gold and silver (right) in the most sophisticated of Japanese patterns. The firm also supplied blanks for china painters (center) and architectural tiles in the Japanese style.

Plate, 1876 (left)
Transfer-printed earthenware
Stoke-on-Trent,
Staffordshire, England
MINTON AND COMPANY
Robert Tuggle and
Paul Jeromack

Art tile, about 1880 (center)
Painted earthenware
Stoke-on-Trent,
Staffordshire, England
MINTON, HOLLINS & COMPANY
Robert Tuggle and
Paul Jeromack

Plate, about 1878 (right)
Gilt, silver, and enameled
decorated porcelain
Stoke-on-Trent,
Staffordshire, England
MINTON AND COMPANY
Wadsworth Atheneum

(147) Tazza and plate, about 1873
Transfer-printed and painted earthenware
Burslem, Staffordshire, England
WEDGWOOD AND SONS
Private Collection

These two forms are the earliest instance of the imitation of Japanese woodblock prints in decorative arts. All of the details flanking the central image are drawn from Hokusai's Manga, *notably his studies of bamboo fencing, flora, and traditional technology. The central image on the plate is based on a print by Ando Hiroshige titled* Tenryu River View, *from his* Fifty-three Views of Tokaido, *first published during the 1840s.*

(148) Teapot, about 1880
Gilt and enamel decorated porcelain
Beleek, County Fermanagh, Ireland
MCBERNEY AND ARMSTRONG
Wadsworth Atheneum

Belleek, the ivory-colored, eggshell-thin porcelain made in Ireland, was one of the few ceramic products to attract a wide following among Americans during the Japan craze. Indeed, the prestige of this ware was so great that American manufacturers like Ott & Brewer developed products that imitated its texture, color, and glaze. This teapot is an example of Irish Beleek marketed as "Kioto ware," owned by a Hartford family during the Japan craze.

160 THE JAPAN IDEA

VIII. Women's Art and Popular Culture

The most visceral and distinctive art produced by Americans during the Japan craze came at the point where that craze intersected with the women's suffrage movement. On the surface, gender politics may not appear to have played a vital role in the arts of Victorian America; but if we scratch beneath the rhetoric and look at some facts and figures, it becomes immediately apparent that the Japan craze, the push behind art education, and, indeed, the entire market for art products in the Japanese taste were byproducts of the changing status of women in Victorian life. In these closing pages I would like to open Pandora's box by summarizing the role of Victorian women in shaping the culture of art in late nineteenth-century America and suggesting why a story of such vigor and interest has been suppressed.

Aspects of class, equal opportunity employment, and the emergence of the home as an incubator for family values were major factors behind the unprecedented ascendancy of art in American life. The period of the Japan craze gave birth to our great museums and schools of art, confirmed for the first time that American artists, architects, and designers could attract international recognition and patronage, and established, as never before or since, a place for art at the center of American life. None of this would have happened without the driving imperative of female politics. From the interrupting of the official July 4th program with a reading of the Declaration of Rights for Women, to the novelty and grandeur of the Women's Pavilion (fig. 149), the Centennial witnessed the arrival, not just of Japan, but of American women.

Regardless of politics or class, women of all stripes treated the social maladies of their sex with the balm of art. On one side were the good housekeepers who elevated to the rank of secular religion the idea of the home as moral retreat. On the other side were feminist reformers, many of them also leaders in the antislavery movement, pressing for women's suffrage and reforms in the divorce, labor, and property laws.[213] One side saw art, particularly that which embodied the Japan idea, as fostering the ideal domestic environment. The other side saw the boom in industrial arts as an opportunity to blaze new trails across the appallingly limited terrain of "women's occupations." Both sides harmonized about the value of art, a fact so unusual amidst the cacophony of nineteenth-century feminist rhetoric that its story also begs to be told – alas, by someone else.

Quick to recognize the potential for consensus, male art-reform critics and women of privilege espoused opening careers in art for women. In an effusive aside in *Modern Dwellings* (1878), the American architect Henry Hudson Holly professed that

efforts on the part of ladies of rank to elevate an employment whereby women may earn a livelihood is philanthropic in the extreme. There is, indeed, no reason why women should not become proficient, and be employed in all the industrial arts. . . . We might then hear less of the tyranny of shopkeepers and manufacturers in compelling girls to be on their feet from morning until night, destroying both mind and body in the endeavor to earn an insignificant stipend. . . . When some of our ladies of wealth have become proficient themselves, what

(149) Women's Pavilion at the Centennial, 1876
Lithograph
Philadelphia, Pennsylvania
THOMAS HUNTER
Courtesy of the Athenaeum of Philadelphia

a field of industry they might establish for a worthy and highly gifted set of women, who simply want instruction to excel in something better and higher than what has hitherto been conceded as woman's sphere of labor![214]

The extent to which support for women's careers in art cut across class lines is epitomized in the role of upper-class women in the formation of decorative art societies, art schools, and museums across America. No one was more centrally involved in these changes than Candace Wheeler, one of the most influential women in the arts during the Japan craze.

Wheeler's story is intriguing because, up to the point of her awakening, her life was comfortable but ordinary. Having mastered the range of traditional domestic arts while growing up on a farm in upstate New York, Wheeler married and raised a family while dabbling in painting and needlework. The exhibit of the Royal School of Art Needlework at the Centennial aroused her idealism and changed her life. In the years immediately following, Wheeler became a persistent advocate for, and the ideal model of, the career woman in the arts. In 1877, backed by a New York society matron, Wheeler founded the Society of Decorative Art of New York City, which became a model for similar societies in cities like Boston and Hartford, Connecticut. More concerned with the plight of women of artistic ability who really needed to work (it is unclear whether she was among them), Wheeler went on to found the Women's Exchange, which placed greater emphasis on marketing than education. She was a gifted designer, painter, and embroiderer (color plate 26) who professionalized her work by pursuing awards, critical acclaim, and sales. In 1879 Wheeler was invited to join Louis Comfort Tiffany's newly-formed interior-decorating business, Associated Artists. As an equal among very distinguished male artists, Wheeler participated in founding what became the leading decorating firm in America. As an artist, designer, and author, Candace Wheeler defined the upper limits of what was possible for a career woman in the arts in Victorian America.[215]

The Societies of Decorative Art in New York, Hartford, Boston, and elsewhere were prototypical women's organizations. Although men were hired as visiting instructors (fig. 150), these societies were run by and for women. A feature article in (Appleton's) *Art Journal* praised the New York Society for covering "ground yet untouched by any of the already established Art-schools in extending facilities for the unfolding of Art-talent in *any and every form* ... [and] securing to the Art-worker a rewarding labour by opening a market ... without the intervention of middle-men." The society, the author explained, was "primarily designed for those who depend upon such employment for a livelihood.... The piece-worker, who has heretofore laboured well for a pittance, now receives an adequate return; ... [while] a lady is encouraged ... to use her talents, and to no longer feel that to lift a finger for herself is to demean herself."[216]

The "ground yet untouched" staked out by the decorative art societies was not less than the whole kit and caboodle of the industrial arts. Even as male painters were attempting to define their professional status as artists by narrowing the range of what qualified as art, and thus controlling entry to their ranks (women need not apply), women and industry (strange bedfellows) joined together to broaden the definition by "extending facilities for the unfolding of Art-talent in any and every form."

The women were onto something big, and whether they ceded control later or whether it was appropriated from them, their work altered the course of art education and museums in America. The Cincinnati Art Museum (1886) was founded as the offspring of the Women's Centennial Executive Committee, which continued to operate after the Centennial "as an Association to advance women's work ... in the field of industrial art." Rechristened the Women's Art Museum Association of Cincinnati, this

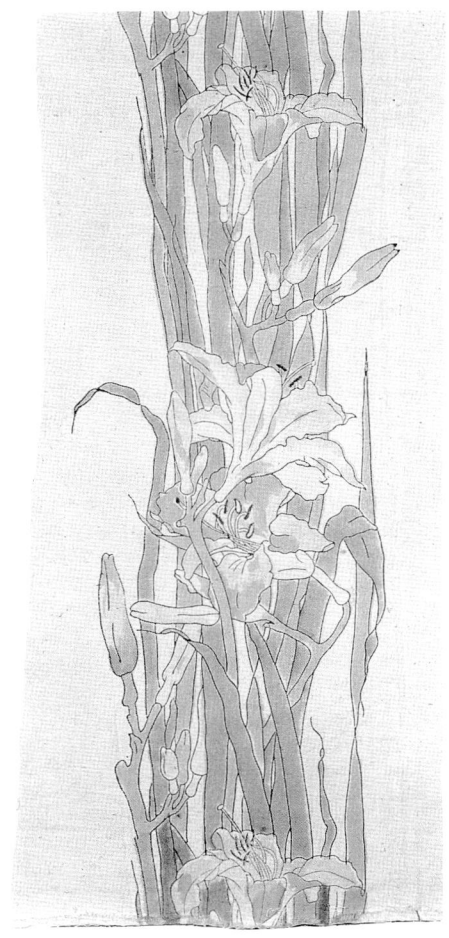

(plate 26-color reproduction, page 198)
Textile fragment, about 1885
Printed cotton
Probably New York, New York
CANDACE WHEELER
Mark Twain Memorial, Hartford, Connecticut

Under the direction of Candace Wheeler, Associated Artists produced limited runs of screen printed cottons. Examples in the Japanese taste, like this panel depicting lemon lilies, were used as furnishing fabrics in Japanesque parlors and reception rooms. Five colors were used to create the design.

(150) Plaque, 1879
Earthenware with underglaze painted decoration
The Cleveland Museum of Art
JOHN BENNETT
John L. Severence Fund

John Bennett was among the most prominent of the many British decorative art masters who relocated to America during the Japan craze. Americans first discovered Bennett's work in the Centennial display of his employer, Doulton & Company. The following year he established himself as a teacher and practitioner of china painting in New York, later serving as the first instructor of china painting at the New York Society of Decorative Art. Although he is best known for his work in the medieval revival style of William Morris, this plaque is one of several examples by Bennett that reflect an interest in the Japanesque.

organization was one of the big engines powering the arts at a time when Cincinnati was leading the nation in art education and career development for women in the arts.[217]

The Society of Decorative Art in Hartford played a smaller but comparable role in resuscitating the city's moribund arts institution, the Wadsworth Atheneum. The society's first president was Elizabeth Colt, heiress to the fortune of firearms impresario Samuel Colt. The society and its descendant organization, the Hartford Art School, renewed the Atheneum's mission and restored its financial solvency by moving the society's flourishing operations there in the 1880s.[218] A similar story can be told about Helen Metcalf and the founding of the Rhode Island School of Design in Providence. It makes you wonder if this just might have been the story everywhere.

In the end, the industrial arts did not prevail, nor were women able to maintain control over organizations they helped found or rehabilitate during the 1880s. More than that, their very notion of art – their art – was eventually banished to a dark corner or tossed back into the market by the very institutions they helped create. Clearly, something had changed. The Japan idea was so malleable and powerful a force that it excited passions and bred conflict. Entrenched and powerful interests – rich men – ultimately seized the idea of Japanese influence in art and reshaped it in their own image. The literature of japonisme has not embraced or even recognized the role of women and manufacturers, or the tastes of the middle class, during the Japan craze. And yet this is the material that I believe best represents the American response to Japan. It was there first; it was vital and distinctive; and it defined the course of the movement. Not to recognize the involvement of women – indeed, their leadership – both as consumers and creators of art in the Japan idea is to miss the phenomenon's richest, thickest point of being.

The segment of American women who turned to art as a career was small compared with the enormous numbers who lived day to day with the anxiety bred out of not being sure they were modern enough, cosmopolitan enough, or simply with it enough. Whatever it was, they needed it badly, and something about art, particularly Japanese art, and most definitely art of their own making, was certain to create the illusion, if not the reality, of being in the vanguard of the modern age.

In 1882 Oscar Wilde, Britain's outrageous high priest of aestheticism, arrived in the United States for a much-heralded, sold-out lecture tour. He spoke on the decorative arts, ethics of art, home furnishings, and related topics. Eighty-five percent of his audiences were women, a fact attributed to the "new excitement over etiquette and Anglomania."[219] Let's face it, most Americans in 1882 were either still on, or had recently left, the farm. To describe their concerns with etiquette and proper art as intense would understate the case. American women who, in fact, were charged with the ugly task of polishing things up were terrified of looking countrified, which, indeed, many of them were.

To get started, women made things. They painted pictures, decorated "china," embroidered table covers, carved wooden vases, collected and arranged scraps of everything, and basically reshaped whole rooms in their homes as monuments to their reflexive individuality. Japanese art conventions and decoration figured so prominently in this activity that, unlike the fine and industrial arts where it was a sideline, women's art put Japan front and center. When critics and pundits referred to "the Japan craze," it was women's work they had in mind.

Demand for training and equipment spawned an entire industry that catered to women's art. The art-supply business boomed. A Boston company advertised ready-made oil paints in dozens of colors with names like *crimson lake* and *flake white*.[220] In St. Louis the A.S. Aloe Co. issued a catalog with the title "How to Paint." It provided color formulas for painting twilight clouds, running brooks, chrysanthemums, cornflowers, and cherries. Subsequent chapters on china painting, watercolor painting, pyrography (fig. 151), tapestry painting, painting on silk, and wood carving were squarely aimed at the female market.[221] There were perhaps hundreds of other publications, some legitimate instructional manuals, others merely trade catalogs with instructional boilerplates. There were books on wood carving and art needlework that instructed "ladies" in the art of Kensington embroidery, crazy patchwork, and worsted cross-stitch patterns (figs. 152, 153, 154).[222] But none of these was as big as what was called, apocryphally, "china painting."

The rapidity with which the china-painting fad

(151) Tray, about 1890
Stained and burned wood
American
Strong Museum

Pyrography, the art of decorating wood by burning with irons, was one of many new crafts that were popularized during the Japan craze. This tray illustrates peach branches composed on a diagonal in the Japanese manner.

(153) Lambrequin, about 1885
Wool with silk embroidery and glass beads
Wisconsin
Helen Allen Textile Collection, University of Wisconsin

(152) Splasher, about 1890
Woven cotton/linen blend silk and cotton embroidery
Vassalboro, Maine
Female member of the Sturges Family
Woolwich, (Maine) Historical Society

Outline stitch embroidery in red on white became fashionable during the Japan craze. Known today as turkey red needlework, this method of decoration was used in making decorative splashers, towels, pillow shams, and other forms suited for use on the bedroom wash stand. This example, with its interwoven ribbon and fringe, is more elaborate than most.

Women's Art and Popular Culture 165

(154) Runner, about 1890
Silk and wool with silk, wool, and cotton embroidery
American
Helen Allen Textile Collection, University of Wisconsin

At the height of the Japan craze, hundreds of thousands of women across the country became involved in the production of "art needlework." They made table covers and runners and decorative skirts for furniture and interior woodwork. This runner is a representative example of art needlework in the Japanese taste.

(156) Vase, 1887-1891
Enameled and painted earthenware
American
CAROLINE SCOTT HARRISON, decorator
D.A.R. Museum

This moon-shaped flask was decorated by Caroline Scott Harrison, the wife of President Benjamin Harrison. It closely resembles a type of art pottery which the Cincinnati Art Pottery Company marketed as "Hungarian Faience."

(155) Interior, Molly Sheafe's Studio
about 1885
Center Harbor, New Hampshire
New Hampshire Historical Society

Once trained, women artists could set up studios for china painting with a minimum of expenditure. Although some women purchased kilns so they could fire their work to completion, others shipped their decorated wares to kilns in nearby cities, thus keeping their operations on a small and intimate scale. Center Harbor on Lake Winnipesaukee in New Hampshire was a popular tourist destination a century ago. Molly Sheafe undoubtedly supplied her work for the tourist market and for neighbors and friends.

swept the nation after the ceramic arts were canonized at the Centennial astonished contemporary observers, one of whom likened it to "a prairie flame across the wide expanse of the land." Before the end of the century as many as one hundred thousand women would try their hand at china painting, twenty-five thousand in the year 1893 alone.[223] (Fig. 155) The ranks of china painters included presidents' wives (fig. 156), renowned artists and literary figures, and farm women anxious to supplement the family income by selling and trading decorated pottery to their neighbors. China-painting clubs were formed from Maine to Texas, as women scrambled to get on board the biggest fad since sewing stockings during the Civil War.

Japanese and Japanese-style pottery so eclipsed everything else of the type at the Centennial that it is no surprise it became the ornamental style of choice for china painters. Of the work produced before 1890, it is the rare example of china painting that does not exhibit Japanese characteristics. The "Japanese ring," or disk-and-flower motif, was ideally suited for execution on plates. But then what wasn't? No other art form drew on a wider vocabulary of Japanese motifs than china painting. Embraced were all of the flowers, all of the insects, marine life and birds, and all of the compositional devices, from fractured overlays to the stark gilt-ground figural and floral portraits. The variety and depth of japanism exhibited by American china painting is staggering (figs. 157 a,b, 158, 159, color plate 27).

Invoking Japan as her inspiration, the New England poet Celia Thaxter, of the Isles of Shoals in New Hampshire, wrote of her new-found passion for china painting in 1877, describing plates, "tinted just pale sea-green [with] a Japanese lady ... in the middle of each, with birds, or butterflies or bats or turtles, swallows, dragon-flies, lizards, beetles, any and everything, on the border, with flowers and grasses or leaves, all copied from the Japanese."[224]

In Wiscasset, Maine, Jane Tucker painted china and furniture (fig. 160), embroidered art needlework, and experimented with molding and decorating art brass. Having studied women's arts in Boston around 1884, she tried unsuccessfully to make a go of teaching art to her neighbors in Maine before returning to Boston where she taught embroidery and china painting at Stearn's department store. She later moved

(157 a) Plate, 1881
Painted earthenware
Hartford, Connecticut
MARY KINGSBURY TALCOTT
The Stowe-Day Foundation, Hartford, Connecticut

Mary Talcott was a china painter and illustrator who probably enrolled in the first classes at the Society of Decorative Art in Hartford, founded in 1878.

(157 b) Pitcher, about 1885
Painted earthenware
Marked L.V.W.
Wadsworth Atheneum

This vase was a gift to Elizabeth Colt, the first president of the Society of Decorative Art in Hartford, and was probably the work of one of the many students enrolled in china painting classes taught by Mrs. Darrow in the Society's studios beginning in 1879. Although not signed by its decorator, this pitcher is representative of the Japanesque aesthetic favored by china painters at the height of the Japan craze.

(158) Teapot and sugar bowl, 1885
Painted earthenware
Probably Boston area
Signed "Arnold"
Wadsworth Atheneum

(plate 27-color reproduction, page 199)
Vase, about 1885
Painted earthenware
Concord, New Hampshire
Attributed to Julia Kimball
Kimball-Jenkins Estate

(159) Plate, 1884
Painted porcelain
Probably Orange, Massachusetts
Orange Historical Society

This plate bears the initials "M.W." of an unidentified china painter. The curled edged porcelain blank was manufactured by Haviland and Company of Limoges, France. The china painter employed the Japanesque convention of naturalistic decoration breaking out of its man-made border, an allusion to nature's power over man.

(160) Painted mirror, about 1885
Wood, mirror glass, paint
Probably Boston, Massachusetts
Jane A. Tucker
Castle Tucker House Museum

Painted decoration was applied to everything from doors and mantlepieces to bureaus and chairs during the Japan craze. Mirrors were well suited to Japanesque ornamentation. This example was the work of Jane Tucker of Wiscasset, Maine, who studied china painting there and in Boston. The mirror bears the label of Charles J. Edmunds, a dealer in picture frames and artists' supplies in Boston.

168 THE JAPAN IDEA

to New York and worked for the importer A.A. Vantine & Co. Castle Tucker, the family home in Wiscasset, contains varied specimens of her work and a cornucopia of Japanesque art products bought at Vantine's.[225]

Minnie Ellsworth Hastings of Windsor, Connecticut, learned china (fig. 161) and oil (fig. 162) painting as a student at Wilbraham Academy, in 1898. Marrying shortly after graduation, she was soon a single mother left to raise children on a sixteen-acre farm. With a reputation as a china painter, Hastings managed by selling decorated dresser sets, hair receivers, pin trays, and vases which she fired in a kiln on the property. She grew tobacco, gladiolas, and tomatoes commercially and taught pastel and charcoal drawing to neighboring children, while feeding her own by keeping cows and livestock and growing fruits and vegetables. That is not exactly the picture of gentility suggested by some accounts of china painters, but it is a good measure of how completely the china-painting craze permeated American society.[226] And, of course, Hastings's work was Japanesque.

(161) Covered pitcher, 1919
Painted earthenware
Windsor, Connecticut
Painted by MINNIE ELIZABETH ELLSWORTH HASTINGS
Earthenware blank manufactured by EDWIN M. KNOWLES
East Liverpool, Ohio
Private Collection

Although dated long after the Japan craze had peaked, this pitcher is included to show the persistent interest in china painting, especially in rural areas. The kimono-clad figure and birdhouse are details lifted straight out of Hokusai's Manga, *demonstrating its wide circulation and use by china painters.*

(162) Still life of flowers, 1897
Oil on canvas
Windsor, Connecticut
MINNIE ELIZABETH ELLSWORTH
Private Collection

This picture of a Japanese vase with flower blossoms was the work of a sixteen-year-old student at Wilbraham Academy in Massachusetts.

Women's Art and Popular Culture

(163) *The Old Garden*, 1888
Embossed paper on boards
Written by Rose Terry Cook
Illustrated by Mary Kingsbury Talcott and Harriet D. Andrews
Published by L. Prang & Co.
Boston, Massachusetts
Stowe-Day Foundation, Hartford, Connecticut

Rose Terry Cook and Mary Kingsbury Talcott were active members of the Hartford literary scene at the time The Old Garden *was published. Cook was best known for her short stories and essays on New England folklife. Her* Huckleberries Gathered from New England Hills *(1891) was one of the most popular books of its genre. Mary Talcott was an illustrator and china painter with a gift for depicting Japanesque flowers.*

(plate 28-color reproduction, page 198)
Folding screen, about 1885
Maple frame, painted canvas panels
Boston, Massachusetts
Painted by Mary Newell Farnam
Private Collection

This screen represents the most ambitious type of painting project undertaken by women during the Japan craze. Folding screen frames could be purchased at art supply stores with canvas panels ready to paint. This example depicts Japanesque hollyhocks and airborne sparrows in the trees. Mary Farnam probably studied painting in one of several Boston art schools that offered courses for middle class and affluent women during the 1880s.

Even with the recent opening of the portentously designated National Museum of Women in the Arts, in Washington, D.C., it will probably still be a long time before anyone gets down in the trenches and really looks at the art of Victorian women. Mary Cassatt makes a nice poster child, but she is not representative and I am not ready to concede that the art of mainstream American women is uninteresting, lacking in aesthetic merit, or devoid of content. Women poured into the arts, and their output was so prodigious that it seems almost astonishing to believe it has all just disappeared. Women's involvement in the art industry expanded dramatically during the 1880s. They illustrated books (fig. 163) and magazines and made, exhibited, and sold paintings like never before. In Philadelphia in 1881, about twenty of the 175 individuals listed as artists in the city directory were women. By 1889 that number had shot up to more than seventy, roughly 25 percent of the total.[227] In 1883 Philadelphia was home to more than half a dozen art schools including the Philadelphia School of Technical Design for Women and the Ladies Decorative Art Club.[228] Some of this work must have survived.

Consider Concord, New Hampshire, where in 1885 a group of "artists and amateurs" organized the "Fireside Art" exhibit for the Grand Army Fair. The oversight committee was composed almost entirely of women, and although a few male artists contributed pictures, most of the work – both oil paintings and decorated pottery – was supplied by young, single women. With titles like "Japanese birds," "cherry study," "Snowballs and peonies," and "Holly-hocks," the popularity of Japanese subject matter is apparent.[229]

Women painted everything from folding screens (color plate 28) and (fig. 164) interior woodwork to

(164) Folding screen, 1881-1882
Painted maple
Probably Providence, Rhode Island
Wadsworth Atheneum

This screen is a remarkable example of the convergence of Japanism, antiquarianism, and literature. Its overlapping images were modelled after the illustrated edition of John Greenleaf Whittier's Snow-Bound, A Winter Idyl, *published in Boston in 1868. Passages of the poem were painted in a style of lettering known as the Mikado script, while the pictures are layered and arranged in a Japanesque manner. The screen has associations with Providence, Rhode Island, and may have been produced by a member of the Providence Art Club, founded in 1880.*

Women's Art and Popular Culture 171

Front   Back

(165) Vase, about 1885
Carved wood
Probably Rhode Island
M. Yarrington
Museum of Art, Rhode Island School of Design

Among the arts popular with Victorian women during the Japan craze, wood carving is one of the lesser known. This vase is decorated with layered leaves, cattails, dragonflies, a bird on a branch, and other Japanesque details on one side, with a profile portrait of an unidentified man over an open hearth on the other. This unusual symbolism speaks of art in the language of antiquarianism and Japan. The carved work is signed by M. Yarrington, probably a woman wood carver and member of a prominent family in Rhode Island and southeastern Connecticut.

(166) "Crazy" patchwork table cover, about 1883
Velvet with silk and satin panels of embroidered patchwork
Probably Wallingford, Connecticut
Wallingford Historical Society

fans and dinner menus. Wood carving (fig. 165) was so popular among the women of Cincinnati that in 1876 Benn Pitman, an instructor at the city's School of Design, could boast that the "160 pupils in his department ... designed and carved 664 separate pieces of work, including the decoration of a piano, an organ, three bedsteads, two cabinets, ... four mantlepieces, five writing desks ... [and] twelve large picture frames." The best of these were exhibited in the Women's Pavilion at the Centennial "where it excited much interest and no small amount of incredulity, certain benighted people having no idea that women could execute work requiring so much skill."[230]

The one uniquely American art form of the Japan craze is also its most essential – the crazy quilt. This one form encapsulates better than any other the complex web of impulses that shaped women's art during the 1880s. The crazy quilt, also known as the patchwork quilt, is a record of family and history, a bond of female friendship, a gallery of collected fabrics, a document of its maker's taste and domestic economy, and, most of all, a virtuoso performance of needlework. That the form is also quintessentially Japanesque is not as immediately apparent as its aesthetic power, which is so enormous that the crazy quilt is one of the few art forms of its period that has elicited admiration continuously since the Japan craze. This is one form of women's art that museums *have* collected; indeed, there are thousands in public collections today.

Reviewing the history of the crazy quilt in 1882, an editorial in the *Art Amateur* said that,

when the present favorite style of quilt was introduced it was called the Japanese, but the national sense of humor has been too keen, and the Japanese is now generally known as the "crazy" quilt. There is method in its madness, however, and put together with a good understanding of color effects, the crazy quilt may prove an artistic piece of work. In its simplest form it is a combination of pieces of silk of every color and shape.... The materials are the waste scraps which collect in every house, too small or too irregular to serve any other possible purpose. These are reinforced by the exchanging of scraps between acquaintances.... One of the ambitions of a young man of fashion nowadays is the possession of a crazy quilt, made up of patches contributed by the ladies of his acquaintance; and his social progress may be reckoned by these patches as an Indian warrior's prowess is reckoned by his scalps.[231]

A trade publication from 1884, describing the varied applications of crazy patchwork, cited everything from table scarfs (fig. 166) and quilts to portieres and window curtains. The Japanesque character of the form was suggested by the arrangement of fabric scraps "in a 'hap-hazard' sort of way, so that the angles may somewhat imitate the craze or crackel of old china, from which all this kind of work derives its name."[232] The crazy quilt is the ultimate statement in the aesthetic of random occurrence and accidental effect (color plate 29).

(plate 29-color reproduction, page 199)
Patchwork "Crazy" quilt, 1884
Silk, satin and velvet face, taffeta lining
Hartford, Connecticut
SIGNORA MAY
Wadsworth Atheneum

Of the many thousands of crazy quilts made, this is one of the most outstanding examples known. Composed of 1,047 individual pieces of fabric, it is the embodiment of the Japanese aesthetic of random occurrence, which made a virtue out of chaos. Its maker, Signora May, was a gifted needleworker.

Women's Art and Popular Culture   173

More popular than crazy quilts and less difficult to make were scrapbooks. This was the ultimate document of a woman's aesthetic stream of consciousness. The seemingly random arrangement of mementos, pictures, and advertising cards with decorative accents and borders guaranteed that no two scrapbooks could ever turn out alike. They were the perfect vehicle for self-expression. Sentimental and highly personal, the scrapbook was at once a work of art and autobiography. As if its Japanesque quality was not apparent enough in the contents and in the aesthetic of randomness, most scrapbooks were bound in commercially made albums (fig. 167) with Japanese-style covers.

As an element of popular art, the scrap had many applications during the Japan craze. Indeed, one might interpret the bric-a-brac interior as scrap art writ large. In the late stages of our field research we stumbled across examples of what the antique trade calls "shard art." These are vases and umbrella stands encrusted with bits of broken glass and ceramic. The umbrella stand, dated 1909, at The Strong Museum in Rochester, New York, is one of the few in a public collection, but it is late. Examples, however, have been seen dating from as early as 1886. The historical and biographical quality of scrap art makes dating easy. A date is usually tucked away in some corner of a crazy quilt, and, more often than not, the shard-art vases are dated.

There were also woven and hooked rugs (fig. 168) in the pattern of crazy quilts. A ceramic pitcher in the Maine State Museum, painted and decoupaged like a crazy quilt, represents another form of this art, and Godey's Lady's Book published an article that taught women how to make scrap screens, described as "in imitation of the Japanese work . . . [with] pictures all pale yellow, Oriental designs artistically arranged."233

Popular culture and art during the Japan craze assumed an extraordinary range of forms. After the Centennial the fever subsided slightly but soared again in 1885 with the American productions of Gilbert and

(167) Scrapbook, 1884
Bound plain paper with stamped hard covers
Patented May 22, 1883
MANUFACTURER UNKNOWN

The Japanesque was the most popular style for scrapbook covers.

Hooked rugs are a genre of home-made folk art that mirrored changing fashions for half a century. During the 1880s, rural women worked loose bits of fabric into patterns resembling crazy quilts and Japanese brocades.

(168) Hooked rug, about 1885
Clipped rag on burlap
American
Robert Tuggle and
Paul Jeromack

174 THE JAPAN IDEA

Sullivan's *The Mikado* (figs. 169). As one notice put it, because of "the absurd attempts to represent the Japanese in the many presentations of *The Mikado* . . . the [creations] of that interesting, faraway people are in great demand . . . so great as to entitle it to the superlative appellation of a veritable 'boom.'"[234] *The Mikado*'s captivating music and incisive lyrics plus its realistic and elaborate costumes and sets proved irresistible. No fewer than five production companies crisscrossed the United States between August 1885 and May 1886, reigniting interest in the Japan craze. The show's three little maids – Pitti-Sing, Yum-Yum, and Peep-Bo – were adopted as an advertising gimmick to sell everything from corsets to soap. Popular songs from *The Mikado* were repackaged as sheet music for the parlor organ and the piano. Demand for lyrics and melodies suggestive of Japan (fig. 170) grew and became staples of the expanding popular-music industry.

With the blossoming of America's consumer culture, advertising got more aggressive. Even in colonial times broadsides and newspaper advertisements used humor, bold type, and catchy phrases to attract interest in everything from the stud service of prized bulls to the sale of furniture and dry goods. But the advent of chromo-lithography and the increasingly competitive market for a widening array of consumer goods made traditional methods of advertising obsolete. As shorthand for all that was stylish and modern, the Japan idea was ideally suited for creating persuasive, life-style evoking images. The notion that a picture or image could say far more than words was not born of the Japan craze, but it flourished then as never before. Modern advertising was shaped by the visual possibilities created by the Japan craze.

(169) Sheet music, about 1886
The Mikado Waltz
Arranged by P. BUCALOSSI
Watkinson Library, Trinity College, Hartford, Connecticut

(170) Sheet music, 1891
Japanese Lullaby
Words by EUGENE FIELD
Music by WILLIAM NEIL
THE JOHN CHURCH COMPANY, publisher
Cincinnati, Ohio
Watkinson Library, Trinity College, Hartford, Connecticut

Women's Art and Popular Culture

As early as 1878, printers like L. Prang & Co., J.H. Bufford & Son, and J.A. Lowell & Co. in Boston, Ballin & Liebler and Donaldson Brothers in New York, and the Onondaga Lithographing Co. in Syracuse incorporated Japanese imagery in the design of printed greeting cards, advertising cards and broadsides (fig. 171). These are some of the most graphic and assertive images (color plate 30) created during the Japan craze. Hundreds of Japanesque advertising cards were produced in an astonishing array of styles. They mark the emergence of advertising in the vanguard of art and popular culture in America.[235] The same industry also produced greeting cards (figs. 172, 173 a,b) for the growing number of state and national holidays spawned by America's leisure culture.

(171) Tea box label, about 1885
Extra Fancy Japan Buds
Imported by Fraser, Farley, and Varnum
Connecticut
Connecticut Historical Society

Japan exported vast quantities of tea. Fraser, Farley, and Varnum was a Connecticut based importer. Labels like this were fastened to boxes shipped to small town grocers throughout America.

(plate 30 a-i-color reproduction, page 200)
A group of advertising cards

(a) Advertising card, 1889
Brown Brothers and Company Mill Supplies
Lithographed paper with attached metal coin on string
Providence, Rhode Island
LIVERMORE AND KNIGHT, lithographers
Graphics Collection, The Rhode Island Historical Society

(b) Advertising card, 1882-1884
GEORGE M. LEE JAPANESE NOVELTIES
Color woodblock print
Japan
Lent by Thomas Beckman

(c) Advertising card, about 1884
"Wide Awake Store"
Lithographed paper
Waterbury, Connecticut
Connecticut Historical Society

(d) Advertising card, 1890
Sapanule, The Glycerin Lotion
Samuel Gerry and Company, Proprietors
Lithographed paper
Providence, Rhode Island
L. SUNDERLAND, lithographers
Graphics Collection, The Rhode Island Historical Society

(e) Advertising card, about 1884
SINGER SEWING MACHINES
Machine-printed cardboard
New London, Connecticut
Stowe-Day Foundation, Hartford, Connecticut

(f) Advertising card, about 1886
THOMSON'S PATENT GLOVE FITTING
Chromolithograph on card stock
American
Lent by Thomas Beckman

(g) Advertising card, 1889-1893
O AND O TEA COMPANY
Lithographed paper
Private Collection

(h) Advertising card, about 1884
J.H. ECKHARDT AND COMPANY FINE ARTS
Lithographed paper
Hartford, Connecticut
Connecticut Historical Society

(i) Advertising card, about 1880
PEERLESS TOBACCO COMPANY
Lithographed paper
Rochester, New York
Watkinson Library, Trinity College, Hartford, Connecticut

(172) Greeting card, about 1880
Chromolithograph on card stock
St. Valentine's Day
Minnesota Historical Society Collection
Donor, Mrs. Falwell Coan

(173 a) New Year's greeting card, 1880
Chromolithograph on card stock
L. PRANG AND COMPANY
Boston, Massachusetts
Concord Museum, Massachusetts

(173 b) Christmas greeting card, 1880
Chromolithograph on card stock
L. PRANG AND COMPANY
Boston, Massachusetts
Concord Museum, Massachusetts

Louis Prang perfected chromolithography in the United States and is regarded as one of the pioneers in the greeting card industry. In 1880 he sponsored a competition for the best Christmas card design. To further American decorative design Prang restricted the competition to Americans. The judges were Samuel Colman, Richard Hunt, and Edward C. Moore of Tiffany and Company.

(174) Mounted photographic portrait, about 1880
Printed cardboard
UNKNOWN MAKER
Robert Tuggle and Paul Jeromack

(175) Menu cover, about 1890
"Bill of Fare"
Orange Historical Society

This menu cover was used at the Mansion House, a hotel restaurant in Orange, Massachusetts. It is made of celluloid, an early type of plastic, that could be molded and colored to resemble ivory.

The Japan craze crackled from every corner of American life. Anything that smacked of fashion or modernity was fair game. Photographers' studios were decked out in Japanese regalia, and photographic portraits were framed with Japanesque mats (fig. 174). Going out for dinner at a fancy hotel? The menu cover (fig. 175) might be Japanesque. Going to a summer party? Expect to find the porch or yard strung with Japanese paper lanterns. Looking for a nice book of poetry, or something for the children to read (fig. 176 a,b)? The Japanesque was the style of choice for book covers and illustrations across wide range of genres, from poetry, art, and travel (fig. 177), to etiquette (fig. 178) and almost anything that smacked of the antique (fig. 179). America's most popular sculptor, John Rogers of New York,[236] produced a somewhat racist but intriguing "figure group" titled "Phrenology" (fig. 180) in 1884. It depicts an American scientist measuring the head of a Japanese man, an act reflective of the West's continued awkwardness with any and everything it considered foreign.

(176 b) *The Matsuyama Mirror*, about 1880
Japanese Fairy Tale Series Number 10
Woodblock printed on rice paper
Tokyo, Japan
Published by KOBUNSHA
Hartford Public Library
Hewins Collection

(177) *Picturesque Rhode Island*, 1881
Bound paper with hard covers
Written by W.H. MUNROE
Published by J.A. & R.A. REID
Providence, Rhode Island
Helen Hersh/Hamish Hog Antiques

The Japanesque was associated with travel and leisure. Picturesque Rhode Island *is a lavishly illustrated book with engravings of historic buildings, Newport Harbor, townscape views, and numerous tourist destinations. Illustrations were supplied by several engravers including the Reids. The cover and many of the illustrations reflect the influence of Japanese art.*

(176 a) *Kachi-Kachi Yama*, about 1880
Japanese Fairy Tale Series Number 5
Woodblock printed on rice paper
Tokyo, Japan
Published by KOBUNSHA
Hartford Public Library
Hewins Collection

Given their role in the making and buying of art in the Japanese taste, it is surprising that women were so slow in incorporating it into dress and bodily ornament. By 1890 that had changed; piled hairdos, the use of lipstick, kimono-cut lounging gowns, and dresses made of Japanese print and brocade fabrics (figs. 181, 182) were the height of fashion.[237] The saturation of Japanese influence was complete.

(178) *Decorum, A Treatise on Etiquette & Dress*, 1883
Bound paper with hard covers
Written by S.L. Louis
Published by Union Publishing House
New York
Wadsworth Atheneum

The Japanesque was naturally associated with etiquette. Decorum is typical of the dozens of advice manuals published at the time. With chapters on making social connections, dinner parties, street etiquette, and courtship and marriage, these books were important in codifying the modes of social interaction for middle class Victorians.

(179) *Grandma's Attic Treasures*, 1887
Bound paper with embossed imitation leather covers
Published by E.P. Dutton & Co.
Written by Mary D. Brine
New York, New York
Private Collection

Grandma's Attic Treasures is a story about conflict and changing values between traditional rural families and their city-bound descendants. The old folks on the farm sold off the family heirlooms to greedy antique dealers. The descendants, now caught up in the antique collecting craze, were unwittingly reunited with their family heirlooms which they bought for their charm, not realizing they had family associations. The moral of the story is that while families may be divided, the higher spirit of good taste lives on in the family antiques. The book was first published in 1881, and remained popular and in print for more than a decade. This is one of two known covers designed for the book in the Japanese taste. The Japanesque was widely associated with antiquarian and colonial themes. Both appealed to the romantic and aesthetic tendencies of the time.

(180) "Phrenology at the Fancy Ball,"
1884
Cast plaster sculpture
New York, New York
John Rogers
Belchertown Historical Society

The figural groups patented, mass produced, and sold by New York sculptor John Rogers made sculpture affordable for the masses for the first time. At the time of the Centennial Exhibition, Rogers was America's most popular sculptor. This is his only known figural group of a Japanese subject. Phrenology was the quasi-scientific study of head anatomy. Aspects of character and intelligence were believed to be measurable based on the size and structure of the human head. This group suggests that, in spite of Victorian America's reverence for Japanese arts, the people of Japan were subject to ridicule and racial stereotyping.

(181) Dress, about 1883
Printed cotton
New England
Plainfield Historical Society, Plainfield, Massachusetts

This dress illustrates how Japanesque print fabrics were used to make stylish clothing for rural New England women during the Japan craze. The dress was owned in the rural town of Plainfield, Massachusetts, and was probably one of the most fashionable articles of clothing in its owner's wardrobe. With a bolt of cotton fabric and a sewing machine, rural women were able to make their own stylish clothes at a relatively small cost.

(182) Dress, 1892
Silk brocade, taffeta, velvet with jet trim
New York, New York
Made by D.A. Nolston
Wadsworth Atheneum

This dress was part of the trousseau worn by Anna C. S. Krumbhaar on her honeymoon following her marriage in 1892.

IX. Aftershocks

Like most rich and evocative concepts, the Japan idea was subject to varying interpretations, then and now. By showing both the Japan idea's fine and popular art manifestations, we are revealing its essential pluralism. Rarely has an art movement been embraced so completely by so wide a spectrum of American society. To a large extent the literature on japanism has failed to take stock of its subject's roots in popular culture. The fact that an idea could cut across lines of class, gender, and even ethnicity seems startling in retrospect. We have grown accustomed to the notion that ideas about art and fashion trickle down, when in fact, at least with the Japan craze, ideas and values clearly moved in both directions. That seems natural.

Like Japan in the 1850s, we face a new world that is beyond our control. The ranting of those currently threatened with dispossession—the managers of America's automobile industry, Wyoming's cattle farmers, and Hawaiian real-estate agents—is a distant echo of Japan's shogunate before the fall. Like it or not, we are entwined with an island nation six thousand miles away. We need to make the best of it by listening, learning, adapting, and, finally, by competing on the new playing field defined by our evolving relationship.

Racism cannot be selectively unacceptable. Our experience with Japan a century ago teaches us so many things. We learn that diversity breeds strength and that competition breeds vitality. We learn that differences among people are never so great that there cannot be common ground. A century ago America rediscovered part of its preindustrial identity embedded in the arts of Japan. That discovery was nurtured and blossomed into an aesthetic culture that strengthed our creative spirit and enriched our humanity. A century ago we confronted the challenge of Japan's foreignness by adapting and improvising, not by knee-jerk reactions or political machinations. Can we afford not to be as open and resourceful today?

X. Color Plates

(color plate 1)
Passing the Rubicon
July 11, 1853
Detail of color lithograph
WILLIAM HEINE
Mystic Seaport Museum

186 THE JAPAN IDEA

(color plate 2)
First Landing of Americans in Japan
July 14, 1853
Detail of color lithograph
WILLIAM HEINE
Mystic Seaport Museum

(color plate 3)
Landing of Commodore Perry, Officers, and Men of the Squadron
March 8, 1854
Detail of color lithograph
WILLIAM HEINE
Mystic Seaport Museum

Color Plates 187

(color plate 4)
Pair of covered jars, 1875
Decorated porcelain
Arita, Japan
Koransha porcelain works
Ichiryusai Uchimatsu, decorator
Wadsworth Atheneum

(color plate 5)
Globe-shaped covered jar, about 1890
Cloisonné enamel
Japan
School of NAMIKAWA YASUYUKI (1845-1927)
Wadsworth Atheneum

(color plate 6)
Wallpaper samples, about 1885
Embossed leather with gold leaf and painted decoration
Japan
George Walter Vincent Smith Art Museum
Springfield, Massachusetts

Color Plates 189

(color plate 7)
Folding screen, 1720-1740
A Beauty Playing the Samisen
Painted paper with gold leaf on lacquered wood frame
Japan
Lent by Smith College Museum of Art, Northampton, Massachusetts
Gift of Catherine H. Ayers (Catherine Spicer Hubley '32) in memory of her mother, Nancy Spicer Hubley, and her grandmother, Nancy West Spicer, 1973

(color plate 8)
Color woodblock print, 1857
Iris At Horikiri
From *One Hundred Views of Famous Sites in Yedo* series
Japan
ANDO HIROSHIGE (1797-1858)
Museum of Fine Arts, Springfield, Massachusetts
The Raymond A. Bidwell Collection

(color plate 9)
Night Owl, 1879
Oil on canvas
American
CHARLES CARYL COLEMAN
Jane Voorhees Zimmerli Art Museum
Rutgers, The State University of New Jersey
In memory of the deceased members of the class of 1954

(color plate 10)
The Ameya, 1893
Oil on canvas
American
ROBERT F. BLUM
The Metropolitan Museum of Art
Gift of the Estate of Alfred Corning Clark, 1904

Color Plates 191

(color plate 12)
Folding screen, about 1885
Wooden lattice core covered with paper under watercolor and metallic painted silk front panels, silk brocade backing
San Francisco, California
Painted by FORAKECHI YATA for the ICHI BAN STUDIOS
Essex Institute

(color plate 11)
The Laundry, Branchville, about 1894
Oil on canvas
American
J. ALDEN WEIR
Private Collection

(color plate 13)
Ceiling fresco, about 1880
Samuel Sparhawk Kimball House, 1876–1882
Possibly painted by WILLIAM HENAY & SON
Concord, New Hampshire
Courtesy of the Kimball-Jenkins Estate

(color plate 14)
Art tiles, about 1881
Glazed earthenware
Chelsea, Massachusetts
J. AND J. G. LOW ART TILES
Private Collection

Color Plates 193

(color plate 15)
Monumental vases, 1883
Enameled earthenware
Cincinnati, Ohio
ROOKWOOD POTTERY, decoration attributed to ALBERT VALENTIEN
Collection of Everson Museum of Art (left)
Wadsworth Atheneum (right)

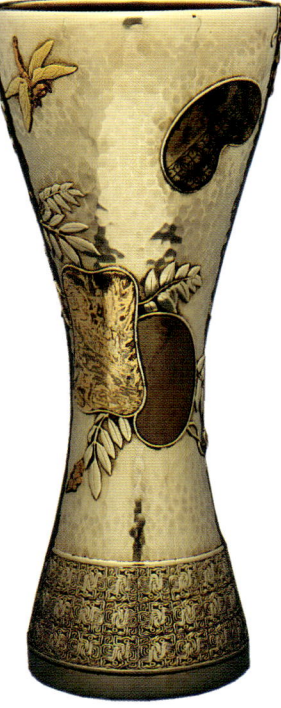

(color plate 16)
Vase, about 1878–1880
Sterling silver with mixed metal and patinated alloy decoration
New York
TIFFANY AND COMPANY
From a friend of the Wadsworth Atheneum

(color plate 17)
Trade catalog, Meriden Britannia Co., 1882
Hartford, Connecticut
Printed by CASE, LOCKWOOD AND BRAINARD
Meriden Historical Society, Inc.

(color plate 18 a)
Wall plaque, 1885
Copper enamel and silverplate
Meriden, Connecticut
MERIDEN BRITANNIA CO.
Collection of Helen Hersh and Charles Sporn

(color plate 18 b)
Clock, about 1885
Copper enamel with silverplate applied decoration, brass and enamel face
Taunton, Massachusetts
Attributed to REED AND BARTON
Collection of Helen Hersh and Charles Sporn

Color Plates 195

(color plate 19)
Center table, 1874
Inlay
New York City
HERTER BROTHERS (stamped)
Wadsworth Atheneum

(color plate 20)
"Verona Ware" pitcher, about 1895
Blown glass with enamel decoration
New Bedford, Massachusetts
PAIRPOINT MANUFACTURING COMPANY
Collection of The New Bedford Glass Museum
New Bedford, Massachusetts

(color plate 21)
Textile fragment, about 1882
Silk damask
Manchester, Connecticut
CANDACE WHEELER (1827-1923)
Cheney Brothers
Mark Twain Memorial, Hartford, Connecticut
Gift of Mrs. Horace B. Learned

(color plate 22)
Wallpaper, about 1884
Composition material, embossed and colored
Stamford, Connecticut
Possibly manufactured by FREDERICK BECK & CO.
Cooper-Hewitt Museum

(color plate 23)
Wallpaper sample, about 1885
American
Henry Ford Museum, Greenfield Village

(color plate 24)
Folding fan, about 1890
Painted satin on wood ribs
East Braintree, Massachusetts
Attributed to the ALLEN FAN COMPANY
New Hampshire Historical Society

(color plate 25)
Tea set, 1878
Gilt and enameled earthenware
Worcester, England
THE WORCESTER ROYAL PORCELAIN COMPANY
Robert Tuggle and Paul Jeromack

(color plate 26)
Textile fragment, about 1885
Printed cotton
Candace Wheeler (1827-1923)
Probably New York, New York
Mark Twain Memorial, Hartford, Connecticut

(color plate 28)
Folding screen, about 1885
Maple frame, painted canvas panels
Boston, Massachusetts
Painted by MARY NEWELL FARNAM
Private Collection

(color plate 27)
Vase, about 1885
Painted earthenware
Concord, New Hampshire
Attributed to JULIA KIMBALL
Kimball-Jenkins Estate

(color plate 29)
Patchwork "Crazy" quilt, 1884
Silk, satin and velvet face, taffeta lining
Hartford, Connecticut
SIGNORA MAY
Wadsworth Atheneum

Color Plates 199

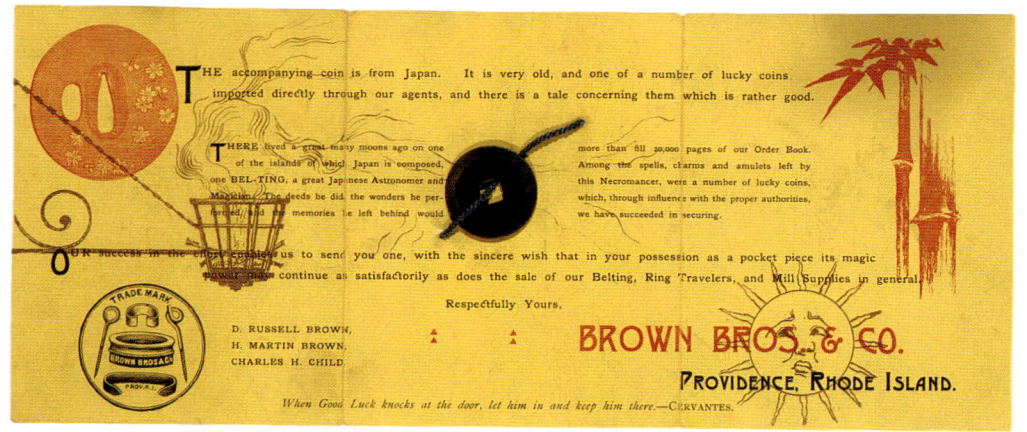

(a)

(f)

(b)

(e)

(g)

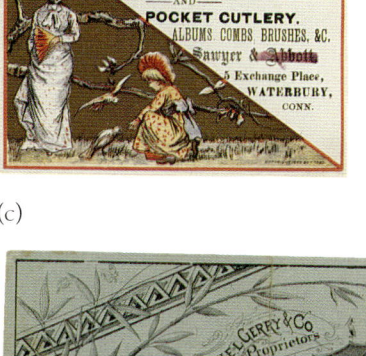

(c)

(d)

(i)

(h)

200 THE JAPAN IDEA

Endnotes

1. William Walton, *World's Columbian Exposition: Art and Architecture* (Philadelphia: George Barrie, 1893), 1, 87.

2. Gabriel P. Weisberg and Yvonne M. L. Weisberg, *Japonisme: An Annotated Bibliography* (New York: Garland Publishing, Inc., 1990). This publication lists over 700 entries of an expanding literature.

3. Samuel Elliot Morrison, *"Old Bruin": Commodore Matthew C. Perry, 1794-1858* (Boston: Little, Brown & Co., 1967).

4. David Murray, *Japan* (New York: G. P. Putnam's Sons, 1894), 318-321.

5. *The Japan Expedition 1852-1855 of Commodore Matthew Calbraith Perry.* Catalog of an exhibition, October 11 to December 11, 1968 (Washington, D.C.: Smithsonian Institution, 1968).

6. Morrison, *"Old Bruin,"* 373-4.

7. Morrison, *"Old Bruin,"* 369.

8. David Hackett Fischer, *Albion's Seed* (New York: Oxford University Press, 1989). This work presents a vast body of scholarship covering all of the sub-regions of colonial America. It all adds up to an unambiguous picture of feudalism's presence in colonial America.

9. William Elliot Griffis, *The Mikado's Empire* (1876; reprint ed., New York: Harper and Bros., 1903), 304.

10. Murray, *Japan*, 361-2.

11. Murray, *Japan*, 372.

12. Yukimasa Hattori, "Foreign Commerce of Japan Since the Restoration, 1869-1900," in *Johns Hopkins University Studies in History and Political Science* 22, nos. 9-10 (October 1904), 12.

13. *Every Saturday* (September 23, 1871), 295.

14. Griffis, *The Mikado's Empire*, 522. Shortly following the Meiji restoration, a national decree was issued instructing each han or regional domain to select two students to be sent abroad for western education. Several hundred young men - among them many of Japan's future leaders - were thus educated. In the United States Rutgers College in New Brunswick, New Jersey was the first and one of the most committed of the many American colleges to receive Japanese students before 1890. *Perspectives of Japonisme: The Japanese Influence on America*, ed. Phillip Dennis Cate (New Brunswick, N.J.: The Jane Voorhees Zimmerli Art Museum, Rutgers, 1988), 8.

15. Robert A. Rosenstone, *Mirror in the Shrine: American Encounters with Meiji Japan* (Cambridge: Harvard University Press, 1988), 31.

16. James Jackson Jarves, *A Glimpse at the Art of Japan* (1876; reprint ed., Rutland, Vt.: Charles E. Tuttle, Co., 1984), 198.

17. Sir Rutherford Alcock, *Catalogue of Works of Industry and Art, Sent from Japan*. International Exhibition Catalog, 1862 (London: William Clowes and Sons, 1862). Although not illustrated, this small publication was the first work in English to survey Japan's progress in the arts of lacquer ware, basketwork, ceramics, metalsmithing, and the related decorative arts media. In what was the first such claim made, Alcock asserted that Japanese pieces "not only bear comparison with the best workmanship of Europe, but, in some particulars, cannot be rivalled."

18. Haga Toru, "The Diplomatic Background of Japonisme: The Case of Sir Rutherford Alcock," in *Japonisme in Art: An International Symposium*, ed. Yamada Chisaburo (Tokyo: Committee for the Year 2001 and Kodansa International Ltd., 1980), 27-42.

19. Haga Toru, "Diplomatic Background," 2.

20. Nancy Burch Wilkinson, "Edward William Godwin and Japonisme in England" (Ph.D. diss., UCLA, 1987), 42.

21. Wilkinson, "Godwin," 29.

22. Edward S. Morse, *Catalogue of the Morse Collection of Japanese Pottery* (Cambridge: Riverside Press, 1901).

23. This was brought out in his bitter review of George A. Audsley's and James L. Bowes's, *Keramic Art of Japan* (London 1875), a deluxe, multi-volume catalog of objects, mostly in Bowes's personal collection. Richard L. Wilson discusses Morse's open attacks on Bowes and Audsley in "Tea Taste in the Era of Japonisme: A Debate," *Chanoyo Quarterly* 50 (1988), 23-39. Morse was the most rabidly anti-industrial of the Japanophiles and believed that western tastes had corrupted Japanese arts. In their highly ethnocentric and aestheticized approach to Japanese ceramics, Audsley and Bowes epitomized everything Morse despised about western collectors. Typical of Morse's sensibility are these comments from *Japan, Day by Day* (1917; reprint ed., Dunwoody, Georgia: Norman S. Berg, 1978), 186-7: "Previous to the demands of the foreigner, the members of the immediate family [of the potter] were leisurely engaged in producing pottery ... Now the whole compound is given up to a feverish activity with ... children slapping it out by the gross ... [which merely] confirms the Japanese that they are dealing with people whose tastes are barbaric."

24. Edward S. Morse, *Japanese Homes and Their Surroundings* (1886; reprint ed., Rutland, Vermont: Charles E. Tuttle, 1972), xxxi-xxxii.

25. Morse, *Japanese Homes*, 114.

26. Morse, *Japanese Homes*, 115 and 117.

27. Morse, *Japanese Homes*, 347.

28. Morse, *Japanese Homes*, xxxvi.

29. Henry Pettit, *Final Report to the United States Centennial Commission on the Structures Erected for the Vienna Universal Exhibition, 1873* (Philadelphia: Centennial Commission, 1873) and J. E. Mitchell and Charles H. T. Collis, *The Vienna Exposition: Report of the Philadelphia Commission to Vienna* (Philadelphia: Centennial Commission, 1873). Both of these rare imprints are in the Philadelphia City Archives.

30. *Philadelphia Inquirer* (November 22, 1876), from Centennial Scrapbook, 36, Archives of the City and County of Philadelphia, np.

31. Dallas Finn, "Japan at the Centennial," *Nineteenth Century* 2, nos. 3-4 (Autumn 1976), 33-40.

32. Sekizaw Akekio to Alfred J. Goshorn, letters, July 19, 1875 and September 14, 1875, Archives of the City and County of Philadelphia, ms. box A-1528.

33. Terashima Nunenori to John A. Bingham, letter, October 11, 1875, Archives of the City and County of Philadelphia, ms. box. A-1528. *Official Catalog of the Japanese Section* (Philadelphia: Japanese Commission, 1876), 4. List of the cost etc. of the Japanese Exhibit, Japanese Commission, July 29, 1876, Archives of the City and County of Philadelphia.

34. Finn, "Centennial," 37.

35. *Frank Leslie's Illustrated Newspaper* (New York) (February 26, 1876), 398 and 404.

36. *The Daily Graphic* (New York) (July 8, 1876), 259. A description of the bazaar ran in *The Weekly Mountaineer* (September 30, 1876), in Centennial Scrapbook 16, Archives of the City and County of Philadelphia, 75.

37. Finn, "Centennial," 39.

38. J. S. Ingram, *The Centennial Exposition* (Philadelphia: Hubbard Bros., 1876), 109.

39. *Public Ledger* (Philadelphia) (August 25, 1876), in Centennial Scrapbook 22, Archives of the City and County of Philadelphia, 3.

40. *Catalog of the Japanese Section*, 51-52.

41. *Catalog of the Japanese Section*, 52.

42. *Philadelphia Evening Bulletin* (November 8, 1876), in Centennial Scrapbook 21, Archives of the City and County of Philadelphia, 91.

43. *The Press* (Philadelphia) (September 26, 1876), in Centennial Scrapbook 22, Archives of the City and County of Philadelphia.

44. Richard R. Nicholai, *Centennial Philadelphia* (Bryn Mawr, PA: Bryn Mawr Press, Inc. 1976), 84.

45. *Evening Bulletin* (Philadelphia) (December 10, 1876), in Centennial Scrapbook 21, Archives of the City and County of Philadelphia, 162.

46. Donald Clive Hardy, *The World's Industrial and Cotton Centennial Exposition* (New Orleans: The Historic New Orleans Collection, 1978). *Frank Leslie's Illustrated Newspaper* (January 24, 1885). Also photographs in The Historic New Orleans Collection.

47. Dorothy Jean Hook, "Fenollosa and Dow: The Effect of an Eastern and Western Dialogue on American Art Education" (Ph.D. diss., Pennsylvania State University, 1987).

48. S. K. Takahaski, *Illustrated Catalogue of the Japanese Exhibits at the Foreign Exhibition, Boston* (Boston: Heliotype Printing Co., 1883), np. Special thanks to Earle Shettleworth, State Historic Preservation Officer of Maine, for making this rare and important document available for study.

49. Takahaski, *Illustrated Catalog*, np.

50. Takahashi, *Illustrated Catalog*, np.

51. Julia Meech-Pekarick, "Early Collectors of Japanese Prints and the Metropolitan Museum of Art," *The Metropolitan Museum Journal* 17 (1984), 107-109.

52. Bill of Sale, First Japanese Manufacturing and Trading Co., New York, to Frederic E. Church, Hudson, N.Y., July 9, 1884, Olana Ms. Collection. My thanks to Joel Sweimler for access to this document.

53. Catalogue of the 17th Annual Exhibition (New York: American Water Color Society, 1884), np.

54. Bill of Sale, Ichi Ban's Japanese Bazaar, San Francisco, to Mrs. Alexander Ramsey, St. Paul, Minnesota, July 28, 1881, Minnesota Historical Society Ms. Collection; Bill of Sale, H. C. Parke, New York to F. E. Church, Hudson, N.Y., December 6, 1884, Olana Ms. Collection; Advertising Broadside, Morimura Bros., New York, 1880s, Peabody Museum of Salem; Advertising Card, A.D. Vorce & Co., Hartford, Connecticut, 1884, Stowe-Day Foundation Library.

55. The following is a list of the billheads for dealers in Japanese art from the Smith Museum Archives in Springfield, Massachusetts. The date merely signifies the date of the document not the years of operation. The archive contains more than one billhead for many of the firms listed. In *New York City*: Artistic Japan, 1898; Edward G. Getz, 1900; A. A. Vantine & Co., 1889; J. P. Woolley, 1892; Y. Fujita & Co., 1902; Tozo Takayanagi, 1892; Fifth Avenue Auction Rooms, 1891; Sypher & Co., 1889; First Japanese Manufacturing & Trading Co., 1890; Kano Oshima, 1900; Rufus E. Moore, 1892; John Wanamaker, 1899; In *California*: Sing Fat & Co., San Francisco, 1897; G. T. Marsh & Co., Japanese Art Repository, San Francisco, 1894; H. B. Kendrick and Co., Los Angeles, 1897; In *New England*: Forbes & Wallace, Springfield, Mass., 1901; Kazanjian & Co., Newport, R.I., 1891; Bunkio Matsuki, Boston, 1895; *International Franchise*: Kan Ko Ba's "Japanese Trading Company" with branch stores in Newport, R.I. and Asbury Park, N.J., 1891; Yamanaka & Co. of Osaka with branches in Kyoto, Nara, London, New York, Boston and the boardwalk in Atlantic City, 1899; Duveen Brothers with branches in London, Paris, and New York, 1899.

56. A. A. Vantine & Co., Trade Catalog, ca. 1880, Winterthur Museum Library, Winterthur, Delaware. My thanks to Arlene Schwind for bringing this apparently unique imprint to my attention.

57. Bill of Sale, A. A. Vantine & Co., New York, to Mrs. S. L. Clemens, Hartford, Connecticut, February 17, 1881, Mark Twain Papers, Bancroft Library, University of California at Berkeley. My thanks to Marianne Curling at the Mark Twain Memorial for furnishing this reference.

58. Vantine, *Trade Catalog*, 5-6.

59. Vantine, *Trade Catalog*, 9-13.

60. Vantine, *Trade Catalog*, 44.

61. *In Pursuit of Beauty: America and the Aesthetic Movement*, Catalog of an exhibition, October 23, 1986 - January 11, 1987 (New York: The Metropolitan Museum of Art, 1986). Expansive, authoritative, and elegantly presented, this book forms one of the milestones on the subject. No comparable work on the arts of Victorian America exists and it has provided a major source of inspiration and point of departure for *The Japan Idea*. While *In Pursuit of Beauty* focuses on aestheticism as an elite ideology, *The Japan Idea* stresses the vitality of the popular cultural manifestations of the same phenomenon. Additionally it argues that Japanism in its rich intersection with middle class taste and culture was much more than merely an example of style "percolating downward." In addition to its many worthy essays and copious illustrations, *In Pursuit of Beauty* includes the best existing bibliography on the subject.

62. Jane Converse Brown, "The 'Japanese Taste:' Its Role in the Mission of the American Home and in the Family's Presentation of Itself to the Public as Expressed in Published Sources, 1876-1916" (Ph.D. diss., University of Wisconsin, 1987). In spite of its title, this is a marvelous piece of literature, eminently suited to publication and far more interesting that the majority of work on "Japonisme." Among the hundreds of books, articles, and documents I read in preparing for *The Japan Idea* this is the one modern work I found most helpful and interesting.

63. Brown, 140.

64. Weisberg and Weisberg, *Japonisme*. Hot off the presses, this book finally provides a quick, handy reference to over 700 books, articles and dissertations on the Japanese art movement. Combined with the bibliographies from Jane Converse Brown's dissertation and *In Pursuit of Beauty*, very little of significance falls through the cracks.

65. Henry Norman, *The Real Japan* (New York: Charles Scribner's Sons, 1893), 136-37.

66. Basil Hall Chamberlain and W. B. Mason, *A Handbook for Travellers in Japan* (London: John Murray, 1903). John Murray began publishing travel guides for Japan as early as 1890.

67. Robert Rosenblum, "Nineteenth-Century Art: A Post-Modern View," in *Sotheby's Preview* (February/March 1990), 7-8, as excerpted from *Paintings in the Musée d'Orsay* (New York: Stewart Tabori & Chang, 1989).

68. Representatives from American and British museums appear to have danced around some of the key objects, complaining about high prices, but eventually buying. The *Doylestown Journal* (June 22, 1876), in Centennial Scrapbook 16, Archives of the City and County of Philadelphia, 43, reporting on a "magnificent bronze incense burner" noted that an "agent of the Pennsylvania University was anxious to get it" but found the price of $4,500 too high. It was subsequently purchased by Prof. Archer of the British Commission for the South Kensington Museum, now the Victoria & Albert. At the height of Centennial fever, Philadelphia's *Public Record* (October 31, 1876), in Centennial Scrapbook 11, Archives of the City and County of Philadelphia, 7, ran an article on the formation of the "new

Pennsylvania museum and school of industrial art" (now Philadelphia Museum of Art) which grew out of the Centennial and, for half a century, occupied the Memorial Hall on the exposition grounds. In response to a lecture the evening before by noted British designer, writer, and industrial arts advocate Dr. Christopher Dresser, numerous benefits were cited for building museums and public collections and for teaching art. The Philadelphia museum was the biggest institutional buyer at the Centennial. About 2,000 objects were acquired in 1876, mostly at the Centennial. Most of this material was deaccessioned during the 1940s and current ownership cannot be established. (Accession Cards, Registration Department). Less depleted but largely inaccessible are the Victorian holdings of Boston's Museum of Fine Arts which organized the first department of Asian Art in the United States. When the distinguished scholar Ernest Fenollosa was appointed as curator in 1890, Boston's collection was unrivalled. It has, however, been purged of many "inferior" works, which usually means Victorian export goods of the type bought at the Centennial. With acquisitions beginning as early as 1871, the collection would be the world's greatest of its type had it remained intact. Many items of extraordinary quality were bought at the Centennial. Others have specific provenance from Japan's Boston trade show of 1884. Boston's campaign to purge itself of these materials was most active between 1927 and 1933 and now appears to be over. (Accession Cards, Department of Asian Art).

69. Rutherford Alcock, *Catalogue of the Works of Industry and Art, Sent from Japan* (London: Willia Clowes & Sons. 1862), 2, 5, 7 and 9.

70. Gillian Walkling, *Antique Bamboo Furniture* (London: Bell & Hyman, 1979), 46. This passage cites a review in the *Gentleman's Magazine*, published at the time of the exposition.

71. "Anent the Japanese," *Crockery and Glass Journal* (March 1885), 100-102.

72. Christopher Dresser, *Japan: Its Architecture, Art and Art Manufactures* (1882; reprint ed., New York: Garland Publishing Inc., 1977), 226-233.

73. George Ashdown Audsley, *The Ornamental Arts of Japan* (New York: Charles Scribner's Sons, 1883), I, iii.

74. Morse, *Japanese Homes*, 36-38.

75. *Official Catalog of the Japanese Section*, 51-52.

76. Dresser, *Japan*, 173-4.

77. Dresser, *Japan*, 180 and 413.

78. Jarves, *A Glimpse at the Art of Japan*, 209.

79. Dresser, *Japan*, 429; Jarves, *Japan*, 107; and Jennie J. Young, *The Ceramic Art* (New York: Harper and Bros., 1878), 182.

80. Jarves, *Japan*, 107, 138, and 142.

81. *Official Catalog of the Japanese Section*, 100.

82. British art lecturer J. W. Tonks as quoted in "Japanesque Decoration," *Art Amateur* 5, no. 4 (September 1881), 79; and "The Japanese Designer," *Art Amateur* 7, no. 3 (August 1882), 53.

83. Morse, *Japanese Homes*, 227.

84. Yamada Chisaburo, "Exchange of Influences in the Fine Arts Between Japan and Europe," in *Japonisme in Art: An International Symposium*, ed. Yamada Chisaburo (Tokyo: Committee for the Year 2001 & Kodansa International Ltd., 1980), 11-23. The importance of cracked ice and fractured picture planes is discussed in a dissertation in progress by Rosemary Torre, at the Fashion Institute of Technology in New York City.

85. Audsley, *Arts of Japan*, I, iii and 1.

86. Julia Meech-Pekarik, "Early Collectors of Japanese Prints and the Metropolitan Museum of Art," *The Metropolitan Museum Journal* 17 (1984). This article is an engaging examination of the interests, personalities and tastes of 19th-century collectors who happen to have donated works to the Metropolitan Museum of Art. Literature on the arts of Keiji Japan, what little there is, tends to be oriented toward production, not consumption, and usually reflects the preferences of contemporary collectors and art historians. Among the best of these is Frederick Baekeland's *Imperial Japan: The Art of the Meiji Era (1868-1912)* (Ithaca, New York: Herbert F. Johnson Museum of Art, Cornell University, 1980).

87. Dresser, *Japan*, 417 and 429.

88. Dresser, *Japan*, 429-430.

89. "The Manufacture of Bronzes and Porcelain in Japan," *Art Journal* (Appleton's) no. 59 (1880), 324.

90. *Doylestown Journal* (June 22, 1876), in Centennial Scrapbook 16, Archives of the City and County of Philadelphia, 43.

91. *New York Daily Tribune* (May 27, 1876), in Centennial Scrapbook 15, Archives of the City and County of Philadelphia, 74.

92. *Japanese Bronzes in the Art Gallery of Edward Greey* (New York: Privately printed, 1888). Greey, who was a member of Commodore Perry's squadron during the historic opening of Japan in 1854, later became an important New York dealer in Japanese goods whose travels to and writing about Japan earned him a reputation as one of the leading Japanophiles in the United States. My thanks to Lee Bruschke-Johnson for sharing this rare and intriguing publication.

93. Jiro Harada as cited by Lee Bruschke-Johnson in "Japanese Cloisonné in The Walters Art Gallery," *The Journal of The Walters Art Gallery* 47 (1989), 5.

94. Harada, "Japanese Cloisonné," 10.

95. F. Brinkley, *Artistic Japan at Chicago* (Yokohama: The Japan Mail, 1893), 17.

96. Brinkley, 18-19. The best English language publication in print on the art of Japanese cloisonné is L. Coben and D. Ferster, *Japanese Cloisonné: History, Technique and Appreciation* (New York, Weatherhill, 1982).

97. "Japanese Lacquers," *Art Amateur* III, no. 5 (October 1880), 100-101. The Dutch were the only Europeans with trading privileges in Japan during the 17th and 18th centuries. In one year during the 18th century 45,000 pieces of Japanese porcelain were exported against only 101 pieces of lacquer. The greatest collection of lacquer in Europe (now at the Louvre) belonged to Madame de Pompadour, who reputedly paid more than 110,000 livres for a piece of Japanese lacquer. Marie Antoinette was also a great collector.

98. Audsley, *Arts of Japan*, v. I, sect. IV, 1.

99. Dresser, *Japan*, 351.

100. Audsley, *Japan*, vol. I, sect. iv, 1.

101. "Japanese Lacquers," *Art Amateur*, 101.

102. "Japanese Lacquers," 101.

103. Morse, *Japanese Homes*, xi.

104. Edward S. Morse, "Old Satsuma," *Harper's New Monthly Magazine* 77, no. 460 (September 1888), 512-529; Christopher Dresser, in *Japan*, 385, argued that, "Here in England we commonly meet with persons who speak of their Satsuma specimens as though this ware were common ... [when actually] 99/100 cases turn out to be Awata ware" which he described as "utterly common, and only suited to the ignorant caprices of a European public." Yet "only a keen eye ... can distinguish between the two." In *Ceramic Art*, 170, Jennie Young stated firmly that "Satsuma ware is imitated at Kioto, Yokohama, and elsewhere." Confusion prevailed!

105. Wilkinson, "Edward William Godwin," 134-141.

106. Dresser, *Japan*, 368-413; Clay Lancaster, *The Japanese Influence in America* (New York: Abbeville Press, 1963), 216.

107. Dresser, *Japan*, 176.

108. Dresser, *Japan*, 411-413.

109. Brinkley, *Artistic Japan*, 27.

110. Brinkley, *Artistic Japan*, 28.

111. Hattori, *Commerce of Japan*, 501.

112. Accession Cards, Asian Art Department, Museum of Fine Arts, Boston.

113. Dresser, *Japan*, 121.

114. Dresser, *Japan*, 454.

115. Accession Cards, 1891.1.2068-2151, Department of Asian Art, Metropolitan Museum of Art.

116. Vantine, *Catalog*, 53. About 1880, a 13-inch paper fan with bright floral design on a red, blue, or silver ground with lacquer handles - toward the upper end of the product line - cost 8 1/2 cents.

117. Morse, *Japanese Homes*, 178.

118. Rafale Fernandez, *Eastern Wind* (Williamstown, Mass: Sterling & Francine Clark Art Institute, 1982).

119. Siegfried Wichmann's *Japonisme* (New York: Harmony Books, 1981) is as good a source as any.

120. *A Timely Encounter: Nineteenth-Century Photographs of Japan* (Cambridge, Mass: Peabody Museum Press and Wellesley College Museum, 1988).

121. Lancaster, *Japanese Influence*, 33; Deborah Jean Johnson, "Japanese Prints in Europe Before 1840," *The Burlington Magazine* 124, no. 951 (June 1982), 343-348; In this essay Johnson establishes the presence and availability of Japanese illustrated books and prints in Europe long before they were embraced by Parisian artists.

122. Stanley Wientraub, *Whistler, A Biography* (New York: Truman Talley Books, 1974).

123. Henry Adams, "A Fish by John La Farge," *The Art Bulletin* 67, no. 2 (June 1980), 269-280; Doreen Bolger Burke, "Painters and Sculptors in a Decorative Age," in *In Pursuit of Beauty*, 306-7.

124. Henry Adams, "John La Farge's Discovery of Japanese Art: A new Perspective on the Origins of Japonisme," *The Art Bulletin* 67, no. 3 (September 1985), 448-485. Published serially between 1814 and 1849, Hokusai's *Manga* bore the full title of *Denshin Kaishu: Hokusai Manga*, which means "the education of beginners by the spirit of things: Hokusai's random sketches." My thanks to Thomas Michie and Helen Nagata at RISD for this information.

125. Thomas S. Michie, "Japanese Illustrated Books and Western Collectors" (Unpublished ms., Museum of Art, Rhode Island School of Design, 1990). Based on his study of a remarkable collection of Japanese pattern books formerly owned by John La Farge, among others, Michie and his colleague Helen Nagata very kindly prepared this eminently publishable essay to fill a gap in the literature.

126. James L. Yarnall, "John La Farge and Henry Adams in Japan," *The American Art Journal* 21, no. 1 (October 1989), 41-77; John La Farge, *An Artist's Letters from Japan* (New York: The Century Co., 1897).

127. Yarnall, "La Farge and Adams in Japan," 72.

128. Michie, "Japanese Illustrated Books," 3; Timothy Hinton, *The Pre-Raphaelites* (New York: Oxford University Press, 1970).

129. *Hartford Daily Times* (June 29, 1876).

130. May Brawley Hill, *Fidelia Bridges, American Pre-Raphaelite*. Catalog of an exhibition, November 15, 1981, to January 3, 1982 (New Britain, Connecticut: New Britain Museum of American Art, 1981).

131. Gertrude Grace Sill, "Two rediscovered paintings by John Haberle," *Antiques* (November 1987), 1120.

132. Christie's, "American Paintings" (New York) (May 31, 1985), lot no. 95; a work by Leavitt, dated 1884, featuring a Japanese Awata, ware vase with flowers; Christie's, "American Paintings" (New York) (December 5, 1986), lot no. 70; a work by Brooks, dated 1889, featuring an example of Japanese-style "china painting."

133. Burke, "Painters and Sculptors," *In Pursuit of Beauty*, 305.

134. Burke, "Painters and Sculptors," *In Pursuit of Beauty*, 296-297.

135. Wayne Craven, "Winckworth Allan Gay, Boston painter of the White Mountains, Paris, the Nile, and Mount Fujiyama," *Antiques* 120 (November 1981), 1222-1224.

136. Doreen Bolger Burke, "Robert Blum, 1857-1903," *American Paintings in the Metropolitan Museum of Art* III (New York, 1980), 301-304.

137. William H. Gerdts, *American Impressionism* (New York: Abbeville Press, 1984); *Connecticut and American Impressionism*. Catalog of three exhibitions, March 17 - June 21, 1980 (Storrs, Connecticut: The William Benton Museum of Art, 1980).

138. Auction catalog, The American Art Galleries, "Works of the Late William Merritt Chase, N.A., His Studio Effects and an Important Collection of Native and Foreign Paintings" (New York) (May 14-17, 1917). Chase's space in the famed Tenth Street Studio building was the subject of some of his best paintings and was illustrated and discussed in contemporary art magazines. At his death, Chase's holdings in Japanese art and Japanesque works by western artists bear noting; there were eight examples of Japanese pottery, dozens of examples of hammered and hand-wrought brass and copper (origin not designated), more than a dozen books and over one hundred Japanese prints by Hokusai, Kiyonaga, Toyokuni, Kunisada, Hiroshige, Kuniyoshi, Koson, Utamaro, and others, a Japanese lacquered chest, and five Japanese folding screens including one described as a "sixfold gilt screen ... by Yusho ... decorated with monkeys, bamboo, flying birds and waterfalls."

139. Albert Ten Eyck Gardner, *Winslow Homer* (New York: Clarkson N. Potter, Inc., 1961), 94-112.

140. Jarves, *Art of Japan*, 21; Morse, *Japanese Homes*, 46.

141. Morse, *Japanese Homes*, 67.

142. Morse, *Japanese Homes*, 108 and 111.

143. Morse, *Japanese Homes*, 114.

144. Morse, *Japanese Homes*, 119.

145. Vincent Scully, *The Stick Style and The Shingle Style* (New Haven: Yale University Press, 1971).

146. Through corresponding with Carol Creutzberg of the Radnor, Pennsylvania Historical Society, (February 2, 1990) I was able to procure a picture of the Strafford station, but no conclusive documentation aside from the fact that local tradition describes it as a "relic of the Philadelphia Centennial ... built by Japanese workmen." True or not - and the story is probably true - it is just as important that the station, a classic example of the Stick Style, was perceived as Japanese work.

147. Vincent Scully, "American Houses: Thomas Jefferson to Frank Lloyd Wright," in *The Rise of an American Architecture*, ed. Edgar Kaufmann, Jr. (New York: Praeger Publishers and the Metropolitan Museum of Art, 1970).

148. Gopsill's Philadelphia Business Directory, 1881 (Philadelphia: James Gopsill's Sons, 1881), 293 and 297, listed eighteen "fresco painters," most with German names, in addition to twenty-one tradesmen who described themselves as "ornamental painters," One of the best and only studies of the fresco painter's trade is included in Jennifer Whitley Smith's "Politics and Professionalism: The Making of the Connecticut State Capital, 1872-1879" (MA: Yale University, 1988), 71-102. In a masterfully researched study of the Boston "fresco painter" William J. McPherson, Smith documented his work as a contractor, designer, stained glass manufacturer, and ornamental painter. Although capable of wearing several hats, McPherson's reputation as a stained glass designer was foremost. With clients stretching from Boston and Hartford to Washington, D.C., and Concord, New Hampshire, McPherson was one of few members of his trade to develop a national market.

149. *The Decorator and Furnisher* 11, no 1 (October 1888), 34 and 64; Pick up almost any city directory from the 1880s and you are likely to find advertisements by architectural millworks producing goods in the Japanese taste. In New Haven, Connecticut, for example, we find D.C. Beardsley, manufacturers of "hard wood mantels, sideboards, doors and church furniture" whose quarter page advertisement illustrates a Japanesque mantlepiece. *Ansonia, Birmingham, Derby, Shelton and Seymour Directory, 1988/9* (New Haven: Price, Lee & Co, 1988), xxv. Catalog of the Porter Manufacturing Co. (Montpelier, Vermont, 1885), courtesy of the Avery Architectural Library, Columbia University.

150. F. W. Beers, *Atlas of Rutland County, Vermont* (New York: F. W. Beers, 1869); William Hosley, "Survey of Historic Buildings in Fair Haven, Vermont," (Montpelier, Vermont: Vermont Division for Historic Preservation, 1977). As the center of Vermont's slate industry, Fair Haven was one of the most prosperous towns in the state during the Japan craze. Many of the more than two hundred houses built there during the last third of the 19th century have locally made slate mantles, several of which were photographed while conducting this survey. Although Vermont was the center of the marbleized slate industry, at least one manufacturer in Philadelphia published a trade catalog that includes Japanesque mantles: Catalog of Charles William's Sons (Philadelphia about 1885), courtesy of Avery Architectural Library, Columbia University.

151. H. Webber Wilson, *Great Glass in American Architecture* (New York: E. P. Dutton, 1986).

152. Catalog of R. S. Groves, Art Stained Glass, (Philadelphia. 1888), 2, 25, and 30.

153. Catalog of Carr, Ryder & Adams Co, (Dubuque, Iowa, 1897), 103, 210, 211, 213, 229, and 242, courtesy of Corning Glass Museum Library.

154. Catalog of John Matthews Decorative Glass, (New York, 1886), 10-12, 16, 19, 24, 25, 27, and 42, courtesy of Corning Glass Museum Library.

155. Jonas Frykman and Orvar Lofgren, *Culture Builders: A Historical Anthropology of Middle-Class Life*, translated by John Gillis (1979: reprint ed., New Brunswick, New Jersey: Rutgers University Press, 1987). This is one of the best in a genre of literature that explores social transformations resulting from the industrial revolution.

156. "About Bric-a-Brac," (Appleton's) *Art Journal* 6 (1878), 313-314.

157. *Public Record* (Philadelphia) (October 31, 1876), in Scrapbook 11, Archives of the City and County of Philadelphia, 7.

158. Charles Wyllys Elliot, "The Porcelain of Japan," (Appleton's) *Art Journal* (1876), 50.

159. Jarves. *Art of Japan*, 144-7.

160. George Ward Nichols, *Art Education Applied to Industry* (New York: Harper & Bros., 1877), 21.

161. "Anent the Japanese," *Crockery and Glass Journal* (March 1885), 101.

162. The hardware and textile manufacturers will be cited further on in the text. With all of the extraordinary artistry behind 19th-century cast-iron stoves, the author was surprised not to have found one in the Japanese taste. Perhaps the style was too widely associated with the revival of the open hearth to have figured convincingly in parlor stove design. A very Japanesque "bamboo" hallstand made of cast iron was documented in a private collection, unmarked by its maker. A remarkable Japanese style cast zinc fountain, dated 1883 and marked as a product of the Monumental Bronze Co. in Bridgeport, Connecticut is on the town green in Stafford Springs, Connecticut. The Hannum family granite marker (1896) in the "Old Quabbin Towns Cemetery" in Ware, Massachusetts is handsomely engraved with Japanesque iris and ferns, a motif not common in Victorian gravestone arts. The bathroom tissue is in the collection of the Adirondack Museum and was issued a patent in 1906.

163. Advertisements illustrating Japanesque products by these firms appear in the following; Prospect Hill, *Crockery and Glass Journal* 19, no. 9 (February 28, 1884), 20 and Willets, *Crockery and Glass Journal* 19, no. 8 (February 14, 1884), 17.

164. *In Pursuit of Beauty*, 426-7.

165. Catalog of J. and J. G. Art Tile Works (Chelsea, Massachusetts, 1881); Catalog of J. G. and J. F. Low Art Tile Works (Chelsea, Massachusetts, 1884); *In Pursuit of Beauty*, 450-451.

166. "Pottery," unsigned essay, about 1887 (attributed to Louise McLaughlin or Laura Fry), Cincinnati Historical Society. This remarkable document, although unsigned, is the best first-hand account of the race to perfect Haviland-style underglaze slip-decorated porcelain in Cincinnati. Evidently written by one of the women involved in the movement, the document is both instructional as historical fact and for its feminist rhetoric, which included the assertion (p. 11) that "the patriotic impulse is always better in woman than in man, so are all good and noble impulses, as for that matter." Kenneth Trapp, "Japanese influence in early Rookwood pottery," *Antiques* 103 (January 1973), 193-197; *In Pursuit of Beauty*, 451-452 and 464-465.

167. Paul Evans, *Art Pottery in the United States* (New York: Feingold & Lewis Publishing Co., 1987), 331-334.

168. Evans, *Art Pottery*, 128-130.

169. Dresser, *Japan*, 221.

170. "Novelties from an Expert's Baggage," *The Graphic*, in Tiffany Scrapbook of News Clippings, vol. IIIA (1877-1885), Tiffany Archives, 408.

171. Auction Catalog, Clinton Hall Sale Rooms, "Dresser Collection of Japanese Curios and Articles Selected for Tiffany & Co." (New York) (June 18, 1877), courtesy of Tiffany Archives.

172. "Glimpses of a Workshop," *The Mail and Express* (New York) (November 1, 1883), in Tiffany Scrapbook of News Clippings, vol. IIIA (1877-1885) Tiffany Archives, 235.

173. Ms. Inventory of Objects and Catalog of Books, Tiffany & Co., ca. 1885, Tiffany Archives.

174. *Springfield (Mass.) Republican* (March 17, 1884), in Tiffany Scrapbook of News Clippings, vol. IIIA (1877-1885) Tiffany Archives, 235.

175. *London Court Circular* (August 18, 1883), in Tiffany Scrapbook of News Clippings, vol. IIIA (1877-1885) Tiffany Archives, 250.

176. "The New Status of American Art," Corporate Memorandum, September 24, 1878, Tiffany & Co., in Tiffany Scrapbook of News Clippings, vol. IIIB (1877-1887), 1e.

177. Translation from Unidentified Japanese Newspaper, 1878, in Tiffany Scrapbook of News Clippings, vol. IIIa (1877-1885) Tiffany Archives, 291; *New York Daily Tribune* (May 16, 1880), in Tiffany Scrapbook of News Clippings, vol. IIIa (1877-1885) Tiffany Archives, 273.

178. Charles H. Carpenter, Jr., *Tiffany Silver* (New York: Dodd, Mead & Co, 1978), 182 and 186.

179. W. Chandler Roberts-Austen, *The Colours of Metals and Alloys, A Lecture* (London: Richard Clay and Sons, 1887), courtesy of Tiffany Archives. The copy cited belonged to Edward C. Moore and is the best period analysis of the metallurgy of Japanese alloys. My thanks to Jeanne Sloane of Christie's for leading me to this document.

180. Elaine Swearengin Draper, *The Wilkinson Family Story* (ca. 1988), p. 100 (Typescript copy at Providence Public Library), as cited in Thomas S. Michie's "Japanese Illustrated Books," p. 6; Charles H. Carpenter, Jr., *Gorham Silver, 1831-1981* (New York: Dodd, Mead & Co., 1982), 103.

181. Gorham Financial Inventory, 1871, Gorham Archives, John Hay Library Ms. Collection, Brown University, 34-35.

182. Carpenter, *Gorham*, 112.

183. "Gorham History of Techniques before 1877," Gorham Manufacturing Co. Archives, John Hay Library Ms. Collection, Brown University.

184. "Gorham History of Techniques," 107-110.

185. J. D. Van Slyck, Representatives of New England Manufacturers (Boston: Van Slyck and Co., 1879), 331.

186. Catalog of Simpson, Hall, Miller Company (Wallingford, Connecticut, 1878), courtesy of Avery Architectural Library, Columbia University; 1879; also 1881 and 1891, courtesy of the Connecticut Historical Society.

187. Leonard E. Padgett, *Pairpoint Glass* (Des Moines, Iowa: Wallace-Homestead, 1979).

188. *The Decorator and Furnisher* 11, no. 1 (October 1887), 32.

189. Catalog, F. H. Lovell & Co., "New Styles of Hitchcock Lamps" (New York 1886), 35, courtesy of Corning Glass Museum Library.

190. The Parker story has been pieced together from a series of advertisements, a company profile, several documented and attributed objects, and from conversations with Helen Hersh who first attributed a well-known group (*In Pursuit of Beauty*, 281) of the most flamboyant brass light stands to the firm. An example in the Wadsworth Atheneum collection has marked Longwy tiles. A small table at The Brooklyn Museum bears a Charles Parker Co. label. Van Slyck, *New England Manufacturers*, 349-350; *The Decorator and Furnisher* 11, no. 1 (October 1887), 38; *Crockery and Glass Journal* (February 14, 1884), 31; and (October 1, 1885), 41.

191. Catalog of The Peck, Stow and Wilcox Co. (Southington, Plantsville and East Berlin, Connecticut, 1890), courtesy of The Connecticut Historical Society; Catalog of Russell & Erwin Manufacturing Co. (New Britain, Connecticut, 1887), courtesy of The Connecticut Historical Society; Catalog of P. F. Corbin (New Britain, Connecticut, 1885), courtesy of Avery Architectural Library, Columbia University; Catalog of Nashua Lock Co., in *Illustrated and Descriptive Catalogue and Price List of Hardware, Tools, Etc.*

192. *In Pursuit of Beauty*, 438-439.

193. Description based on an analysis of the following works signed or attributed to Herter Brothers: Sideboard and Reception chair, Art Institute of Chicago; Looking Glass, Philadelphia Museum of Art; Wardrobe, The Metropolitan Museum of Art; Reception chair, The Currier Gallery of Art; Reception Room Suite, Wadsworth Atheneum.

194. William Hosley, "Goodwin Reception Room, A Gallery Guide," (Hartford, Connecticut: Wadsworth Atheneum, 1990); Phillip L. Goodwin, *Rooftrees, or the Architectural History of an American Family* (Philadelphia: J. B. Lippincott Co., 1933), 45-51; From conversations with Katherine S. Howe, project director for the upcoming Herter Brothers retrospective, The Museum of Fine Arts, Houston, I learned that the serial numbers branded on the legs of Herter Brothers chairs almost certainly designate the sequence in which various items were made. James Goodwin's mansion "Woodlands," was completed in 1874 and occupied early in 1875. The reception room, where the Herter suite was used, was being painted and papered during the summer of 1874. The furniture probably arrived from New York late the following fall. It is almost identical to a suite made for the Red Room in the White House around the middle of 1875. The White House furniture bears 3,200 series numbers, while the Goodwin furniture is branded as the 3,000 series.

195. My thanks to William G. Allman, Assistant Curator of the White House, for providing valuable documentation on one of Herter's earliest Japanesque designs. A voucher dated December 23, 1875 contains a complete summary of work billed by Herter Brothers (Voucher, Government Accounting Office, no. 202.494, Voucher 36, as cited in Letter, William G. Allman to William Hosley, August 30, 1989 (Herter File, Wadsworth Atheneum).

196. Donald C. Peirce, "Mitchell and Rammelsberg" Cincinnati Furniture Manufacturers 1847-1881," in *American Furniture and its Makers*, *Wintherthur Portfolio* 13, ed. Ian M. G. Quimby (Chicago: University of Chicago Press, 1979), 209-229; *Catalogue of the University of Cincinnati for the Academic Year, 1877-1878* (Cincinnati, 1877), np. A description of the accomplishments of the University's art school boasted of the placement of former students as lithographers, sculptors, potters, landscape painters, architects, stonecutters, fresco painters, and one individual described as a "woodcarver, Mitchell and Rammelsberg."

197. *The Decorator and Furnisher* 3, no. 3 (December 1883), 107; also, 11, no. 1 (October 1887), 3; *The Manufacturers of the United States for Domestic and Foreign Trade* (New York: Armstrong & Knauer, 1887), np.

198. Wendy Kaplan, *"The Art that is Life:" The Arts & Crafts Movement in America, 1875-1920* (Boston: Little, Brown and Company and the Museum of Fine Arts, Boston, 1987); Craig Gilborn, *Adirondack Furniture and the Rustic Tradition* (New York: Harry N. Abrams, Inc., 1987). A dressing bureau at The Brooklyn Museum is the work of Nimura & Sato Co., of Brooklyn. Made about 1915, it incorporates ukiyo-e prints, reed matting, and split bamboo in its construction.

199. Kenneth M. Wilson, *New England Glass and Glassmaking* (New York: Thomas Y. Crowell Co., 1972), 353-356; Padgett, *Pairpoint Glass*, 27-8, 37-40; Albert Christian Revi, *Nineteenth Century Glass* (New York: Thomas Nelson & Sons, 1959), 14-15, 40-44, 50-51, 69-74, 202-203; John A. Shuman III, *The Collector's Encyclopedia of American Art Glass* (Paducah, KY: Collector Books, 1988), 12, 15, 56, 58, 104.

200. Padgett, *Pairpoint Glass*, 51-58; Wilson, *New England Glass*, 342-347.

201. William Heacock and Fred Bickenheuser, *Encyclopedia of Victorian Colored Pattern Glass* (Marietta, Ohio: Richardson Printing Corp., 1978); Neila M. Bredehoft, George A. Fogg and Francis C. Maloney, *Early Duncan Glassware* (Boston: Privately printed, 1987), 56.

202. Albert Christian Revi, *American Pressed Glass and Figure Bottles* (New York: Thomas Nelson, Inc., 1970), 225-228.

203. *China, Glass & Lamps* 6, no. 9 (August 9, 1893), 37. Neville claimed to have worked in pressed and blown glass decorated by etching, engraving, and cutting.

204. Antoinette Cheney Crocker, *Frank Woodbridge Cheney, Two Years in China and Japan* (Westwood, Massachusetts: Privately printed, 1970).

205. Lloyd Lewis and Henry Justin Smith, *Oscar Wilde Discovers America* (1936; reprint ed., New York: Harcourt, Brace & Co., 1967), 150.

206. My thanks to Robert Tuggle and Paul Jeromack, whose insights into this material and whose tenacious collecting enabled me to understand one of the great events in nineteenth-century design. Tuggle's argument is that if you look at enough material it basically documents itself and tells its own story. More than one art museum curator with whom I discussed *The Japan Idea* acknowledged that the art world's vestigial prejudice against mass produced objects had blocked them from acquiring Victorian transfer-printed earthenwares for their museums, even though work of extraordinary quality was available and extremely affordable and they collect it themselves. It is a sad day when museums only approve of things they increasingly cannot afford.

207. Information on the crockery trade is not readily available. A few snippets of information encountered during research for *The Japan Idea* suggest that a great story awaits further research. A lavishly illustrated trade catalog issued in 1882 by Jones, McDuffee & Stratton of Boston (Stowe-Day Foundation Library, Hartford) documents the complex and highly sophisticated nature of their importing and retail business. An aside in the 1878 edition of (Appleton's) *Art Journal*, 352, noted that Gilman Collamore, of Boston's Davis, Collamore & Co. had recently returned from Japan. The idea of American crockery merchants visiting Japan on buying excursions as early as 1878 suggests an intensity of involvement with Japan that surely merits further investigation.

208. *Crockery and Glass Journal* 21, no. 7 (February 12, 1885), 9; and 19, no. 9 (February 28, 1884), 11; and 19, no. 8 (February 14, 1884), 11; and 21, no. 20 (May 14, 1885). My thanks to Robert Tuggle for identifying the range of color combinations based on extensive firsthand observation.

209. *The Decorator and Furnisher* 2, no. 1 (April 1883), 4.

210. "Tonquin" was registered by Edge, Malkin & Co. of Burslem in 1883; "Kioto" was registered by Brownhills Pottery Co. in Tunstall in 1883; Two similar versions of "Warwick" have been identified, one dated 1878 (Orange, Massachusetts Historical Society) and a pattern dated 1880 that was so popular that Jones, McDuffee & Stratton used it to illustrate a company advertising card (Tuggle Collection). Both were manufactured by J. Dimmock & Co. in Hanley; "Excelsior" was registered by the Old Hall Earthenware Co. in Hanley in 1880. More than sixty Japanesque patterns of British transfer-printed earthenware were photographed and identified during the course of research for *The Japan Idea*.

211. Stuart Durant and Hannah Oorthuys, *The Aesthetic Movement and the Cult of Japan* (London: The Fine Art Society, Ltd., 1972), 22.

212. "Centennial Exhibition, part 7" (Appleton's) *Art Journal* 4 (1876), 371. The account noted that Royal Worcester's Japanesque work had "attained such excellence as to excite astonishment even in Japan."

213. Mabel Collins Donnelly, *The American Victorian Woman* (New York: Greenwood Press, 1986). A cogent summary of women's politics and culture in Victorian America, told with passion but without rancor.

214. H. Hudson Holly, *Modern Dwellings* (New York: Harper & Brothers, 1878), 216-217.

215. *In Pursuit of Beauty*, 481; Candace Wheeler, *Yesterdays in a Busy Life* (New York: Harper and Brothers, 1918).

216. Arthur B. Turnure, "The Society of Decorative Art," (Appleton's) *Art Journal* 6 (1878), 50-52.

217. *Art Palace of the West* (Cincinnati: Cincinnati Art Museum, 1981).

218. *Report of the Society of Decorative Art of the City of Hartford, Connecticut* (New York: Studio Press, 1883), courtesy of the Stowe-Day Foundation. In describing the Society's origin this report noted that it "grew out of the stimulus given to all industrial and decorative art by the great Philadelphia Exhibition of 1876. Its object was especially to give employment to women, for it was believed that there existed much undeveloped and unremunerated talent." John W. Teahan and Eugene R. Gaddis, "Two Families Save The Atheneum from Decent Burial," *Atheneum* (Autumn, 1990), 8.

219. Lewis and Smith, *Oscar Wilde*, 137.

220. Catalog of Charles J. Edmunds Artist's Materials (Boston, ca. 1880), np., courtesy of The Strong Museum, Rochester, New York; Lacroix's colors for tile and china painting and a growing list of books on "china painting" and related women's arts were part of an inventory that included everything from brushes and palettes, to easels, sketching umbrellas and seats, and porcelain blanks for china painting.

221. *How to Paint* (St. Louis: A.S. Aloe Co., 1894), 9-16 and 55-78, courtesy of The Strong Museum.

222. *Ladies' Book of Fancy Work* (Lynn, Massachusetts: J. F. Ingalls, 1885).

223. Cynthia A. Brandimarte, "Somebody's Aunt and Nobody's Mother: The American China Painter and Her Work, 1870-1920," *Winterthur Portfolio* 23, no. 4 (Winter 1988), 204-205.

224. Celia Thaxter to Annie Fields, letter, 1877, as quoted in "Aesthetic Forms in Ceramics and Glass," in *In Pursuit of Beauty*, 221.

225. Interview with Jane Tucker, August 1989. This remarkable family-run house museum is virtually unaltered since the turn of the century.

226. Interviews with Laura Hastings Banta, Windsor, Connecticut, December 1988 and July 1990. Brandimarte, "Somebody's Aunt," 219, notes that china painting was "perceived as a genteel profession." Although the work had more status than operating a spinning jenny in some filthy mill, the fact that women's arts were practiced across a wide spectrum of class is critical to understanding its political ramifications. Even if most china painters did not need the work, the fact that many did begs a broader interpretation of its significance.

227. *Gopsill's Philadelphia Directory, 1881* (Philadelphia: James Gopsill's Sons, 1889), 87-88; also, 1889, 90-92.

228. "Art Schools in Philadelphia," *The Decorator and Furnisher* 1, no. 4 (February 1883), 148.

229. *Fireside Art Catalog*. Catalog of an exhibition, 1885 (Concord, New Hampshire: Grand Army Fair, 1885), courtesy of the New Hampshire Historical Society.

230. *Cincinnati Daily Enquirer* (June 11, 1876), 11, courtesy of the Cincinnati Historical Society.

231. "'Crazy' Quilts," *Art Amateur* 7, No. 5 (October 1882), 108.

232. *Crazy Patchwork with Instructions* (C. W. Richardson & Co., 1884); my thanks Dr. Charles Burden of Bath, Maine and the Woolwich, Maine Historical Society for sharing this rare document.

233. "Scrap Screens," *Godey's Lady's Book* (May 1876), 465-466.

234. "Anent the Japanese," *Crockery and Glass Journal*, 100.

235. My thanks to Thomas Beckman of Wilmington, Delaware for photocopies of dozens of images from his collection which he annotated with notes and interpretation which I have found most valuable.

236. Ingram, *The Centennial*, 371. In describing Roger's plaster cast figure groups at the Centennial the author noted that "there were no works of American sculpture more interesting..." Roger's brilliant innovation in developing the figure group - mass produced sculpture for parlor use - enabled him to invest far more in crafting and designing the original models than if he were producing one of a kind. It is noteworthy that Centennial-era Victorians did not apply abstract notions of value in assessing a work of art.

237. Lancaster, *The Japanese Influence*, 230.

Index

Page numbers in *italics* refer to illustrations or captions.

A

Abstraction, 82, 87, 100
Adams, Henry, 88-90
Advertising, 44, 62, 156, 175-176; *Advertising Broadside* (Moore), *62, 176, 177*
Advertising Cards, A Group of, 176; *176-177, 200*
"Albertine" Vase, about 1887, 144; *145*
Album of Fan Designs after Chinese Patterns, (Gafu); *89*
Alcock, Henry, and Company, 156
Alcock, Sir Rutherford, 29, 30; *Catalogue of Works of Industry and Art Sent from Japan, 48*
Allen and Leonard, 109
Allen Fan Company; *Folding Fan, about 1890, 152, 197*
Amateis, Louis; *Bust of Japanese Maiden, "Okamoto",* 100; *101*
American Bamboo Company, 142-143
American painting, 87-88, 90-100; impressionist, 87, 96-98
Ameya, The, (Blum), *95, 191*
Andrews, Harriet D., *170*
Anti-modernism, 39
Antique Japanese art, 28, 56, 72; *78*
Appleton and Company, D., *39*; Appleton's *Art Journal*, 111, 162; *39*
Architectural fragment (Earle); *109*
Architecture, 31, 72, 103-116; *105-107*
  at Centennial exposition, 33, 104
Arita ware, 63, 66, 158
Arnold, Sir Edwin, 94; *Japonica, 94*
Art critics, 29, 31
Art education, 118
Art goods. *See* Decorative arts; Industrial art
Art history, as a western device, 79
Art tiles, 94, 120-121; *122, 159, 193*
Art-supply industry, 164; *170*
Arts-and-crafts movement, 143
Associated Artists, 101, 148, 162
Audsley, George, 49
Audubon, John James; *23*
Avery, Samuel P., 61
Awata ware, 63

B

Ballin and Liebler, 176
Baluster Jar, 65
Bamboo, 73, 142; *73, 75-76*; imitation, *142-143*; as a motif, 51, 146; *53, 132*
"Bamboo" Creamer and Covered Butter Dish, (La Belle Glass Company), 146; *147*
Basket, 75
Basketry, 72; *75*
Bassett, George F., and Company, 156
Beauty Playing the Samisen, A, 78, 190
Beck and Company, Frederick, *150, 197*
Bedstead (Mitchell and Rammelsberg Furniture Co.), *142*
Belleek. *See* Irish Belleek
Bennett, John, *163*

Bicknell, Frank Alfred, 94
Bigelow, William Sturgis, 42
Bingham, John A., 33
Binns, R. W., 157
Birds of America Folio, The (Audubon), *23*
Birdseye View of Centennial Exhibition (Poleni), *34*
Blue Kimono, The (Chase), 96; *97*
Blum, Robert F., 94-95; *Ameya, The, 95; Japonica, 94, 191*
Bowie and Company Decorators, S. R., 146; *146*
Bowl (Meizan), *64*
Bowl with Scalloped Rim, 64
Box, 24
Bracquemond, Felix, 32, 87
Bradstreet and Company, John S., 143; *143*
Brass, 135; *137, 151*
Bric-a-brac, 93, 111, 174; *141*
Bridges, Fidelia, 91; *Cherry Twig, 91; Grapevines, 91*
Briggs, Richard, 156
Brinckley, Captain Frank, 66, 67
Brine, Mary D., 180
Britannia. *See* Electroplating
British aesthetic style, 104
British pottery, 154-160
Bronze, 44, 55-56; *53, 55, 100, 130, 136*; and brass plating, 136
Brooks, Nicholas Alden, 93
Brownhills Pottery Company, 156; *156*
Brown, Jane Converse, 45
Brown, Westhead, Moore and Company, 156
Buddhism, 48, 80
Bufford, J. H. and Son, 176
Burges, William, 30, 48, 91
Burgess and Goddard, 156
Burne-Jones, Edward, *101*
Bust of Japanese Maiden, "Okamoto" (Amateis), *100*

C

Capital of the Tycoon: A Narrative of a Three Years' Residence in Japan, The (Alcock), 30
Card case, 72
Carr, Ryder and Adams Company, 110
Carved Tray, about 1880, 67
Carved Vase, 73
Cassatt, Mary, 87, 99; *Fitting, The, 99*
Catalogue of Works of Industry and Arts Sent from Japan (Alcock), *48*
Ceiling decoration, 106-109
Ceiling Fresco (William Henay and Son), *106, 193*
Centennial Exhibition (United States' International Exhibition of Arts, Manufacturers, and Products of the Soil and Mines) of 1876, 32-42; *Exhibition Catalog, 15, 39*
Center table, *139, 196*
Ceramics, 44, 61-66, 118-125; *64, 66, 119-126*. *See also* Earthenware; Porcelain; Pottery
Charger, 60
Chase, William Merritt, 94, 96; *Blue Kimono, The, 97*

Chelsea Keramic Art Works, 119; *119*
Cheney Brothers Mills, 148; *Textile Fragment, 150*
Cherry Twig (Bridges), *91*
Chigoi-dana, 115
China painting, 164-169; *166-169*; of Maria Nichols, 123-125; *123, 124*
China painting: A Practical Manual for the Use of Amateurs in the Decoration of Hard Porcelain, (McLaughlin), 121
Christmas Greeting Card (Prang), *178*
Cincinnati, art pottery, 121-125; Cincinnati Pottery Club, 121
Clock, 134, 195
Cloisonné, 56-58; *40, 54, 56, 155, 189*. *See also* Shippo ware
Cocheco Mills Manufacturing Company, 148; *Engraver's Sheet, 1886, 148*
Coffee pot (Tiffany and Co.), *129*
Coleman, Charles Caryl, *Night Owl, 93, 191*
Colt, Elizabeth, 164; *167*
Colt, Samuel, 24; *24, 25*
Columbia Glass Company, 146
Commode (Orin Hooper and Son), *140*
Composition, 51-52; *123*
Cook, Clarence, 142
Cook, Rose Terry, *170*
Copper, 130-131, 135-137; *129, 134, 135, 195*
Corbin, P. F., *136*
Corning Museum of Glass, 109
Cosmetic box (Kobako), 60
Cotton, 152; *163, 165, 174, 181, 198*
Covered Box, 66
Covered Jar, 58
Covered Pitcher (Hastings), *169*
Crackled ware, 66
Crane, Walter, 158
"Crazy" Patchwork Table Cover, about 1883, *172*
Crazy quilts, 152, 172-174; *172, 173, 174, 199*
Creamer and Covered Butter Dish (La Belle Glass Co.), *147*
Critics, and the selling of Japan, 29, 47-50
"Crown Milano" Vase (Mount Washington Glass Co.), *144*
Cutting and Delaney, 109

D

Daimyo, 18, 20, 27
Davis, Collamore and Company, 156
Decorative art, 42, 48, 93, 118
Decorum, A Treatise on Etiquette and Dress (Louis), *180*
Dedham pottery. *See* Chelsea Keramic Art Works
"Depose" pattern, 156
Derby Silver Company, 131; *Pitcher, 131; Tray, 131*
Desk, 142
Diagonal, as a compositional device, 81, 99
Diapers, 50
Dimmock and Company, 156
Donaldson Brothers, 176

Door Handle and Escutcheon, (Nashua Lock Co.), *136*
Door panel, *110*
Doorknobs (Russell and Erwin Co.), *137*
Dormitory room, *112*
Dormitory room of John C. Coolidge, *112*
Doulton and Company, 154, 163
Dow, Arthur Wesley, 99-100; *The Lily*, *100*
Dress, *181*
Dress, (Nolston), *181*
Dresser, Christopher, 48, 63, 126-127, 158
Duncan and Sons, George, 146

E

Earle, Stephen C.; *Architectural fragment, about 1885*, *109*
Earthenware, 44; *163*; art tiles, *122*, *159*, *193*; British, 154-160; *156-160*; china painting, *167*, *168*, *169*; tableware, 64, *120*, *123*, *126*, *156-160*; vases, *119*, *121*, *123-125*, *166*, *194*, *199*. See also Ceramics; Satsuma ware
Eastlake, Charles, 140
Edge, Malkin and Company, 156
Edo Bay (Tokyo), *17*, *23*, *28*
Electroplating. See Silversmithing
Elkington and Company, 154; *155*
Elliot, Charles Wyllys, 29, 117
Ellsworth, Minnie Elizabeth, *169*
Embroidery, *165*, *166*
Emperors, in Japan, 27
Empire of Japan Exhibit, Philadelphia Centennial Exposition, *37*
Engraved glass, 146
Engraver's Sheet (Coheco Manufacturing Co.), *148*
Erving House Parlor, *114*
Etagere (Lejambre), *141*
Etruria Pottery. See Ott and Brewer
Exhibition Catalog, *39*
Export goods, 32-33, 41, 43-44, 47, 52, 67, 72

F

Fabyan House Office, *113*
Faience. See Satsuma ware
Faience Manufacturing Company, 120; *Vase* (Lycett), *121*
Fans, 44-45, 75, 76; *36*, *75*, *76*, *89*
Farnham, Mary Newell, *170*, *198*
Fashion, 180; *181*
Fenollosa, Ernest F., 42
Feudalism, in Japan, 27-28
Finn, Dallas, 32
Firearms, 24; *24*, *25*
First Japanese Manufacturing and Trading Company, 43
First Landing of Americans in Japan (Heine), *20*, *187*
Fitting, The (Cassatt), *99*
Flat Fan, *75*
Folding Fan, *36*, *76*
Folding Fan (Allen Fan Co.), *152*, *197*
Folding Reception Chair (New Haven Folding Chair Company), *140*
Folding Screen, *79*, *100*, *102*, *170-171*, *192*, *198*
Folding Screen, A Beauty Playing the Samisen, *78*, *190*
Folding Screen (Farnham), *170*
Folding screens, 45, 68, 76-79, 100, 171; *78-79*, *101-102*, *192*; gilded, 76; in Japanese homes, 104
Forbes and Wallace, 44
Foreigners, in Japan, 17, 27
French ceramics, 159
French Impressionists, 80
Fresco painting, 106-109; *Ceiling Fresco*, *106*
Fukusa, 70; *69*
Furniture, 103-104, 137-143; *138-143*

G

Gardner, Albert, 99
Gay, Winckworth Allen, 94
General Grant's Parlor, *115*
Gildea and Walker, 156; *156*
Glass, 109, 135, 144-147; *110*, *144-7*, *196*
Globe-shaped covered jar, *57*, *189*
Glyptic arts. See Wood carving
Godwin, Edward, 90, 138
Gold and silver, 55; *53*
Goodwin Brothers Pottery Company, 119; *119*
Goodwin Building (Kimball and Wisedell), *106*
Gorham Manufacturing Company, 126, 127-130; *130*
Goshorn, Major Alfred T., 118
Gothic style, 104, 108; *108*
Government in Japan, 18-20
Grandma's Attic Treasures (Brine), *180*
Grapevines (Bridges), *91*
Greene and Greene, 143
Greeting card, *178*
Griffis, William Elliot, 27, 29
Groves Company, R. S., 109; *110*

H

Haberle, John, 92; *Japanese Corner*, *93*
Hamilton Manufacturing Company, 148; *Pattern Book*, *149*
Hammered copper and brass, 135, 136
Hammond's Japanese Bedroom, Doctor William A., *115*
Hampshire Pottery, 125; *126*
Hanger and Company, R., 109
Hanging Lantern, *77*
Harrison, Caroline Scott, 166
Hassam, Childe, 96
Hastings, Minnie Elizabeth Ellsworth, 167; *169*
Hawthorne earthenware, 44
Heine, William, 19, 20; *First Landing of Americans in Japan*, *20*, *187*; *Landing of Commodore Perry, Men of the Squadron*, *22*, *187*; *Passing the Rubicon*, *19*, *186*
Henay and Son, William; *Ceiling Fresco*, *106*, *193*
Herter, Albert, 94
Herter Brothers, 137-138; *138*, *139*, *196*
Hill, John William, 91
Hiromichi, Shugio, 43
Hiroshige, 82, 158, 160; from *Eight Views of Lake Biwa Series*, *81*; *Iris at Horikiri*, *84*, *191*; *Plum Trees Flower Garden at Kameido*; *82*
Hizen ware. See Imari porcelain
Hokusai, Katsushika; *Manga*, *88*, *160*
Holloware. See Silversmithing
Holly, Henry Hudson, 161
Holmes and Edwards, 131
Homer, Winslow, 94, 96-99; *Wild Geese in Flight*, *99*
Hooked Rug, *174*
Hooper and Son, Orin; *Commode*, *140*
Hosada, Eishi; *Beauty with Samisen*, *83*
Huet, S., *109*
Hunter, Thomas; *Birdseye View of Centennial Exposition*, *34*; *Japanese Bazaar, Philadelphia Centennial Exposition*, *35*; *Japanese Dwelling, Philadelphia Exposition*, *35*
Hyde, Helen, 100

I

Iceland Falcon (Audubon), *23*
Ichi Ban Studios, *102*
Ichi Bangi's Japanese Bazaar, 43
Imari porcelain, 63
Impressionism, 80, 87, 96-98
Industrial art, 48, 117-153

Inlays, in metal work, 52
Interior, Camp Cedars, *113*
Interior design and furnishings, 111-115; *112-116*
Interior, Molly Sheafe's Studio, *166*
Interior woodwork, 103-104, 108, 110
International expositions, 30, 32, 42
International Silver Company. See Meriden Britannia
Iris at Horikiri (Hiroshige), *84*, *191*
Irish Belleek, 159; *160*
Isolation of Japan, 17
Ivory, 72; *72*

J

Japanese art collections, loss of, 47-48
Japanese Bazaar, Philadelphia Centennial Exposition, 1876, *35*, *37*
Japanese composition, 65; in American paintings, 97, 98
Japanese Corner (Haberle), *93*
Japanese Court (Alcock), *30*
Japanese Court at London Exposition of 1862, *48*
Japanese Dwelling, Philadelphia Centennial Exposition (Hunter), *35*
Japanese Homes and Their Surroundings (Morse), *30*
Japanese lifestyle, 91, 103-104; and artisanry, 39, 48-49; and government, 17-23, 27-28
Japanese Lullaby (Field/Neil), *175*
"*Japanese*" *Pattern Flatware Set* (Tiffany and Co.), *146*; *128*
Japanese Pavilion, Philadelphia Centennial, *36*
Japanese prints, 80-87. See also Woodblock printing
Japanese Winter Landscape (Twachtman), *96*; *97*
Japanned work. See Lacquer ware
Japonica (Arnold), *94*
Japanophile, definition of, 29-30
Jars, 38, 65; *38*, *57-8*, *65*
Jarves, James Jackson, 29, 49, 117
Jeromak, Paul, *132*, *152*, *178*
Ji-maki, 59
Jin-di-sugi, 143; *143*
Jones, McDuffee and Stratton, 156
Jones, Owen, 90

K

Kachi-Kachi Yama, (Kobunsha), *179*
Kaga ware, 63
Kamakura-bori, 67
Kan Ko Ba's Japanese Trading Company, 44
Katagammi, 71
Kenzoa, Ichidsuka, 123
Kerosene Lamp, *135*
Kerosene Lamp (S. R. Bowie and Co. Decorators), *146*
Kimball and Cabus, 137
Kimball and Wisedell; *Goodwin Building*, *106*
Kimball, Julia; *168*
Kimonos, 68; *Kimono, 19th Century*, *68*
"Kioto" pattern, 156; *156*
Kioto ware, 160
Kirigane, 59
Kiriu Koshu Kuarsha Trading Company, 43
Kobunsha, *179*
Kodzukas, 130
Koransha Porcelain Works, *38*
Koyama, 65
Kunihiko, Takenaka; *Samurai Sword*, *25*
Kunisada, 82; *Woman on a Boat in a Snowy Landscape*, *83*
Kuniyoshi, 82
Kyoto school, 58

Index 209

L

La Belle Glass Company, 146; *147*
Lacquer work, 58-61; *24, 59-61, 67, 78*; Kamakura-bori, 67; ornamentation of, 59, 61; *72*
Lacquered Ostrich Egg on Stand, 61
Ladies Desk, 143
La Farge Decorative Art Company, 92
La Farge, John, 88-90, 94; *An Artist's Letters from Japan in 1897, 90; Water Lily and Moth, 90*
Lambrequin, 165
Lamp Globe, 147
Landing of Commodore Perry, Officers, and Men of the Squadron (Heine), *22, 187*
Landscape features, as motifs, 51
Laundry, Branchville, The (Weir), *96; 98, 192*
Lava glass, 144
"Lava" Vase, (Mount Washington Glass Co.), *144*
Lavezzo and Brothers, J., 142
Leather, *72; 79;* wallpaper; *74, 189*
Leavitt, Edward C., 93
Lejambre, A. and H.; *Etagere, 141*
Letter opener, 72
Lily, The (Dow), *100*
Lincrusta Walton, *74, 150*
Lithographs, *19-20, 22, 34-35, 76, 186*
Lock and hardware industry, 136-137; *136-137*
"Lotus" Center Table (Bradstreet), *143*
Louis, S. L., *186*
Lovell, F. H., and Company, 135
Lowell and Coon, J. A., 176
Low, John Gardner, 120; Low Art Tile Works, J. and J. G., 120-121; *Art Tiles, 122, 193*
Lycett, Edward, 120; *Vase* (Faience Manufacturing Company), *121*

M

McBerney and Armstrong; *160*
McLaughlin, Louise, 121
Magazines, 45; *39;* subsidizing artists' travels to Japan, 87, 94-95
Majolica-type pottery, 125
Manga (Hokusai), *87, 127, 169; 88;* as a source for patterns, 158; *123, 127, 160*
Mantel Clock (New Haven Clock Company), *151*
Map of Japan, 15
Marketing, of Japanese art, 30-32, 41-46, 62; at international expositions, 32-41. *See also* Advertising; Export goods
Mass production, of export goods, 32-33, 41, 43
Matchlock guns, 25
Matsuyama Mirror, The (Kobunsha), *179*
Matthews, John, 110
May, Signora; *173, 199*
Medieval idealism and Japan, 48-49, 91
Meiji Restoration, 28, 33, 56, 67
Meizan, Yabu, 64
"Melbourne" pattern, 156; *156*
Menu Cover, 178
Mercer China Company, 120
Meriden Britannia Company, 131-134; *133-5, 195*
Meriden Glass Company, 135
Message of the Admiral of the United States to the Shogun, 21
Metalworking, 44, 52-56, 125-137; mixed metals and alloys, 52-54, 130; *129, 130. See also* Silversmithing
Metcalf, Helen, 164
Metropolitan Museum of Art, 47
Mikado script, 171
Mikado, The (Gilbert and Sullivan), 68, 148, 174-175; *68, 175*
Mikado Waltz, The (Bucalossi), *175*
Minton and Company, 154-156, 158; *159*
Mitchell and Rammelsberg, 137, 140-142; *142*
Modern Dwellings (Holly), 161
Modernism, 29, 47-48
Modernization of Japan, 27-29
Mokume, 127, 130; *129*
Moore, Edward C., 72, 126; *73, 75*
Moore, H. Humphrey, 94
Moore, H. R., and Company; *Advertising Broadside, 62*
Monumental Vases (Rookwood Pottery), *124, 194*
Morimura Brothers and Company, 44
Morse, Edward S., 29, 30-31, 42, 49, 76, 103-104, 111; collections of, 30, 62-63; on Victorian lifestyle, 104, 111
Moths and Blossoms (Vedder), 92
Motifs, in Japanese art, 50, 64, 70; *129*
Mounted Photographic Portrait, 178
Mount Washington Glass Company, 135, 144-145; *144-5*
Museum of Fine Arts (Boston), 42, 62
Mythical figures, in Japanese art, 56

N

Nashiji, 59
Nashua Lock Company, 136; *Door Handle and Escutcheon, 136*
Natural motifs, in Japanese art, 39, 50-51, 82, 133; *129, 133, 147, 172;* stork, 50; *140, 144, 157;* weather, 51, 83
Nature and realism in art, 90
Navy pistol (Colt), *24*
Necklace, 153
Netsuke, 70-72
Neville Glass Company, Asa G., 146
New England Glass Company, 135
New Haven Clock Company; *Mantel Clock, 151*
New Year's Greeting Card, (Prang), *178*
Nichols, George Ward, 118
Nichols, Maria Longworth, 118, 121-125
Night Owl (Coleman), *93, 191*
Nolston, D. A., *182*
Nut Bowl, 135

O

Obi, 69
Oil painting; *92-3, 95, 97-9, 119, 169, 191-192*
Old Garden, The (Cook), *170*
Old Hall Earthenware Company, 156
Onandaga Lithographing Company, 176
Opera House or Village Hall, 105
Osborn, Arthur, 120
Ott and Brewer (Etruria Pottery), 120; *120*
Ovoid Jar with Cover, 65

P

Painted Mirror (Tucker), *168*
Pair of Covered Jars (Uchimatsu), *38, 188*
Pair of Monumental Vases, 40
Pairpoint Manufacturing Company, 133, 135, 145; *Selection of Hollowware Forms, A, 132;* "Verona Ware" Pitcher, *145, 196. See also* Mount Washington Glass Company
Palliser, George and Charles; *Frank H. Underwood House, 105*
Palmer Manufacturing Company, 135
Paper; fans, 44-45, 75-76; *36, 75-76, 89;* lanterns, 77
Parasols, 76
Paris Exposition of 1867, 32, 63, 127
Parke, H. C., 43, 44
Parker, Charles, 136
Parlor interior, 114
Parson, Albert, 94
Passing the Rubicon (Heine), *19, 186*
Patchwork "Crazy" Quilt (May), *173, 199*

Pattern Book (Hamilton Manufacturing Company), *149*
Patterned Fabric Stencils (Katagami), *71*
Peabody and Stearns, 105
Peabody Museum (Salem, Massachusetts), 62
"Peach Blow" pattern, 144
Peck, Stow and Wilcox Company, 136
Perry, Commodore Matthew C., 17-27
Perspective, use in Japanese art, 84
Philadelphia exposition. *See* Centennial Exposition of 1876
Philadelphia Museum of Art, 117
Photography, 100; *37, 85-6;* American, 179; *178;* Japanese, 83-90; *85, 86*
"Phrenology at the Fancy Ball" (Rogers), *181*
Picturesque Rhode Island (Munroe), *179*
Pilgrim Flask (Koyama), 65
Pine Tree Point Camp, 107
Pitcher, 167
Pitcher (Derby Silver Co.), *131*
Pitcher (Ott and Brewer), *120*
Pitcher (Whiting Manufacturing Company), *131*
Pitcher (Worcester Royal Porcelain Company), *157*
Pitman, Benn, 118, 121, 172
Plaque (Bennett), *163*
Plate, 168
Plate (Minton and Company), *159*
Plate (Rookwood Pottery), *123*
Plate (Worcester Royal Porcelain Company), *157*
Plate, "Tropics" (Willetts Manufacturing Company), *120*
Platter ("Melbourne", Gildea and Walker), *156*
Platter ("Kioto", Brownhills Pottery Company), *156*
Poleni, Theodore, *34*
Porcelain, 63, 159; *38, 66, 120, 156, 159-60, 168, 188*
Porter Manufacturing Company, 109
Portraiture, 88, 97, 101; *102, 178;* of rooms, 111-115; *112-116*
Post-and-beam construction. *See* Stick style
Post-impressionists, 80
Pottery, 39, 61-66, 118; British, 154-160; Japanese, 31, 63. *See also* Ceramics
Pottery Decoration Patterns, 119
Prang and Company, L., 176; *170, 178*
Pressed glass, 110, 147
Pressed leather, 72. *See also* Lincrusta Walton
Printing styles, 171, 175, 176
Prints, 80-87; *81-86, 99. See also* Lithographs; Photography; Ukiyo-e prints; Woodblock printing
Prospect Hill Pottery, 120
Publishing, 30, 45; *179, 180*

Q

Queen Anne style, 104-106; *105-106*
Quilts, 172-173; *172-3*

R

Ramma, 72; *73*
Randomness, as a compositional convention, 51-52, 173
Religion and Japanese art, 48, 80
Reed and Barton, 133; *134, 195*
Rhode Island School of Design, 164
Robertson, Hugh C.; *Vase, 119*
Rogers, John; *181*
Romanticism, 30
Rookwood Pottery, 123-125; *123-4*
Room portraits; *112-116*
Rosenblum, Robert, 47
Royal Worcester Porcelain Company, 120, 157-158

Runner, 166
Ruskin, John, 90, 104
Russell and Erwin Manufacturing Company, 136; *Doorknobs*, 137
Rustic style, 113

S

Saint Louis World Fair, 42
Samurai swords (Kunihiko), 25
Sandblasted glass, 110, 147
Sargent, John Singer, 91
Satsuma ware, 44, 63; *64-65*
 imitations of, 63, 158; *158*
Scalloped Fish Plate (Kyoku-Ho-En), 66
Scrapbook, 174
Scrapbooks, 174
Scully, Vincent, 104
Sculpture; *101, 181*
Sculpture and stand, 55
Seido, 56
Selection of Hollowware Forms, A (Pairpoint Manufacturing Co.), 132
Selections from the Japanese Exhibit, 39
Shaku-do, 56, 127, 130, 134
Shard art, 174
Sheafe, Molly, 166
Sheet Music (Bucalossi), 175
Sheet Music (Field/Neil), 175
Shibu-ichi, 56, 127, 130
Shingle style, 104
Shintoism, and art, 48
Shippo Kuwaisha of Owari, 43
Shippo ware. *See* Cloisonné
Shirayamadani, Kataro, 123
Shirley, Frederick, 144
Shoguns, in Japanese society, 17-23, 27-28
Side chair, (Herter Brothers), 138
Silks, 45, 68-70, 148; *68-69, 166, 181*; brocade, *26, 69*; damask, *150, 196*; raw, 68
Silversmithing, 125-135; *128-131, 153, 194*; hollowware, 127; *129, 132*; mixed metals, 56, 127, 130, 134; *129, 134-5*;
 silverplate, 130-135; *131-132, 135, 195*; sterling, *129, 153*; with gold, 55; *53*
Simpson, Hall and Miller Company, 133, 134-135; *Nut Bowl*, 135
Small Cabinet on Stand, 60
Smith Brothers (Alfred and Harry), 145
Smith, George Walter Vincent, 44, 55
Society of Decorative Arts (Hartford, CT), 164
Society of Decorative Arts (New York), 162
Soft-haired Squirrel (Audubon), 23
South Kensington Museum (London), 39
Splasher, 165
Stanley, Thomas, 125
Steichen, Edward, 100
Stenciled towels (Tenugi), 110; *70*
Stencils, 70; *71*
Stick style, 104-105; *105*
Still Life of Flowers (Ellsworth), 169
Still lifes, 92-93
Sturgis, William, 42
Sword guards (Tsuba), 53-54, *54, 55*
Symbolism in Japanese art, 50. *See also* Mythical figures; Natural motifs

T

Taft Company, J. S.; *Teapot and two creamers*, 125
Takahashi, S. K., 43
Takamakie, 59
Talcott, Mary Kingsbury, 172; *167, 170*
Tazza and plate (Wedgwood and Sons), 160

Tea Box Label, 176
Teapot (McBerney and Armstrong), 160
Teapot and Sugar Bowl, 168
Teapot and two creamers, 126
Tea Set (James W. Tufts Co.), 132
Tea Set (Worcester Royal Porcelain Company), *158, 198*
Tenugi, 110; *70*
Terra cotta industry, 106
Textile Fragment, 163, *198*
Textile Fragment (Cheney Brothers), *150, 196*
Textile Retailer's Sample Book, 89
Textiles, 148, 163. *See also* Cotton; Silks; Wool
Thaxter, Celia, 167
Tiffany and Company, 126-130, 158; *Coffee Pot*, *129*; *"Japanese" Pattern Flatware Set*, *128*; *Tea Caddy*, *129*; *Vase*, *129, 194*
Tiffany, Louis Comfort, 92, 93, 148
Tile Club, 92-93
Tonzaku, 146
Toyokuni III, Kunisada; *Autumn Rain and Leaves*, 83
Trade catalog (Meriden Brittannia Company), *133, 195*
Transfer-printing, 123, 155-159; *156-159*
Transom (Ramma), 73
Travel to Japan, 46, 94-95, 126-127
Tray, 165
Tray (Derby Silver Co.), 131
Tray (Gorham Manufacturing Co.), 130
Trompe l'oeil, 92; *Japanese Corner* (Haberle), *93*
Tsuba, 44, 55; *54*
Tucker, Jane A., 167; *168*
Tufts and Company, James W., 133; *Tea Set*, 132
Tuggle, Robert, 152; *152, 178*
Turkey red needlework, 165
Twachtman, 94, 96; *Japanese Winter Landscape*, 97

U

Uchimatsu, Ichiryusai, 38, *188*
Ukiyo-e prints, 52, 80-83, 87; for designs in pottery, 159
Umbrella, 77
Underglaze slip decoration, 121-123; *66, 163*
Underwood House, Frank H., 105
United States International Exhibition of Arts, Manufacturers, and Products of the Soil and Mines. *See* Centennial Exhibition of 1876
Utamaro, 82

V

Valentien, Albert; *Monumental Vases* (Rookwood Pottery), 124
Vanderbilt's Japanese Room, Mr. William H; 116
Vantine and Company, A. A., 44-45, 169
Vase, 53, 92, 166
Vase (Elkington), 155
Vase (Harrison), 166
Vase (Kimball), 168, *199*
Vase (Lycett), 121
Vase (Roberston), 119
Vase (Rookwood Pottery), 123-124, *194*
Vase (T. J. Wheatley and Company), 125
Vase (Yarrington), 172
Vase in Shape of Bamboo, 53
Vases, 40, 65; *53, 92, 119, 121, 123-125, 166, 168, 194, 199*
Vedder, Elihu, 92, 94; *Moths and Blossoms*, 92
"Verona ware" Pitcher (Pairpont Manufacturing Company), 145, *196*
Victorian life, 30, 110; and collecting, 42, 44-45, 46, 93, 111, 174; *141*; disillusionment with, 29-30, 39-42, 48-49, 117-118
Viviparous Quadrupeds of North America, The (Audubon), 23

W

Wadsworth Atheneum (Hartford, CT), 164
Wall, J. E., 142
Wallhanging, 26
Wall plaque, 53, 56, 134
Wallpaper, 148; *74, 150-1, 189, 197*
Wallpaper (Frederick Beck and Company), *150, 197*
Wallpaper samples, 74, 151, 189, 197
Walters, William T. and Henry, 55
Warren, Fuller, and Lange, 148
Watercolor, 91-92; *90-1*
Water Drop earthenware, 44
Water Lily and Moth (La Farge), 90
Wedgwood, Josiah and Sons, Ltd., 154, 156, 158-159; *160*
Weir, J. Alden, 94, 96; *Laundry, Branchville, The*, 98, *192*
Weldon, Charles Dater, 94
Westernization of Japan, 28, 31, 41, 52, 62-67; export goods, 41, 56-57, 62. *See also* Meiji Restoration
Wheatley, Thomas J., 121, 125; *125*
Wheatley and Company, T. J., 125; *125*
Wheeler, Candace, 148, 162; *150, 163, 196, 198*
Whistler, James McNeill, 87, 91
White, Stanford, 94, 105
Whiting Manufacturing Company, 130; *Pitcher*, 131
Wilde, Oscar, 164
Wild Geese in Flight (Homer), 99
Wilkinson, George, 130
Wilcox Silverplate Company, 133
Willets Manufacturing Company, 120; *120*
Window Pane, 110
Women, in Victorian America, 161-182; *166*
Women's Art Museum Association of Cincinnati, 163
Women's Exchange, 162
Women's Pavilion at the Centennial, 161; *162*
Wood burning, 165
Wood carving, 70, 172; *67, 70, 73, 109, 143, 172*
Woodblock printing, 21, 80-83, 87, 99-100, 160; *81-84, 100, 191*
Wool, 165, 166
Worcester Royal Porcelain Company, The, 154, 157-158; *157-158, 198*
Wores, Theodore, 94
World Colombian Exposition in 1893, 58; *40*
World fairs, 42
Woven tapestry, 152
Wright, Frank Lloyd, 103, 143
Writing Box (Suzuribako), 59

Y

Yamanaka and Company, 44
Yarrington, M., 172
Yasuyuki, Namikawa; *Cloisonné jar*, 57, *189*
Yata, Forakechi; *Folding Screen*, 102, *192*

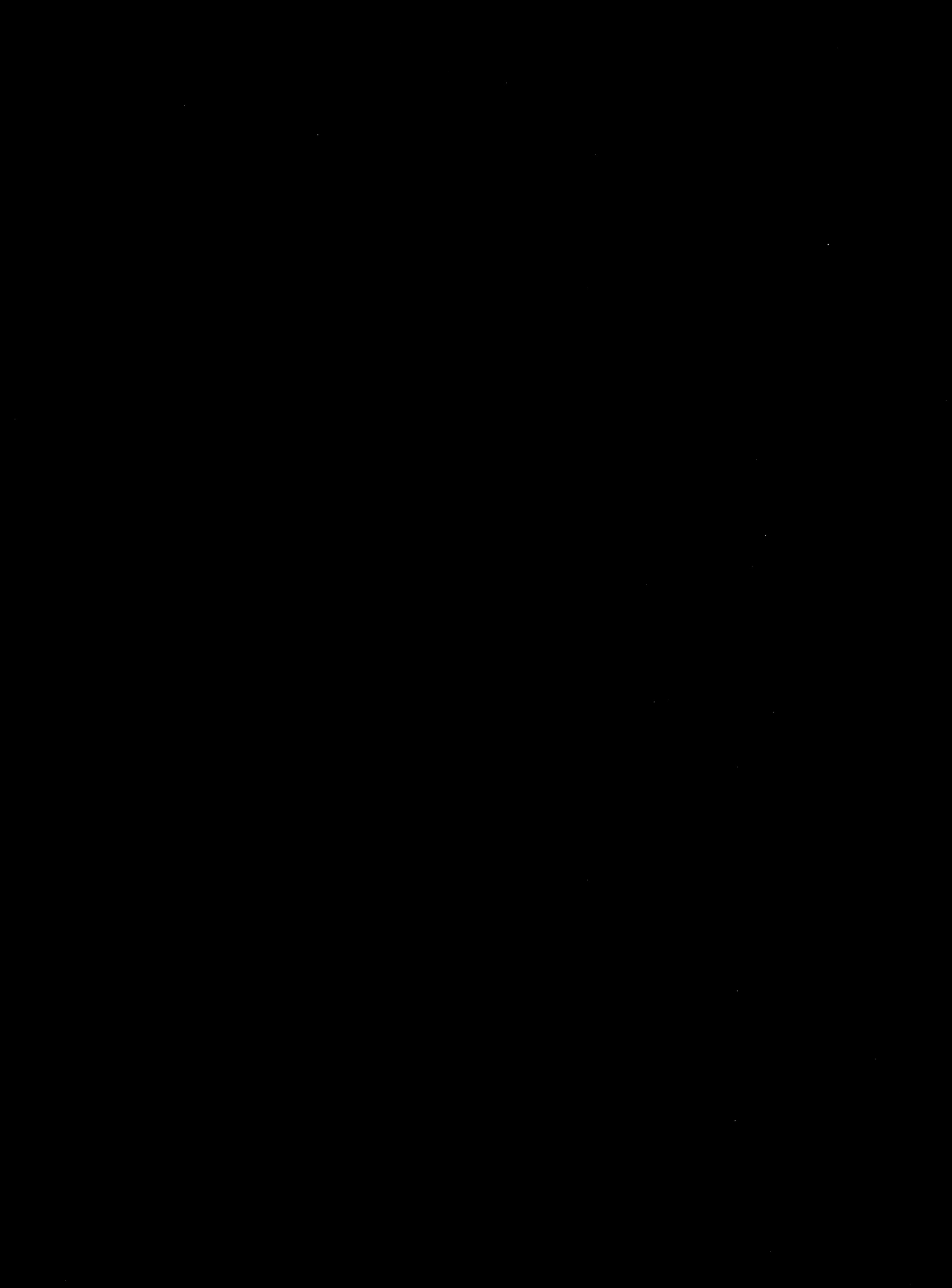